A Practical
View of
CHRISTIANITY

A Practical View of CHRISTIANITY

WILLIAM WILBERFORCE

EDITED BY
Kevin Charles Belmonte

WITH AN INTRODUCTION BY
CHARLES COLSON
and a foreword by
GARTH M. ROSELL

© 1996 by Hendrickson Publishers, Inc.
P. O. Box 3473
Peabody, Massachusetts 01961–3473
All rights reserved
Printed in the United States of America

ISBN 1–56563–176–5

Second Printing — June 1996

An annotated reissue of the First British edition of 1797, *A Practical View of the Prevailing Religious System of Professed Christians, in the Higher and Middle Classes in This Country, Contrasted with Real Christianity,* by William Wilberforce.

Library of Congress Cataloging-in-Publication Data

Wilberforce, William, 1759–1833.
    [Practical view of the prevailing religious system of professed Christians, in the higher and middle classes in this country, contrasted with real Christianity]
    A practical view of Christianity: an annotated critical reissue of the 1st British edition of 1797 / William Wilberforce; edited by Kevin Charles Belmonte; with an introduction by Charles Colson; and a foreword by Garth M. Rosell.
    Includes bibliographical references and index.
    ISBN 1–56563–176–5 (alk. paper)
    1. Christianity—Early works to 1800. 2. Great Britain—Church history—18th century.—3. Evangelicalism—Early works to 1800. 4. Vocation—Early works to 1800. I. Belmonte, Kevin Charles. II. Title.
BR120.W5   1996
274.1'07—dc20

                        96–4139
                           CIP

~Table of Contents

Yes, I trust that the Lord, by raising up such an incontestable witness to the truth and power of the gospel, has a gracious purpose to honour him as an instrument of reviving and strengthening the sense of real religion where it already is, and of communicating it where it is not.

—John Newton

§

If I live, I shall thank Wilberforce for having sent such a book into the world.

—Edmund Burke

§

[I]t is a great relief to my mind to have published what I may call my manifesto. . . . I shall at least feel a solid satisfaction from having openly declared myself as it were on the side of Christ . . .

—William Wilberforce

Foreword

by Garth M. Rosell

THIS SPLENDID NEW EDITION OF WILLIAM WILBER-force's classic work, *A Practical View of Christianity,* deserves to be read as eagerly today as it was by the thousands of Londoners who made it an immediate best-seller nearly two centuries ago. Its author, then a prominent member of Parliament, is now largely forgotten. His message, however, is as fresh and relevant for readers today as it was for his contemporaries in late eighteenth-century England.

Troubled by what he considered to be a dangerous decline in public and private morality, Wilberforce determined in 1787 to focus his remaining time and energy on the two great tasks which he believed God had given him to do: namely, "the abolition of the slave trade and the reformation of manners." Realizing that neither objective was possible without the other, he gave himself unstintingly to the task of moral reform—calling an often balky nation to clean up its hospitals, to reform its prisons, to provide food and clothing for the poor, to protect its children from the brutal practices of the industrial workplace, to promote Christian missions at home and abroad, to distribute the Bible to a needy world and, most especially, to shut down the slave trade and bring an end to the tragic and vicious evil of slavery.

To achieve these ends, Wilberforce and his colleagues adopted a wide variety of strategies from moral suasion to political action. Among the most important of these strategies, however, was the power of the pen—and nowhere is this demonstrated more clearly than in the widespread influence which for more than half a century was enjoyed by *A Practical View.* Clearly declaring himself "on the side of Christ," Wilberforce sought in its pages to persuade his readers that the only hope for the nation rested in a return to biblical principles and the shared morality which flowed so naturally from them. If they could be persuaded of the truth and power of "real Christianity," he was convinced, then they might be ready to join hands with those who sought like Wilberforce himself to free their beloved England from the blight of slavery and to restore its basic institutions to their intended purpose and power.

Some contemporary readers might find it surprising to discover that Wilberforce was not alone in his commitment to political action and social reform. Indeed, throughout the eighteenth and nineteenth centuries, literally tens of thousands of evangelical Christians, on both sides of the Atlantic, sought to apply the teachings of the Bible to every arena of life. The remarkable social reforms which emerged from that era, I suspect, could never have been achieved without their efforts. And no more wholesome example of the healthy interaction of religion and reform within that historic period can be found than in the work of William Wilberforce and his colleagues.

Dubbed the Clapham Sect by later historians—a designation taken from the section of London in which many of them lived—an array of talented men and women such as Henry Thornton, Hannah More, Isaac Milner, John Venn, and others joined with Wilberforce in the spreading of the Gospel and work of reform. Their diligent efforts helped significantly in securing a number of important achievements, including the establishment of the Church Missionary Society and the British and Foreign Bible Society, the legalization of missionary outreach in India, the ending of the slave trade, the establishment of a colony in Sierra Leone for ex-slaves and, of course, the abolition of slavery within the British colonies.

The world in which we live is very different, of course, from the world which Wilberforce and his Clapham colleagues faced in eighteenth-century England. Yet, these fascinating men and women have much to teach those of us who must live and work at the close of the twentieth century. To those of us who have abandoned the public square, they remind us of Christ's command to be salt and light in the world. To those of us who have given up on the political process, they remind us that genuine change is possible through wise and wholesome laws. To those of us who expect immediate results, they remind us of the need for hard work over many years. To those of us who think we can achieve great goals by ourselves, they remind us of the importance of Christian community. To those of us who have grown cynical and pessimistic, they remind us that the power of the Gospel is still gloriously able to transform individual lives, to renew decaying institutions, to motivate individuals for a lifetime of benevolence, and to provide hope in a world of despair.

William Wilberforce came to be known in his day as the "conscience of a nation." Now that his most important writings are available once again, perhaps they will inspire a whole new generation to follow his lead. Perhaps, as John Newton once phrased it, his words will once again become "an instrument of reviving and strengthening the sense of real religion" throughout a very needy world.

Editorial Preface

It has been nearly two hundred years since *A Practical View of Christianity* was first published on April 12, 1797. In keeping with the custom of the day of devising long titles, William Wilberforce chose to call his book *A Practical View of the Prevailing Religious System of Professed Christians, in the Higher and Middle Classes in This Country, Contrasted with Real Christianity.* Though it might be difficult for the modern reader to see how a book with such an imposing title could sell well, *A Practical View* did just that. Indeed, the story of how it came to be published and its subsequent success is a fascinating one.

Initially, *A Practical View* was thought to have so little public appeal that its publisher, Thomas Cadell, was dubious as to whether Wilberforce would want to affix his name to it. Several of his friends tried to discourage him from writing the book at all, stating that such works never sold well.[1] Furthermore, they wondered who would want to buy a religious book by a politician. Cadell was convinced that he would be fortunate to sell five hundred copies of the book. Everyone's fears proved to be entirely unfounded. The first five hundred copies were purchased in a few days, and six months later, 7,500 copies had been sold. *A Practical View* went on to become a best seller, and by 1826, seven years before Wilberforce's death, fifteen editions had been printed in Britain and twenty-five in the United States.[2] It was translated into Dutch, French,

German, Italian, and Spanish. In time, it came to be regarded as the manifesto of the Evangelical movement.[3]

Many prominent persons of the day lauded Wilberforce for his achievement. John Newton, author of the immortal hymn "Amazing Grace," proclaimed: "I deem it the most valuable and important publication of the present age . . . I shall be glad to look to you (at least to your book) . . . to strengthen my motives for running the uncertain remainder of my race with alacrity."[4] The brilliant orator and politician Edmund Burke spent the last two days of his life reading *A Practical View*. Not long before he died, Burke stated, "If I live, I shall thank Wilberforce for having sent such a book into the world."[5] In their five-volume *Life of William Wilberforce*, sons Robert and Samuel wrote: "Not a year passed throughout his after-life, in which he did not receive fresh testimonies to the blessed effects which it pleased God to produce through his publication."[6]

When I became acquainted with the extent of the sales and acclaim that *A Practical View* enjoyed, it seemed very strange and unfortunate that this classic declaration of the Christian faith was no longer in print. The book is of value for the historian and scholar, but it is also a work of great significance by virtue of its stature as a manifesto of the Evangelical movement in Britain during the late eighteenth and early nineteenth centuries. A work which represents such an important part of the church's heritage greatly deserved to be republished.

In 1994, a series of events occurred which led to publication of this book. While conducting preliminary research for my master's thesis, "William Wilberforce: The Making of an Evangelical Reformer," I began to search for a copy of *A Practical View*. Through the kindness of John Beauregard, Director of the Jenks Learning Resource Center at my alma mater, Gordon College, I was allowed to electronically scan the pages of an edition which appeared to date from the early 1800s and store the text on my notebook computer. A few weeks later, when comparing my computer text with a fragile first American edition of 1798 housed in the rare book room at Gordon-Conwell Theological Seminary, I was surprised to find that the 1798 American edition contained sentences, paragraphs, and even pages worth of material that the later Gordon College edition lacked. This prompted me to search for the first British edition of 1797, and eventually I located a microfilmed copy at St. Michael's College in Colchester, Vermont.

During the same period, John Beauregard suggested that I try to get the book republished. "After all," he said, "you've already invested so much work in generating a computerized text." Encouraged, I began to discuss the idea with friends and professors at Gordon-Conwell. Everyone I talked to showed enthusiasm for such a project. I became convinced that a critical edition of *A Practical View* was long overdue.

One classmate, Christopher Armstrong, suggested I approach Hendrickson Publishers. Hendrickson accepted my proposal and offered me a contract. As I reflect on this series of events, I am amazed that such an opportunity materialized before I had completed my master's thesis.

After I completed my thesis, I posted a copy of it to Chuck Colson. I had contacted him several months earlier, knowing that he possessed an abiding interest in William Wilberforce. In the letter sent with my thesis, I asked him if he would be interested in writing a foreword to this reissue of *A Practical View*. He wrote back saying that he would be interested in writing an *introduction!* I believe I have ample cause to think that seldom has a first-time editor been so fortunate in his initial publishing experience.

As this project has progressed, my indebtedness to many special people has increased. Patrick Alexander, David Townsley, and everyone at Hendrickson Publishers have constantly exhibited dedication to the highest standards throughout this project. Thank you for giving me this wonderful opportunity.

Chuck Colson has honoured me with the gift of his collaboration. This book has been greatly enriched by the inclusion of an introduction that so masterfully describes the legacy bequeathed to Christendom by William Wilberforce. I also wish to thank his research assistant Ann Morris for her contributions and the board of Prison Fellowship for its support.

The Right Honourable Richard Lord Wilberforce, C.M.G., O.B.E., P.C. sent me a moving letter expressing his enthusiasm for this new edition of *A Practical View of Christianity*. His encouragement of my studies into William Wilberforce's life and achievements is something I will always treasure.

Garth Rosell of Gordon-Conwell Theological Seminary has constantly encouraged my desire to become a Wilberforce scholar—especially during the writing of my master's thesis, when he provided me with a wealth of advice and guidance. His dedication to excellence in the execution of the historian's craft has influenced me profoundly and I am delighted that he has written the foreword for this book. I am grateful as well for the instruction, encouragement, and dedication to scholarship modelled to me by my other professors at Gordon-Conwell Theological Seminary.

I have received much encouragement and kind correspondence from the Reverend John Pollock. I owe a tremendous debt to his scholarship, which has done so much to shape my understanding of William Wilberforce. I will always treasure his gift of an inscribed copy of his masterful biography, *Wilberforce*.

Os Guinness has been a faithful correspondent and source of support during the last several months. He has helped me to understand and appreciate how much William Wilberforce's life and achievements have to say to us today. The Hon. Sir Alexander Hoyos has provided me with research advice and encouragement while I have been finishing this book in Barbados. I am privileged to have made his acquaintance and to have been shown such kindness.

John Beauregard has been a friend and ally from the start—thank you John for being the first one to encourage me to get *A Practical View of Christianity* published. Chris Armstrong deserves hearty thanks for aiding me in my initial contact with the folks at Hendrickson Publishers. Norman Anderson of the Goddard Library at Gordon-Conwell Theological Seminary graciously allowed me to use the seminary's copy of the first American edition of *A Practical View*. He and his staff provided able assistance which also expedited the research connected with writing the footnotes for this book. St. Michael's College in Colchester, Vermont, provided indispensable assistance by furnishing me with a copy of the first British edition of *A Practical View* to use as an authoritative text for this reissue.

Melissa Kummerer of EBSCO Publishing kindly allowed me access to a flatbed scanner to generate the first electronic text for *A Practical View*. Betty Carillo-Shannon and her colleagues at the Barbados Museum offered kind and efficient assistance while I used their research facilities. Thanks to Derrick F. Bowen, Maria Boyce, and Suzanne Durant for all their help during my stay in Barbados.

My high school Latin teacher, Martha Niver, offered me invaluable assistance in deciphering the Latin passages contained in *A Practical View*. I would also like to thank Harold Small, the Senior Pastor of Fellowship in Christ Church in Raymond, New Hampshire, for bringing me to Congress '83 in Haverhill, Massachusetts. It was at Congress '83 that I first heard about William Wilberforce via an article in *The New England Correspondent.*

My family has supported me in countless ways. In particular, I would like to thank my parents Dianne and Charles Belmonte. To Daniel and Tammi Griswold, Tim and Pam Griswold, and Alice and David Martin, thank you for welcoming me into the family and for assisting Kelly and me in so many ways.

My wife Kelly's love, encouragement, sacrifice, and patience throughout this project has meant more than I can say. I could not have done it without her.

It is a profound honour to have been given the chance to serve as the editor of William Wilberforce's magnum opus. Though the duties associated with doing so have presented a number of challenges, the labour expended to meet each of them has been well worth the effort. In closing, I would like to say that working on this book has been instructive and inspirational. It is my hope that those who read this work will come away with the same sense of having been enriched.

ᔅ

Dedicated to Kelly,

and to my grandparents Doris and William Young—
who always believed that someday
their grandson would become a writer.

ᔅ

Notes ᐱ

1. See appendix 1 for Wilberforce's own list of reasons for and against publishing *A Practical View.*

2. Robin Furneaux, *William Wilberforce* (London: Hamish Hamilton, 1974), p. 151.

3. See appendix 2 for a description of the impact of *A Practical View,* following its initial publication.

4. Robert Isaac Wilberforce and Samuel Wilberforce, *The Life of William Wilberforce* Vol. 2 (London: John Murray, 1838), p. 207.

5. Furneaux, *Wilberforce,* p. 152.

6. Wilberforce, *Life of Wilberforce,* Vol. II, p. 207.

Introduction

by Charles Colson

THE CONGRESSMAN'S FACE BETRAYED HIS ANGER. "THE Republicans accept the religious right and their tactics at their own peril," he thundered. "These activists are demanding their rightful seat at the table—and that is what the American people fear most." And then Representative Vic Fazio[1] ominously asked, "Should they attempt to impose their personal religious views and ethical beliefs on the party system?"

Sounds pretty scary, doesn't it? You can almost see "these activists" tossing the Constitution into the trash with one hand while shoving other people's kids into Sunday School with the other. How intolerant. How dogmatic. And how utterly ridiculous.

As we enter the twenty-first century, Christians are increasingly—and rightfully—taking their place in the public square. But we're discovering that plenty of people want to roll up the sidewalk when they see us coming. "Bigot." "Zealot." "Extremist." Many sling these verbal stones at us whenever we invade what they consider *their* turf.

But this is not new. These strident voices echo those of an earlier generation of politicians—politicians who accused the Christians of *their* day of "imposing their morality" when they dared to carry their faith into public life. And at no one did they hurl that accusation more vociferously than the great abolitionist, William Wilberforce.

Old Palace Yard, London, October 25, 1787: A slight young man sat at his oak desk in the second-floor library. As he adjusted the flame of his lamp, the warm light shone on his piercing blue eyes, oversized nose, and high wrinkled forehead. His eyes fell on the jumble of pamphlets on the cluttered desk. They were all on the same subject: the horrors of the slave trade, grisly accounts of human flesh being sold, like so much cattle, for the profit of his countrymen.

The young man would begin this day, as was his custom, with a time of personal prayer and scripture reading. But his thoughts kept returning to those pamphlets. Something inside him—that insistent conviction he'd felt before—was telling him that all that had happened in his life had been for a purpose, preparing him to meet that barbaric evil head-on. . . .

Wilberforce was born in Hull, England, in 1759, the only son of prosperous merchant parents. Though an average student at Cambridge, his quick wit had made him a favorite among his fellows, including William Pitt, with whom he shared an interest in politics.

After graduation Wilberforce ran as a conservative for a seat in Parliament from his home county of Hull. Though Wilberforce was only twenty-one at the time, the prominence of his family, his speaking ability, and a generous feast he sponsored for voters on election day carried the contest.

The London of 1780, when Wilberforce arrived to take office, was described as "one vast casino" where the rich counted their profits through a fog of claret. Fortunes were lost and won over gaming tables, and duels of honor were the order of the day. The city's elegant private clubs welcomed young Wilberforce, and Wilberforce happily concentrated on pursuing both political advancement and social pleasure.

Far from the homes of the rich, the poor were crammed together in grimy cobblestoned neighborhoods. They were living cogs in Britain's emerging industrial machines. Pale children worked as many as eighteen hours a day in the cotton mills or coal mines, bringing home a few shillings a month to their parents, who often wasted it on cheap gin.

Newgate and other infamous prisons overflowed with debtors, murderers, children, and rapists. Frequent executions provided a form of public amusement. In short, London was a city where unchecked passions and desires ran their course. Few raised their voices in opposition.

So it is not surprising that few argued against one of the nation's most bountiful sources of wealth—the slave trade. Political alliances revolved around commitments to it. In a celebrated case in England's high court only four years earlier, slaves had been deemed "goods and chattels." They could be thrown overboard and drowned by sea captains, all within the law.

Government corruption was so widespread that few members of Parliament thought twice about the usual practice of accepting bribes for their votes. The same attitude reigned in the House of Lords. Their political influence in Parliament grew until a large voting bloc was controlled by the vested influence of the slave trade.

The horrors of the trade were remote and unseen, the cotton and sugar profits they yielded very tangible. So most consciences were not troubled about the black men and women suffering far away on remote Caribbean plantations.

Early in 1784 Wilberforce's friend William Pitt was elected prime minister at the age of twenty-four. This inspired Wilberforce to take a big political gamble. He surrendered his safe seat in Hull and stood for election in Yorkshire, the largest and most influential constituency in the country. Thanks in part to the power of his oratory, Wilberforce was elected.

Shortly afterward, Wilberforce agreed to take a tour of the continent with his mother, sister and several cousins. When he happened to run into his old schoolmaster from Hull, Isaac Milner, Wilberforce impulsively invited him to join the traveling party. That invitation was to change Wilberforce's life.

Isaac Milner was a large, jovial man whose forceful personality had contributed to the spread of Christian influence at Cambridge. Not unnaturally, then, he raised the matter of faith to his former pupil as their carriage ran over the rutted roads connecting Nice and the Swiss Alps. Wilberforce initially treated the subject flippantly, but eventually agreed to read the scriptures daily.

The summer session of Parliament forced Wilberforce to make a break in his travels. When he and Milner continued their Continental tour in the fall of 1785, Wilberforce was no longer the same frivolous young man. He returned to London in early November, feeling weary and confused. In need of counsel, he sought advice from John Newton, the former captain of a slave ship and now a committed Christian.

By the time Wilberforce knew of him, Newton was a clergyman in the Church of England, renowned for his outspokenness on spiritual matters. He counseled Wilberforce to follow Christ but not to abandon public office: "The Lord has raised you up to the good of His church and for the good of the nation," he told the younger man. Wilberforce heeded his advice.

Thus Wilberforce sat at his desk at that foggy Sunday morning in 1787 thinking about his conversion and his calling. Had God saved him only to rescue his own soul from hell? He could not accept that. If Christianity was true and meaningful, it must not only save but serve. It must bring God's compassion to the oppressed as well as oppose the oppressors.

Wilberforce dipped his pen into the inkwell. "Almighty God has set before me two great objectives," he wrote, his heart suddenly pumping with passion, "the abolition of the slave trade and the reformation of manners."

Wilberforce knew the slavery issue had to be faced head-on in Parliament. Throughout the damp fall of 1787 he worked late into the nights on his investigation of slavery, joined by others who saw in him a champion for their cause.

But in February of 1788, Wilberforce suddenly fell gravely ill. Doctors predicted he would not live more than two weeks; however, Wilberforce recovered. And though not yet well enough to return to Parliament, in March he asked Pitt to introduce the abolition issue in the House for him. On the basis of their friendship, the prime minister agreed.

Pitt moved that a resolution be passed binding the House to discuss the slave trade in the next session. The motion was passed. But then another of Wilberforce's friends, Sir William Dolben, introduced a one-year experimental bill to regulate the number of slaves that could be transported per ship.

Now sensing a threat, the West Indian bloc rose up in opposition. Tales of cruelty in the slave trade were mere fiction, they said. Besides, warned Lord Penrhyn ominously, the proposed measure would abolish the trade upon which "two thirds of the commerce of this country depends." Angered by Penrhyn's hyperbole, Pitt pushed Dolben's regulation through both houses in June of 1788.

By the time a recovered Wilberforce returned to the legislative scene, the slave traders were furious and ready to fight, shocked that politicians had the audacity to press for morally based reforms in the political arena. "Humanity is a private feeling, not a public principle to act upon," sniffed the Earl of Abingdon. Lord Melborne angrily agreed. "Things have come to a pretty pass when religion is allowed to invade public life," he thundered.

But Wilberforce and the band of abolitionists knew that a private faith that did not act in the face of oppression was no faith at all. Nonetheless, despite the passionate advocacy of Wilberforce, Pitt, and others, the House of Commons voted not to decide.

Early in 1791 Wilberforce again filled the House of Commons with his stirring eloquence. "Never, never will we desist till we . . . extinguish every trace of this bloody traffic," he declared. The opposition was equally determined, pointing to the jobs and exports that would be lost. And when the votes were cast, "commerce clinked its purse," as one observer commented, and Wilberforce was again defeated.

As the abolitionists analyzed their battle in 1792, they were painfully aware that many of their colleagues were puppets, unable or unwilling to stand against the powerful economic forces of their day. So Wilberforce and his friends decided to go to the people, believing, "it is on the general impression and feeling of the nation we must rely . . . so let the flame be fanned." The abolitionists distributed thousands of pamphlets detailing the evils of slavery, spoke at public meetings, and circulated petitions.

Later in 1792, Wilberforce brought to the House of Commons 519 petitions for the total abolition of the slave trade, signed by thousands of British subjects. But again the slavers exercised their political muscle, and the House moved that Wilberforce's motion be qualified by the word GRADUALLY. And so it was carried.

Though Wilberforce was wounded by yet another defeat, he retained a glimmer of hope. For the first time the House had actually voted for an abolition motion. That hope was soon smashed by events across the English Channel. The fall of the Bastille in 1789 had heralded the people's revolution in France. By 1792 all idealism had vanished. The September massacres loosed a tide of bloodshed as the mob and the guillotine ruled France.

Fears of a similar revolt abounded in England until any type of public agitation for reform was suspiciously labeled "Jacobinic," after the radicals who had fanned the flames of

France's Reign of Terror. Sensing the shift in the public mood, the House of Commons rejected Wilberforce's motion.

Weary with grief and frustration, Wilberforce wondered whether he should abandon his seemingly hopeless campaign. One night as he sat at his desk, flipping through his Bible, a letter fluttered from between the pages. The writer was John Wesley. Wilberforce had read it dozens of times, but never had he needed its message as much as he did now. "Unless God has raised you up . . . you will be worn out by the opposition of men and devils, but if God be for you who can be against you? Oh, be not weary of well-doing," Wesley wrote. Wilberforce's resolution returned, and for the next several years he doggedly reintroduced, each year, the motion for abolition; and each year Parliament threw it out.

And so it went—1797, 1798, 1799, 1800, 1801—the years passed with Wilberforce's motions thwarted and sabotaged by political pressures, compromise, personal illness, and the continuing war in France. During those long years of struggle, however, Wilberforce and his friends never lost sight of their equally pressing objective: "the reformation of manners," or the effort to clean up society's blights. It was the great genius of Wilberforce that he realized that attempts at political reform without, at the same time changing the hearts and minds of people, were futile. The abolitionists realized that they could never succeed in eliminating slavery without addressing the greater problems of cultural malaise and decay.

But it was a difficult concept to explain. As Garth Lean writes in his book, *God's Politician*, "It was largely in the hope of reaching Pitt and others of his friends—some of whom had strange ideas of what he really thought—that Wilberforce wrote his book." Wilberforce finished the book in 1797 and called it *A Practical View of the Prevailing Religious System of Professed Christians in the Higher and Middle Classes in this Country Contrasted with Real Christianity.*

The title itself was a scandal to the established religion, a direct challenge to the corrupted church of his day. But the book's impact can scarcely be overstated. It became an instant bestseller, and remained one for the next fifty years. Lean quotes one observer who wrote: "[the book] was read at the same moment, by all the leading persons in the nation. An electric shock could not be felt more vividly and instantaneously."

A Practical View is credited with helping spark the second Great Awakening (the first was begun by Wesley) and its influence was felt throughout Europe and rippled across the ocean to America.

In 1806 Wilberforce's decades-long efforts finally began to pay off. His friend Pitt died that year, and William Grenville, a strong abolitionist, became prime minister. Reversing the pattern of the previous twenty years, Grenville introduced Wilberforce's bill into the House of Lords first. After a bitter, month-long fight, the bill was passed on February 4, 1807.

On February 22, the second reading was held in the House of Commons. There was a sense that a moment in history had arrived. One by one, members jumped to their feet to decry the evils of the slave trade and praised the men who had worked so hard to end it. The entire House rose, cheering and applauding Wilberforce. Realizing that his long battle had come to an end, Wilberforce sat bent in his chair, his head in his hands, tears streaming down his face.

The motion carried, 283 to 16.

Later, at Wilberforce's home, the old friends exuberantly crowded into the library, recalling the weary years of battle and rejoicing for their African brothers and sisters. Wilberforce looked into the lined face of his old friend Henry Thornton. "Well, Henry," Wilberforce said with joy in his eyes, "what do we abolish next?"

In the years that followed that night of triumph, a great spiritual movement swept across England, launched in great part by Wilberforce's book. With the outlawing of the slave trade came Wilberforce's eighteen-year battle toward the total emancipation of the slaves. Social reforms swept beyond abolition to clean up child labor laws, poorhouses, prisons, to institute education and health care for the poor. Evangelism flourished, and later in the century missionary movements sent Christians fanning across the globe.

The eminent historian Will Durant once wrote that the great turning point of history was when "Christ met Caesar in the arena—and Christ won." Well might he have added that fifteen centuries later, Christ met vice and vested interests in Britain—and Christ won.

Wilberforce's success is all the more amazing when we consider that in his day, Britain was, spiritually speaking, sinking sand. The church was apostate, and the whole nation wallowed in self-indulgent decadence. But it was there that Wilberforce and his companions took their stand, clinging to biblical truth, resisting barbaric injustice, and striving to change the heart of a nation.

That's the rich heritage of Christian activism in the public square. And it's one we ought to recall whenever today's politicians accuse Christians of wanting to "impose their personal religious views" or when they claim, as the *New York Times* recently did, that conservative Christians involved in politics pose "a far greater threat to democracy than was presented by communism."

In America as in England, it was Christians who led the fight against slavery. It was Christians who enacted child labor laws, opened hospitals, and ran charitable societies to aid widows and orphans, alcoholics, and prostitutes. And it is Christians who are acting as salt and light in our culture today.

Have we really "come to a pretty pass when religion is allowed to invade public life?" as Lord Melborne complained more than two hundred years ago? Is Christian influence truly "a far greater threat to democracy than was posed by communism?" Nonsense.

William Wilberforce is a great hero of mine, because I have come to see the same thing he saw: That you can't get rid of social scourges without the reformation of manners. In Wilberforce's day, that scourge was slavery. Today, it's crime. We have to understand that we'll never clean up the crime problem without reversing the rot of our own decaying culture. And we have to recognize that a decaying church that has lost its vibrancy can never be an effective tool in reforming our own society.

William Wilberforce is a special inspiration for today's politically incorrect, "religious right activists": To stay in the public square, to keep fighting the battles despite debasement, derision, and defeat, as long as we believe that's where God wants us.

As the aging Wilberforce wrote in the conclusion to *A Practical View of Christianity*: "I must confess equally boldly that my own solid hopes for the well-being of my country depend, not so much on her navies and armies, nor on the wisdom of her rulers, nor on the spirit of her people, as on the persuasion that she still contains many who love and obey the Gospel of Christ. I believe that their prayers may yet prevail."

Wilberforce's confidence was not misplaced. May the same hope prevail for us today, and this book, as you read it, inspire you to action—to a bold affirmation of your faith, as it did for tens of thousands of Christians in Wilberforce's day.

Washington, D.C.
December 1995

Notes ‿

1. Representative Vic Fazio (D-Calif.), "Democrat Fazio Assails Religious Right in GOP," *Washington Post,* June 22, 1994, p. A-6.

# Introduction

to the First British Edition of 1797

Search the Scriptures![1]

  —John 5:39

How charming is divine philosophy!
Not harsh and crabbed, as dull fools suppose,
But musical as is Apollo's lute,
And a perpetual feast of nectar'd sweets,
Where no crude surfeit reigns.[2]

  —John Milton

IT HAS BEEN, FOR SEVERAL YEARS, THE EARNEST WISH OF the writer of the following pages to address his countrymen on the important subject of Religion; but the various duties of his public station, and a constitution incapable of much labour, have obstructed the execution of his purpose. Long has he been looking forward to some vacant season, in which he might devote his whole time and attention to this interesting service, free from the interruption of all other concerns; and he has rather wished for this opportunity of undistracted and mature reflection, from a desire that what he might send into the world might thus be rendered less undeserving of the public eye. Meanwhile life is wearing away, and he daily becomes more and more convinced, that he might wait in vain for this season of complete vacancy. He must, therefore, improve such occasional intervals of leisure as may occur to him in the course of a busy life, and throw himself on the Reader's indulgence for the pardon of such imperfections, as the opportunity of undiverted and more mature attention might have enabled him to discover and correct.

But the plea here suggested is by no means intended as an excuse for the opinions which he shall express, if they be found mistaken. Here, if he be in an error, it is however a deliberate error. He would indeed account himself unpardonable, if he were to intrude his first thoughts upon the Public on a question of such importance; and he can truly declare, that what he shall offer will be the result of much reading, observation, and inquiry, and of long, serious, and repeated consideration.

It is not improbable that he may be accused of deviating from his proper line, and of impertinently interfering in the concerns of a profession to which he does not belong. If it were necessary, however, to defend himself against this charge, he might shelter himself under the authority of many most respectable examples. But surely to such an accusation it may be sufficient to reply, that it is the true duty of every man to promote the happiness of his fellow-creatures to the utmost of his power; and that he who thinks he sees many around him, whom he esteems and loves, laboring under a fatal error, must have a cold heart, or a most confined notion of benevolence, if he could refrain from endeavouring to set them right, lest in so doing he should be accused of stepping out of his proper walk, and expose himself on that ground to the imputation of officiousness.

But he might also allege as a full justification, not only that Religion is the business of every one, but that its advancement or decline in any country is so intimately connected with the temporal interests of society, as to render it the peculiar concern of a political man; and that what he may presume to offer on the subject of Religion may perhaps be perused with less jealousy and more candour, from the very circumstance of its having been written by a Layman, which must at least exclude the idea (an idea sometimes illiberally suggested to take off the effect of the works of Ecclesiastics) that it is prompted by motives of self-interest, or of professional prejudice.

But if the writer's apology may not be found in the work itself, and in his avowed motive for undertaking it, he would in vain endeavour to satisfy his readers by any excuses he might assign; therefore, without farther preamble, he will proceed to the statement and execution of his purpose.

The main object which he has in view is, not to convince the Sceptic [one who doubts the truth of religious doctrines], or to answer the arguments of persons who avowedly oppose the fundamental doctrines of our Religion; but to point out the scanty and erroneous system of the bulk of those who belong to the class of orthodox Christians, and to contrast their defective scheme with a representation of what the author apprehends to be real Christianity. Often has it filled him with deep concern, to observe in this description of persons, scarcely any distinct knowledge of the real nature and principles of the religion which they profess. The subject is of infinite importance; let it not be driven out of our minds by the bustle or dissipations of life. This present scene, and all its cares and all its gaieties, will soon be rolled away, and "we must stand before the judgment seat of Christ" [Romans 14:10]. This aweful consideration will prompt the writer to express himself with greater freedom than he should otherwise be disposed to use. This consideration he trusts, also, will justify his frankness, and will secure him a serious and patient perusal. But it would be trespassing on the indulgence of the reader to detain him with introductory remarks. Let it only be farther premised, that if what shall be stated should to any appear needlessly austere and rigid, the writer must lay in his claim not to be condemned without a fair inquiry whether or not his statements accord with the language of the sacred writings. To that test he refers with confidence; and it must be conceded by those who admit the authority of Scripture (such only he is addressing) that from the decision of the word of God there can be no appeal.

Notes ↵

1. The force of the Greek text for John 5:39 is such that this phrase at the beginning of the verse can be rendered as an imperative command. Wilberforce knew this, for he was fluent in the classical languages (Greek and Latin) and often read the New Testament in Greek. This scripture reference and the quote from John Milton that follows it originally appeared on the title page of the second British edition of *A Practical View of Christianity*.

2. See John Carey and Alastair Fowler, eds., *The Poems of John Milton* (London: Longmans, Green, & Co. Ltd., 1968), p. 200. Wilberforce has cited lines 475–479 of Milton's "Comus. A Masque Presented at Ludlow Castle," written in 1634. The edition that Wilber-

force cited appears to be slightly different from the more authoritative text used by Carey and Fowler. The text they have used reads:

> How charming is divine philosophy!
> Not harsh, and crabbed as dull fools suppose,
> But musical as is Apollo's lute,
> And a perpetual feast of nectared sweets,
> Where no crude surfeit reigns.

Chapter One

Inadequate Conceptions of the
Importance of Christianity

Popular Notions—Scripture Account—
Ignorance in This Case Criminal—
Two False Maxims Exposed

BEFORE WE PROCEED TO THE CONSIDERATION OF ANY
particular defects in the religious system of the bulk of professed Christians, it may be proper to point out the very
inadequate conception which they entertain of the importance
of Christianity in general, of its peculiar nature, and superior
excellence. If we listen to their conversation, virtue is praised,
and vice is censured; piety is perhaps applauded, and profaneness condemned. So far all is well. But let any one, who would
not be deceived by these "barren generalities" examine a little
more closely, and he will find, that not to Christianity in
particular, but at best to Religion in general, perhaps to mere
Morality, their homage is intended to be paid. With Christianity, as distinct from these, they are little acquainted; their views
of it have been so cursory and superficial, that far from discerning its characteristic essence, they have little more than perceived those exterior circumstances which distinguish it from
other forms of religion. There are some few facts, and perhaps
some leading doctrines and principles, of which they cannot be
wholly ignorant; but of the consequences, and relations, and
practical uses of these they have few ideas, or none at all.

Does this seem too strong? View their plan of life and
their ordinary conduct; and not to speak at present of their

1

general inattention to things of a religious nature, let us ask wherein we can discern the points of discrimination between them and professed unbelievers. In an age wherein it is confessed and lamented that infidelity abounds, do we observe in them any remarkable care to instruct their children in the principles of the faith which they profess, and to furnish them with arguments for the defence of it? They would blush, on their child's coming out into the world, to think him defective in any branch of that knowledge, or of those accomplishments which belong to his station in life, and accordingly these are cultivated with becoming assiduity. But he is left to collect his religion as he may; the study of Christianity has formed no part of his education, and his attachment to it (where any attachment to it exists at all) is, too often, not the preference of sober reason, but merely the result of early prejudice and groundless prepossession. He was born in a Christian country, of course he is a Christian; his father was the member of the church of England, so is he. When such is the hereditary religion handed down from generation to generation, it cannot surprise us to observe young men of sense and spirit beginning to doubt altogether of the truth of the system in which they have been brought up, and ready to abandon a station which they are unable to defend. Knowing Christianity chiefly in the difficulties which it contains, and in the impossibilities which are falsely imputed to it, they fall perhaps into the company of infidels; and, as might be expected, they are shaken by frivolous objections and profane cavils [petty objections], which, had they been grounded and bottomed in reason and argument, would have passed them "as the idle wind," and scarcely have seemed worthy of serious notice.

Let us beware before it be too late. No one can say into what discredit Christianity might hereby grow, at a time when the free and unrestrained intercourse subsisting amongst the several ranks and classes of society, so much favours the general diffusion of the sentiments of the higher orders. To a similar ignorance is perhaps in no small degree to be ascribed the success with which Christianity has been attacked of late years in a neighboring country [France]. Had she not been wholly unarmed for the contest, however she might have been forced from her untenable posts, and compelled to disembarass herself from her load of incumbrances, she never could have been driven altogether out of the field by her puny assailants, with all their cavils [petty objections], and gibes, and sarcasms; for in these consisted the main strength of their petty artillery. Let us beware, lest we also suffer from a like cause; nor let it be our crime and our reproach, that in schools, perhaps even in Colleges, Christianity is almost if not altogether neglected.

It cannot be expected, that they who are so little attentive to this great object in the education of their children, should be more so in other parts of their conduct, where less strongly stimulated by affection, and less obviously loaded with responsibility. They are of course therefore, little regardful of the state of Christianity in their own country; and still more indifferent about communicating the light of divine truth to the nations which "still sit in darkness" [Luke 1:79].

But Religion, it may be replied, is not noisy and ostentatious; it is modest and private in its nature; it resides in a man's own bosom, and shuns the observation of the multitude. Be it so.

From this transient and distant view then, which we have been taking of these unassuming Christians, let us approach a little nearer, and listen to the unreserved conversation of their confidential hours. Here, if any where, the interior of the heart is laid open, and we may ascertain the true principles of their regards and aversions; the scale by which they measure the good and evil of life. Here, however, you will discover few or no traces of Christianity. She scarcely finds herself a place amidst the many objects of their hopes, and fears, and joys and sorrows. Grateful, perhaps (as well indeed they may be grateful) for health, and talents, and affluence, and other blessings belonging to their persons and conditions in life, they scarcely reckon in the number this grand distinguishing mark of the bounty of Providence [God's care and protection]; or if they mention it at all, it is noticed coldly and formally, like one of those obsolete claims to which, though but of small account in the estimate of our wealth or power, we think it as well to put in our title from considerations of family decorum or of national usage.

But what more than all the rest establishes the point in question: let their conversation take a graver turn: here at length their religion, modest and retired as it is, must be expected to disclose itself; here however you will look in vain for the religion of Jesus. Their standard of right and wrong is not the standard of the gospel: they approve and condemn by a different rule; they advance principles and maintain opinions altogether opposite to the genius and character of Christianity.

You would fancy yourself rather amongst the followers of the old philosophy; nor is it easy to guess how any one could satisfy himself to the contrary, unless, by mentioning the name of some acknowledged heretic, he should afford them an occasion of demonstrating their zeal for the religion of their country.

The truth is, their opinions on these subjects are not formed from the perusal of the word of God. The Bible lies on the shelf unopened; and they would be wholly ignorant of its contents, except for what they hear occasionally at church, or for the faint traces which their memories may still retain of the lessons of their earliest infancy.

How different, nay, in many respects, how contradictory, would be the two systems of mere morals, of which the one should be formed from the commonly received maxims of the Christian world, and the other from the study of the holy Scriptures! It would be curious to remark in any one, who had hitherto satisfied himself with the former, the astonishment which would be excited on his first introduction to the latter. We are not left here to bare conjecture. This was, in fact, the effect produced on the mind of a late ingenious writer,[1] of whose little work, though it bear perhaps some marks of his customary love of paradox, we must at least confess, that it exposes, in a strong point of view, the *poverty* of that superficial religion which has been above condemned; and that it every where displays that happy perspicuity [clarity of expression] and grace, which so eminently characterize all the compositions of its author. But after this willing tribute of commendation, we are reluctantly compelled to remark, that the work in question discredits the cause which it was meant to serve, by many crude and extravagant positions; from which no one can be secure who forms a hasty judgement of a deep and comprehensive subject, the several bearings and relations of which have been imperfectly surveyed; and above all, it must be lamented, that it treats the great question which it professes to discuss, rather as a matter of mere speculation, than as one wherein our everlasting interests are involved. Surely the writer's object should have been, to convince his readers of their guilt still more than of their ignorance, and to leave them impressed rather with a sense of their danger than of their folly.

It were almost a waste of time to multiply arguments in order to prove how criminal the voluntary ignorance, of which we have been speaking, must appear in the sight of God. It must be confessed by all who believe that we are accountable creatures, and to such only the writer is addressing himself, that we shall have to answer hereafter to the Almighty for all the means and occasions we have here enjoyed of improving ourselves, or of promoting the happiness of others. And if, when summoned to give an account of our stewardship, we shall be called upon to answer for the use which we have made of our bodily organs, and of the means of relieving the wants and necessities of our fellow-creatures; how much more for the exercise of the nobler and more exalted faculties of our nature, of invention, and judgment, and memory, and for our employment of all the instruments and opportunities of diligent application, and serious reflection, and honest decision. And to what subject might we in all reason be expected to apply more earnestly, than to that wherein our eternal interests are at issue? When God has of his goodness vouchsafed [deigned] to grant us such abundant means of instruction in that which we are most concerned to know, how great must be the guilt, and how awful the punishment of voluntary ignorance!

And why, it may be asked, are we in this pursuit alone to expect knowledge without inquiry, and success without endeavour? The whole analogy of nature inculcates on us a different lesson, and our own judgments in matters of temporal interest and worldly policy confirm the truth of her suggestions. Bountiful as is the hand of Providence, its gifts are not so bestowed as to seduce us into indolence, but to rouse us to exertion; and no one expects to attain to the height of learning, or arts, or power, or wealth, or military glory, without vigorous resolution, and strenuous diligence, and steady perseverance. Yet we expect to be Christians without labour, study, or inquiry. This is the more preposterous, because Christianity, being a revelation from God, and not the invention of man, discovering to us new relations, with their correspondent duties; containing also doctrines, and motives, and practical principles, and rules, peculiar to itself, and almost as new in their nature as supreme in their excellence, we cannot reasonably expect to become proficients in it by the accidental intercourses of life, as one might learn insensibly the maxims of worldly policy, or a scheme of mere morals.

The diligent perusal of the Holy Scriptures would discover to us our past ignorance. We should cease to be deceived by superficial appearances, and to confound the Gospel of Christ with the systems of philosophers; we should become impressed with that weighty truth, so much forgotten, and never to be too strongly insisted on, that Christianity calls on us, as we value our immortal souls, not merely in *general,* to be *religious* and *moral,* but *specially* to believe the doctrines, and imbibe the principles, and practice the precepts of Christ. It might be to run into too great length to confirm this position beyond dispute by express quotations from Scripture. And (not to anticipate what belongs more properly to a subsequent part of the work) it may be sufficient here to remark in general, that Christianity is always represented in Scripture as the grand, the unparalleled instance of God's bounty to mankind. It was graciously held forth in the original promise to our first parents; it was predicted by a long continued series of prophets; the subject of their prayers, inquiries, and longing expectations. In a world which opposed and persecuted them, it was their source of peace, and hope, and consolation. At length it approached—the Desire of all Nations—The long expected Star announced its presence—A multitude of the heavenly host hailed its introduction, and proclaimed its character; "Glory to God in the highest, on earth peace, good will towards men" [Luke 2:4]. It is every where represented in Scripture by such figures as may most deeply impress on us a sense of its value; it is spoken of as light from darkness, as release from prison, as deliverance from captivity, as life from death. "Lord, now lettest thou thy servant depart in peace, for mine eyes have seen thy salvation" [Luke 2:29–30], was the exclamation with which it was welcomed by the pious Simeon; and it was universally received and professed among the early converts with thankfulness and joy. At one time, the communication of it is promised as a reward, at another, the loss of it is threatened as a punishment. And, short as is the form of prayer taught us by our blessed Saviour, the more general extension of the kingdom of Christ constitutes one of its leading petitions [Matthew 6:9–13].

With what exalted conceptions of the importance of Christianity ought we to be filled by such descriptions as these? Yet, in vain have we, "line upon line, and precept upon precept" [Isaiah 28:13].—Thus predicted, thus prayed and longed for, thus announced and characterized and rejoiced in, this heavenly treasure poured into our lap in rich abundance we scarce accept. We turn from it coldly, or at best profess it negligently, as a thing of no account or estimation. But a due sense of its value would be assuredly impressed on us by the diligent study of the Word of God, that blessed repository of divine truth and consolation. Thence it is that we are to learn our obligations and our duty, what we are to believe and what to practice. And, surely, one would think it could not be required to press men to the perusal of the sacred volume. Reason dictates, Revelation commands; "Faith comes by hearing, and hearing by the word of God" [Romans 10:17]—"Search the Scriptures" [John 5:39]—"Be ready to give to every one a reason of the hope that is in you" [1 Peter 3:15]. Such are the declarations and injunctions of the inspired writers; injunctions confirmed by commendations of those who obey the admonition. Yet, is it not undeniable that with the Bible in our houses, we are ignorant of its contents; and that hence, in a great measure, it arises, that the bulk of the Christian world know so little, and mistake so greatly, in what regards the religion which they profess?

This is not the place for enquiring at large, whence it is that those who assent to the position, that the Bible is the word of God, and who profess to rest their hopes on the Christian basis, contentedly acquiesce in a state of such lamentable ignorance. But it may not be improper here to touch on two kindred opinions, from which, in the minds of the more thoughtful and serious, this acquiescence appears to derive much secret support. The one is, that it signifies little what a man believes; *look to his practice.* The other (of the same family) *that sincerity is all in all.* Let a man's opinions and conduct be what they may, yet, provided he be sincerely convinced that they are right, however the exigencies of civil society may require him to be dealt with amongst men, in the sight of God he cannot be criminal.

It would detain us too long to set forth the various merits of these favorite positions, of which it is surely not the smallest excellence, that they are of unbounded application, comprehending within their capacious limits all the errors which have been believed, and many of the most desperate crimes which have been perpetrated among men. The former of them is founded altogether on that grossly fallacious assumption, that a man's opinions will not influence his practice. The latter proceeds on this groundless supposition, that the Supreme Being has not afforded us sufficient means for discriminating truth from falsehood, right from wrong: and it implies, that be a man's opinions or conduct ever so wild and extravagant, we are to presume, that they are as much the result of impartial inquiry and honest conviction; as if his sentiments and actions had been strictly conformable to the rules of reason and sobriety. Never indeed was there a principle more general in its use, more sovereign in its potency. How does its beautiful simplicity also, and compendious brevity, give it rank before the laborious subtleties of Bellarmin![2] Clement,[3] and Ravaillac,[4] and other worthies of a similar stamp, from whose purity of intention the world has hitherto withheld its due tribute of applause, would here have found a ready plea, and their injured innocence shall now at length receive its full though tardy vindication. "These, however," it may be replied, "are excepted cases." Certainly they are cases of which any one who maintains the opinion in question would be glad to disencumber himself; because they clearly expose the unsoundness of his principle. But it will be incumbent on such a one, first to explain with precision why they are to be exempted from its operation, and this he will find an impossible task; for sincerity, in its popular sense, so shamefully is the term misapplied, can be made the criterion of guilt and innocence on no grounds which will not equally serve to justify the assassins who have been instanced. The conclusion cannot be eluded; no man was ever more fully persuaded of the innocence of any action, than these men were, that the horrid deed they were about to perpetrate was not lawful merely, but highly meritorious. Thus Clement and Ravaillac being unquestionably sincere, they were therefore indubitably innocent. Nay, the absurdity of this principle might be shewn to be even greater than what has yet been stated. It would not be going too far to assert, that whilst it scorns the defence of petty villains, of those who still retain the sense of good and evil, it holds forth, like some well frequented sanctuary, a secure asylum to those more finished criminals, who, from long habits of wickedness, are lost alike to the perception as to the practice of virtue; and that it selects a seared conscience and a heart become callous to all moral distinctions as the special objects of its care. Nor is it only in profane history that instances like these are to be found, of persons committing the greatest crimes with a sincere conviction of the rectitude of their conduct. Scripture will afford us parallels; and it was surely to guard us against the very error which we have been now exposing, that our blessed Saviour forewarned his disciples: "The time cometh, that whosoever killeth you will think that he doeth God service" [John 16:2].

A principle like this must then be abandoned, and the advocates for sincerity must be compelled to restore this abused term to its genuine signification, and to acknowledge that it must imply honesty of mind, and the faithful use of the means of knowledge and of improvement, the desire of being instructed, humble inquiry, impartial consideration, and unprejudiced judgment. It is to these we would earnestly call you; to these (ever to be accompanied with fervent prayers for the divine blessing) Scripture every where holds forth the most animating promises. "Ask, and ye shall receive; seek, and ye shall find; knock, and it shall be opened unto you" [Matthew 7:7]. "Ho! every one that thirsteth, come ye to the waters" [Isaiah 55:1]; such are the comfortable assurances, such the gracious encouragements to the truly sincere inquirer. How deep will be our guilt, if we slight all these benevolent offers. "How many prophets and kings have desired to hear the things that we hear, and have not heard them" [Matthew 13:17]. Great indeed are our opportunities, great also is our responsibility. Let us awaken to a true sense of our situation. We have every consideration to alarm our fears, or to animate our industry. How soon may the brightness of our meridian sun be darkened! Or, should the long-suffering of God still continue to us the mercies which we so much abuse, it will only aggravate our crime, and in the end enhance our punishment. The time of reckoning will at length arrive. And when finally summoned to the bar [the railing in a law court behind which persons on trial are stationed] of God, to give an account of our stewardship, what plea can we have to urge in our defence, if we remain willingly, and obstinately ignorant of the way which leads to life, with such transcendent means of knowing it, and such urgent motives to its pursuit?

Notes 〰

1. Wilberforce writes, "It is almost superfluous to name Mr. Soame Jenyns." Jenyns (1704–87) was a writer of verse and prose. In his younger years he was regarded as a religious skeptic, but in later life he embraced orthodox Christianity. In 1776, he published what was perhaps his most famous work, *View of the Internal Evidence of the Christian Religion.*

2. Cardinal Robert Bellarmine (1542–1621) was a scholar, theologian, and controversialist during the period known as the Counter-Reformation. He was an opposer of Protestants and he sought to refute them by the use of reason and argument, as opposed to dogmatic assertion and abuse.

3. Pope Clement VIII (Ippolito Aldobrandini, 1536–1605) pursued ecclesiastical policies of reform, sought to convert James I of England to Roman Catholicism, undertook a revision of the service books, and issued new editions of the Vulgate, the Missal, the Breviary, the Caeremoniale Episcoporum, and the Pontifical.

4. Wilberforce is referring to Franciois Ravaillac (1578–1610). Lawyer, teacher, and assassin of Henry IV of France, Ravaillac was regarded as a visionary mystic. He sought and was refused admission to the Society of Jesus (the Jesuits). It is commonly thought that this disappointment in life fostered his fanatical temperament. In addition, it is thought that he assassinated the king because of rumors that Henry intended to make war on the pope.

$\curvearrowright$Chapter Two

Corruption of Human Nature

SECTION ONE $\curvearrowleft$

*Inadequate Conceptions of the
Corruption of Human Nature*

AFTER CONSIDERING THE DEFECTIVE NOTIONS OF THE importance of Christianity *in general,* which prevail among the higher orders of the Christian world, the particular misconceptions which first come under our notice respect the corruption and weakness of human nature. This is a topic on which it is possible that many of those, into whose hands the present work shall fall, may not have bestowed much attention. If the case be so, it may be requisite to intreat them to lend a patient and serious ear. The subject is of the deepest import. We should not go too far if we were to assert that it lies at the very root of all true Religion, and still more, it is eminently the basis and ground-work of Christianity.

So far as the writer has had an opportunity of remarking, the generality of professed Christians among the higher classes, either altogether overlook or deny, or at least greatly extenuate the corruption and weakness here in question. They acknowledge indeed that there is, and ever has been in the world, a great portion of vice and wickedness; that mankind have been ever prone to sensuality and selfishness, in disobedience to the more refined and liberal principles of their nature; that in all ages and countries, in public and in private life, innumerable instances have been afforded of oppression, of rapacity, of cruelty, of fraud, of envy, and of malice. They own that it is too often in vain that you inform the understanding, and convince the judgment. They admit that you do not thereby reform the hearts of men. Though they *know* their duty, they will not practice it; no not even when you have forced them to acknowledge that the path of virtue is that also of real interest and of solid enjoyment.

These facts are certain; they cannot be disputed; and they are at the same time so obvious, that one would have thought that the celebrated apophthegm [a pithy saying] of the Grecian sage, "the majority are wicked," would scarcely have established his claim to intellectual superiority.

But though these effects of human depravity are every where acknowledged and lamented, we must not expect to find them traced to their true origin.

> Causa latet, vis est notissima [fontis].
>
> [The cause is hidden, but the enfeebling
> power of the fountain is well known.
>
> —Ovid][1]

Prepare yourself to hear rather of frailty and infirmity, of petty transgressions, of occasional failings, of sudden surprisals, and of such other qualifying terms as may serve to keep out of view the true source of the evil, and, without shocking the understanding, may administer consolation to the pride of human nature. The bulk of professed Christians are used to speak of man as of a being, who naturally pure, and inclined to all virtue, is sometimes, almost involuntarily, drawn out of the right course, or is overpowered by the violence of temptation. Vice with them is rather an accidental and temporary, than a constitutional and habitual distemper; a noxious plant, which, though found to live and even to thrive in the human mind, is not the natural growth and production of the soil.

Far different is the humiliating language of Christianity. From it we learn that man is an apostate creature, fallen from his high original, degraded in his nature, and depraved in his faculties; indisposed to good, and disposed to evil; prone to vice, it is natural and easy to him; disinclined to virtue, it is difficult and laborious; that he is tainted with sin, not slightly and superficially, but radically and to the very core. These are truths which, however mortifying to our pride, one would think (if this very corruption itself did not warp the judgment) none would be hardy enough to attempt to controvert. I know not any thing which brings them home so forcibly to my own feelings, as the consideration of what still remains to us of our primitive dignity, when contrasted with our present state of moral degradation.

> Into what depth thou seest,
> From what height fallen!

Examine first with attention the natural powers and faculties of man; invention, reason, judgment, memory; a mind "of large discourse," "looking before and after," reviewing the past, and thence determining for the present, and anticipating the future; discerning, collecting, combining, comparing: capable not merely of apprehending but of admiring the beauty of moral excellence: with fear and hope to warn and animate; with joy and sorrow to solace and soften; with love to attach, with sympathy to harmonize, with courage to attempt, with patience to endure, and with the power of conscience, that faithful monitor within the breast, to enforce the conclusions of reason, and direct and regulate the passions of the soul. Truly we must pronounce him "majestic though in ruin,"[2] "Happy, happy world," would be the exclamation of the inhabitant of some other planet, on being told of a globe like ours, peopled with such creatures as these,[3] and abounding with situations and occasions to call forth the multiplied excellences of their nature. "Happy, happy world," with what delight must your great Creator and Governor witness your conduct, and what large and merited rewards await you when your term of probation shall have expired."

> I, bone, quo virtus tua te vocat, i pede fausto,
> Grandia laturus meritorum proemia.

> [Go, good man, whither your courage calls you,
> go on auspicious foot.
> You will carry off great rewards of merits—
> what are you waiting for?

> —Horace]

But we have indulged too long in these delightful speculations; a sad reverse presents itself on our survey of the *actual* state of man, when, from viewing his *natural* powers, we follow him into *practice*, and see the uses to which he applies them. Take in the whole of the prospect, view him in every age, and climate, and nation, in every condition and period of society. Where now do you discover the characters of his exalted nature? "How is the gold become dim, and the fine gold changed?" How is his reason clouded, his affections perverted, his conscience stupefied! How do anger, and envy, and hatred, and revenge, spring up in his wretched bosom! How is he a slave to the meanest of his appetites! What fatal propensities does he discover to evil! What inaptitude to good!

Dwell awhile on the state of the ancient world; not merely on that benighted part of it where all lay buried in brutish ignorance and barbarism, but on the seats of civilized and polished nations, on the empire of taste, and learning and philosophy: yet in these chosen regions, with whatever luster the sun of science poured forth its rays, the moral darkness was so thick "that it might be felt" [Exodus 10:21]. Behold their sottish [drunken] idolatries, their absurd superstitions, their want of natural affection, their brutal excesses, their unfeeling oppression, their savage cruelty! Look not to the illiterate and the vulgar, but to the learned and refined. Form not your ideas from the conduct of the less restrained and more licentious; you will turn away with disgust and shame from the allowed and familiar habits of the decent and the moral. St. Paul best states the facts, and furnishes the explanation; "Because they did not like to retain God in their knowledge, he gave them over to a reprobate mind" [Romans 1:28].[4]

Now direct your view to another quarter, to the inhabitants of a new hemisphere, where the baneful practices and contagious example of the old world had never traveled. Surely, among these children of nature we may expect to find those virtuous tendencies for which we have hitherto looked in vain. Alas! our search will still be fruitless! They are represented by the historian of America,[5] (whose account is more favourable than those of some other great authorities) as being a compound of pride, and indolence, and selfishness, and cunning, and cruelty;[6] full of a revenge which nothing could satiate, of a ferocity which nothing could soften; strangers to the most amiable sensibilities of nature.[7] They appeared incapable of conjugal affection, or parental fondness, or filial reverence, or social attachments; uniting too with their state of barbarism, many of the vices and weaknesses of polished society. Their horrid treatment of captives taken in war, on whose bodies they feasted, after putting them to death by the most cruel tortures, is so well known, that we may spare the disgusting recital. No commendable qualities relieve this gloomy picture, except fortitude, and perseverance, and zeal for the welfare of their little community, if this last quality, exercised and directed as it was, can be thought deserving of commendation.

But you give up the heathen nations as indefensible, and wish rather to form your estimate of man from a view of countries which have been blessed with the light of revelation.—True it is, and with joy let us record the concession, Christianity has set the general tone of morals much higher than it was ever found in the Pagan world. She has every where improved the character and multiplied the comforts of society, particularly to the poor and the weak, whom from the beginning she professed to take under her special patronage. Like her divine Author, "who sends his rain on the evil and on the good" [Matthew 5:45], she showers down unnumbered blessings on thousands who profit from her bounty, while they forget or deny her power, and set at nought her authority. Yet, even in this more favoured situation we shall discover too many lamentable proofs of the depravity of man. Nay, this depravity will now become even more apparent and less deniable. For what bars does it not now overleap? Over what motives is it not now victorious? Consider well the superior light and advantages which we enjoy, and then appreciate the superior obligations which are imposed on us. Consider in how many cases our evil propensities are now kept from breaking forth, by the superior restraints under which vice is laid among us by positive laws, and by the amended standard of public opinion; And we may be assisted in conjecturing what force is to be assigned to these motives, by the dreadful proofs which have been lately exhibited in a neighboring country [France], that when their influence is withdrawn, the most atrocious crimes can be perpetrated shamelessly and in the face of day. Consider then the superior excellence of our moral code, the new principles of obedience furnished by the gospel, and above all, the awful sanction which the doctrines and precepts of Christianity derive from the clear discovery of a future state of retribution, and from the annunciation of that tremendous day "when we shall stand before the judgment seat of Christ" [Romans 14:10]. Yet, in spite of all our knowledge, thus enforced and pressed home by this solemn notice, how little has been our progress in virtue? It has been by no means such as to prevent the adoption, in our days, of various maxims of antiquity, which, when well considered, too clearly establish the depravity of man. It may not be amiss to adduce a few instances in proof of this assertion. It is now no less acknowledged than heretofore, that prosperity hardens the heart: that unlimited power is ever abused, instead of being rendered the instrument of diffusing happiness: that habits of vice grow up of themselves, whilst those of virtue, if to be obtained at all, are of slow and difficult formation: that they who draw the finest pictures of virtue, and seem most enamoured of her charms, are often the least under her influence, and by the merest trifles are drawn aside from that line of conduct, which they most strongly and seriously recommend to others; that all this takes place, though most of the pleasures of vice are to be found with less alloy in the paths of virtue; whilst at the same time, these paths afford superior and more exquisite delights, peculiar to themselves, and are free from the diseases and bitter remorse, at the price of which vicious gratifications are so often purchased.

It may suffice to touch very slightly on some other arguments, which it would hardly be right to leave altogether unnoticed: one of these (the justice of which, however denied by superficial moralists, parents of strict principles can abundantly testify) may be drawn from the perverse and froward dispositions perceivable in children, which it is the business and sometimes the ineffectual attempt of education to reform. Another may be drawn from the various deceits we are apt to practice on ourselves, to which no one can be a stranger, who has ever contemplated the operations of his own mind with serious attention. To the influence of this species of corruption it has been in a great degree owing, that Christianity itself has been too often disgraced. It has been turned into an engine of cruelty, and, amidst the bitterness of persecution, every trace has disappeared of the mild and beneficent spirit of the religion of Jesus. In what degree must the taint have worked itself into the frame, and have corrupted the habit, when the most wholesome nutriment can be thus converted into the deadliest poison! Wishing always to argue from such premises as are not only really sound, but from such as cannot even be questioned by those to whom this work is addressed, little was said in representing the deplorable state of the Heathen world, respecting their defective and unworthy conceptions in what regards the Supreme Being, who even then however "left not himself without witness, but gave them rain and fruitful seasons, filling their hearts with food and gladness" [Acts 14:17].

But surely to any who call themselves Christians, it may be justly urged as an astonishing instance of human depravity, that we ourselves, who enjoy the full light of Revelation; to whom God has vouchsafed [condescended to give] such clear discoveries of what it concerns us to know of his being and attributes; who profess to believe "that in him we live, and move, and have our being" [Acts 17:28]; that to him we owe all the comforts we here enjoy, and the offer of eternal Glory purchased for us by the atoning blood of his own Son; ("thanks be to God for his unspeakable gift" [2 Corinthians 9:15]) that we, thus loaded with mercies, should every one of us be continually chargeable with forgetting his authority, and being ungrateful for his benefits; with slighting his gracious proposals, or receiving them at best but heartlessly and coldly.

But to put the question concerning the natural depravity of man to the severest test: take the best of the human species, the watchful diligent self-denying Christian, and let *him* decide the controversy; and that, not by inferences drawn from the practices of a thoughtless and dissolute world, but by an appeal to his personal experience. Go with him into his closet, ask him *his* opinion of the corruption of the heart, and he will tell you that he is deeply sensible of its power, for that he has learned it from much self-observation and long acquaintance with the workings of his own mind. He will tell you, that every day strengthens this conviction; yea, that hourly he sees fresh reason to deplore his want of simplicity in intention, his infirmity of purpose, his low views, his selfish, unworthy desires, his backwardness to set about his duty, his languor and coldness in performing it: that he finds himself obliged continually to confess, that he feels within him two opposite principles, and that "he cannot do the things that he would" [cf. Romans 7:19]. He cries out in the language of the excellent Hooker, "The little fruit which we have in holiness, it is, God knoweth, corrupt and unsound: we put no confidence at all in it, we challenge nothing in the world for it, we dare not call God to reckoning, as if we had him in our debt books; our continual suit to him is, and must be, to bear with our infirmities, and pardon our offences."[8]

Such is the moral history, such the condition of man. The figures of the piece may vary, and the colouring is sometimes of a darker, sometimes lighter hue; but the principles of the composition, the grand outlines, are every where the same. Wherever we direct our view, we discover the melancholy proofs of our depravity; whether we look to ancient or modern times, to barbarous or civilized nations, to the conduct of the world around us, or to the monitor within the breast; whether we read, or hear, or act, or think, or feel, the same humiliating lesson is forced upon us,

> Jupiter est quodcunque vides, quodcunque
> moveris.
>
> [All that we see is God; every motion we make is
> God also.
>
> —Lucan][9]

Now when we look back to the picture which was formerly drawn of the *natural powers* of man, and compare this his *actual* state with that for which, from a consideration of those powers, he seems to have been originally calculated, how are we to account for the astonishing contrast! will frailty or infirmity, or occasional lapses, or sudden surprisals, or any such qualifying terms, convey an adequate idea of the nature, or point out the cause of the distemper? How on any principles of common reasoning, can we account for it, but by conceiving that man, since he came out of the hands of his Creator, has contracted a taint, and that the venom of this subtle poison has been communicated throughout the race of Adam, every where exhibiting incontestable marks of its fatal malignity [a desire to harm others]? Hence it has arisen, that the appetites deriving new strength, and the powers of reason and conscience being weakened, the latter have feebly and impotently pleaded against those forbidden indulgences which the former have solicited. Sensual gratifications and illicit affections have debased our nobler powers, and indisposed our hearts to the discovery of God, and to the consideration of his perfections; to a constant willing submission to his authority, and obedience to his laws. By a repetition of vicious acts, evil habits have been formed within us, and have rivetted the fetters of sin. Left to the consequences of our own folly, the understanding has grown darker, and the heart more obdurate: reason has at length altogether betrayed her trust, and even conscience herself has aided the delusion, till, instead of deploring our miserable slavery, we have too often hugged, and even gloried in our chains.
    Such is the general account of the progress of vice, where it is suffered to attain to its full growth in the human

heart. The circumstances of individuals will be found indeed to differ; the servitude of some, if it may be allowed us to continue a figure so exactly descriptive of the case, is more rigorous than that of others, their bonds more galling, their degradation more complete. Some too (it will be remembered that we are speaking of the natural state of man, without taking Christianity into question) have for a while appeared almost to have escaped from their confinement; but none are altogether free; all without exception, in a greater of less degree, bear about them, more visible or more concealed, the ignominious marks of their captivity.

Such on a full and fair investigation must be confessed to be the state of facts; and how can this he accounted for on any other supposition, than that of some original taint, some radical principle of corruption? All other solutions are unsatisfactory, whilst the potent cause which has been assigned does abundantly, and can alone sufficiently account for the effect. Thus then it appears, that the corruption of human nature is proved by the same mode of reasoning, as has been deemed conclusive in establishing the existence, and ascertaining the laws of the principle of gravitation. That the doctrine rests on the same solid basis as the sublime philosophy of Newton:[10] that it is not a mere speculation, and therefore an uncertain, though perhaps an ingenious theory, but the sure result of a large and actual experiment; deduced from incontestable facts, and still more fully approving its truth by harmonizing with parts and accounting for the various phaenomena, jarring otherwise and inexplicable, of the great system of the universe.

Revelation, however, here comes in, and sustains the fallible conjectures of our unassisted reason. The Holy Scriptures speak of us as fallen creatures; in almost every page we shall find something that is calculated to abate the loftiness and silence the pretensions of man. "The imagination of man's heart is evil, from his youth" [Genesis 8:21]. "What is man, that he should be clean? and he which is born of a woman, that he should be righteous?" [Job 15:14]. "How much more abominable and filthy is man, which drinketh iniquity like water?" [Job 15:16]. "The LORD looked down from heaven upon the children of men, to see if there were any that did understand, and seek God. They are all gone aside; they are altogether become filthy: there is none that doeth good, no not one" [Psalm 14:2–3]. "Who can say, I have made my heart clean, I am pure from my sin?" [Proverbs 20:9]. "The *heart* is deceitful above all things, and desperately wicked, who can know it?" [Jeremiah 17:9]. "Behold, I was shapen in wickedness, and in sin hath my mother conceived me" [Psalm 51:5]. "We were by nature the children of wrath, even as others, fulfilling the desire of the flesh and of the mind" [Ephesians 2:3]. "O wretched man that I am, who shall deliver me from the body of this death!" [Romans 7:24].—Passages might be multiplied upon passages, which speak the same language, and these again might be illustrated and confirmed at large by various other considerations, drawn from the same sacred source; such as those which represent a thorough change, a renovation of our nature, as being necessary to our becoming true Christians; or as those also which are suggested by observing that holy men refer their good dispositions and affections to the immediate agency of the Supreme Being.

SECTION TWO ᣘ

Evil Spirit—Natural State of Man

But in addition to all which has been yet stated, the word of God instructs us that we have to contend not only with our own natural depravity, but with the power of darkness, the Evil Spirit, who rules in the hearts of the wicked, and whose dominion we learn from Scripture to be so general, as to entitle him to the denomination of "the Prince of this world." There cannot be a stronger proof of the difference which exists between the religious system of the Scriptures, and that of the bulk of nominal Christians, than the proof which is afforded by the subject now in question. The existence and agency of the Evil Spirit, though so distinctly and repeatedly affirmed in Scripture, are almost universally exploded in a country which professes to admit the authority of the sacred volume. Some other Doctrines of Revelation, the force and real meaning of which are commonly in a great degree explained away, are yet conceded in general terms. But this seems almost by universal consent to have been abandoned, as a post no longer tenable. It is regarded as an evanescent [quickly fading] prejudice, which it would now be a discredit to any man of understanding to believe. Like ghosts and witches and other phantoms, which haunted the night of superstition, it cannot in these more enlightened times stand the test of our severer scrutiny. To be suffered to pass away quietly, is as much as it can hope for; and it might rather expect to be laughed off the stage as a just object of contempt and derision.

But although the Scripture doctrine concerning the Evil Spirit, is thus generally exploded, yet were we to consider the matter seriously and fairly, we should probably find ground for believing that there is no better reason for its being abandoned, than that many absurd stories, concerning spirits and apparitions, have been used to be believed and propagated amongst weak and credulous people; and that the Evil Spirit not being the object of our bodily eyes, it would be an instance of the same weakness to give credit to the doctrine of its existence and agency. But to be consistent with ourselves, we might almost as well, on the same principle, deny the reality of all other incorporeal beings. What is there, in truth, in the doctrine, which is in itself improbable, or which is not confirmed by analogy? We see, in fact, that there are wicked men, enemies to God, and malignant towards their fellow-creatures, who take pleasure, and often succeed, in drawing in others to the commission of evil. Why then should it be deemed incredible, that there may be one or more spiritual intelligences of similar natures and propensities, who may in like manner be permitted to tempt men to the practice of sin? Surely we may retort upon our opponents the charge of absurdity, and justly accuse them of gross inconsistency, in admitting, without difficulty, the existence and operation of these qualities in a material being, and yet denying them in an immaterial one (in direct contradiction to the authority of Scripture, which they allow to be conclusive) when they cannot, and will not pretend for a moment, that there is any thing belonging to the nature of matter, to which these qualities naturally adhere.

But to dilate no farther on a topic which, however it may excite the ridicule of the inconsiderate, will suggest matter of serious apprehension to all who form their opinions on the authority of the word of God: thus brought as we are into captivity, and exposed to danger; depraved and weakened within, and tempted from without, it might well fill our hearts with anxiety to reflect, "that the day will come," when "the Heavens, being on fire, shall be dissolved, and the elements shall melt with fervent heat;" when the dead, small and great, shall stand before "the tribunal of God" [2 Corinthians 5:10], and we shall have to give account of all things done in the body.

We are naturally prompted to turn over the page of revelation with solicitude, in order to discover the qualities and character of our Judge, and the probable principles of his determination: but this only serves to turn painful apprehension into fixed and certain terror.—First of the qualities of our Judge. As all nature bears witness to his irresistible power, so we read in Scripture that nothing can escape his observation, or elude his discovery; not our actions only, but our most secret cogitations [thoughts or reflections] are open to his view. "He is about our path and about our bed, and spieth out all our ways" [Psalm 139:3], "The Lord searcheth all hearts, and understandeth all the imaginations of the thoughts" [1 Chronicles 28:9].—"And he will bring to light the hidden things of darkness, and will make manifest the counsels of the heart" [1 Corinthians 4:5].

Now, hear his description and character, and the rule of his award: "The Lord our God is a consuming fire, even a jealous God" [Deuteronomy 4:24].—"He is of purer eyes than to behold iniquity" [Habakkuk 1:13].—"The soul that sinneth, it shall die" [Ezekiel 18:4].—"The wages of sin is death" [Romans 6:23]. These positive declarations are enforced by the accounts which, for our warning, we read in sacred history, of the terrible vengeance of the Almighty: his punishment of "the angels who kept not their first estate, and whom he hath reserved in everlasting chains under darkness unto the judgment of the great day" [Jude 1:6]. The fate of Sodom and Gomorrah [ancient Middle Eastern cities which were destroyed by God; see Genesis 18:17–19:29]; the sentence issued against the idolatrous nations of Canaan [the region of the ancient Middle East which encompassed the territory of the present nation of Israel, and much of Jordan, Lebanon and Syria], and of which the execution was assigned to the Israelites, by the express command of God, at their own peril in case of disobedience: The ruin of Babylon, and of Tyre, and of Nineveh [other ancient Near Eastern cities which were objects of divine judgment in the Old Testament], and of Jerusalem, prophetically denounced as the punishment of their crimes, and taking place in an exact and terrible accordance with the divine predictions: These are indeed matter[s] of awful perusal, sufficient surely to confound the fallacious confidence of any who, on the ground that our Creator must be aware of our natural weakness, and must be of course disposed to allow for it, should allege that, though unable indeed to justify ourselves in the sight of God, we need not give way to such gloomy apprehensions, but might throw ourselves, with assured hope, on the infinite benevolence of the Supreme Being. It is indeed true, that with the threatenings of the word of God, there are mixed many gracious declarations of pardon, on repentance, and thorough amendment. But, alas! which of us is there, whose conscience must not reproach him with having trifled with the long-suffering of God, and with having but ill kept the resolutions of amendment, which he had some time or other formed in the seasons of recollection and remorse?—And how is the disquietude naturally excited by such a retrospect, confirmed and heightened by passages like these? "Because I have called, and ye refused; I have stretched out my hand, and no man regarded; but ye have set at naught all my counsel, and would none of my reproof: I also will laugh at your calamity; I will mock when your fear cometh: when your fear cometh as desolation, and your destruction cometh as a whirlwind; when distress and anguish cometh upon you: then shall they call upon me, but I will not answer; they shall seek me early, but they shall not find me: for that they hated knowledge, and did not chuse the fear of the Lord" [Proverbs 1:24–29]. The apprehensions which must be excited by thus reading the recorded judgments and aweful language of Scripture, are confirmed to the inquisitive and attentive mind, by a close observation of the moral constitution of the world. Such a one will find occasion to remark, that all, which has been suggested of the final consequences of vice, is in strict analogy to what we may observe in the ordinary course of human affairs, wherein it will appear, on a careful survey, that God has assigned to things their general tendencies, and established such an order of causes and effects, as (however interrupted here below by hindrances and obstructions apparently of a temporary nature) loudly proclaim the principles of his moral government, and strongly suggest that vice and imprudence will finally terminate in misery.[11] Not that this species of proof was wanted; for that which we must acknowledge, on weighing the evidence, to be a revelation from God requires not the aid of such a confirmation: but yet, as this accordance might be expected between the words and the works, the past and the future ordinations of the same Almighty Being, it is no idle speculation to remark, that the visible constitution of things in the world around us falls in with the representations here given from Scripture of the dreadful consequences of vice, nay even of what is commonly termed inconsiderateness and imprudence.

If such then be indeed our sad condition, what is to be done? Is there no hope? Nothing left for us, "but a fearful looking for of judgment, and fiery indignation, which shall devour the adversaries?" [Hebrews 10:27]. Blessed be God! we are not shut up irrecoverably in this sad condition: "Turn you to the strong hold, ye prisoners of hope" [Zechariah 9:12]; hear one who proclaims his designation, "to heal the broken-hearted, to preach liberty to the captives, and recovering of sight to the blind" [Luke 4:18]. Those who have formed a true notion of their lost and helpless state, will most gladly listen to the sound, and most justly estimate the value of such a deliverance. And this is the cause, which renders it of such pressing moment not to pass cursorily over those important topics of the original and superinduced corruption and weakness of man; a discussion painful and humiliating to the pride of human nature, to which the mind lends itself with difficulty, and hearkens with a mixture of anger and disgust; but well suited to our case, and like the distasteful lessons of adversity, permanently useful in its consequences. It is here, never let it be forgotten, that our foundation must be laid; otherwise our superstructure, whatever we may think of it, will one day or other prove tottering and insecure. This is therefore no metaphysical [the nature of existence, truth, and knowledge] speculation, but a practical matter. Slight and superficial conceptions of our state of natural degradation, and of our insufficiency to recover from it of ourselves, fall in too well with our natural inconsiderateness, and produce that fatal insensibility to the divine warning to "flee from the wrath to come" [Matthew 3:7; cf. Luke 3:7], which we cannot but observe to prevail so generally. Having no due sense of the malignity of our disease, and of its dreadful issue, we do not set ourselves to work in earnest to obtain the remedy, as to a business arduous indeed, but indispensable: for, it must ever be carefully remembered, that this deliverance is *not forced on us*, but *offered to us;* we are furnished indeed with every help, and are always to bear in mind, that we are unable of ourselves to will or to do rightly; but we are plainly admonished to "work out our own salvation with fear and trembling" [Philippians 2:12].—Watchful, for we are encompassed with dangers; "putting on the whole armour of God" [Ephesians 6:11], for "we are beset with enemies" [cf. Psalm 22:12].

May we be enabled to shake off that lethargy which is so apt to creep upon us! For this end, a deep practical conviction of our natural depravity and weakness, will be found of eminent advantage. As it is by this we must at first be rouzed from our fallacious security, so by this we must be kept wakeful and active unto the end. Let us therefore make it our business to have this doctrine firmly seated in our understandings, and radically worked into our hearts. With a view to the former of these objects, we should often seriously and attentively consider the firm ground on which it rests. It is plainly made known to us by the light of nature, and irresistibly enforced on us by the dictates of our unassisted understandings. But lest there should be any so obstinately dull, as not to discern the force of the evidence suggested to our reason, and confirmed by all experience, or rather so heedless as not to notice it, the authoritative stamp of Revelation is superadded, as we have seen, to complete the proof; and we must therefore be altogether inexcusable, if we still remain unconvinced by such an accumulated mass of argument.

But we must not only *assent* to the doctrine clearly, but *feel* it strongly. To this end, let the power of habit be called in to our aid. Let us accustom ourselves to refer to our natural depravity, as to their primary cause, the sad instances of vice and folly of which we read, or which we see around us, or to which we feel the propensities in our own bosoms; ever vigilant and distrustful of ourselves, and looking with an eye of kindness and pity on the faults and infirmities of others, whom we should learn to regard with the same tender concern as that with which the sick are used to sympathize with those who are suffering under the same distemper as themselves. This lesson, once well acquired, we shall feel the benefit of it in all our future progress; and though it be a lesson which we are slow to learn, it is one in which study and experience, the incidents of every day, and every fresh observation of the workings of our own hearts, will gradually concur to perfect us. Let it not, after all then, be our reproach, and at length our ruin, that these abundant means of instruction are possessed in vain.

SECTION THREE ↲

Corruption of Human Nature—Objection

But there is one difficulty still behind, more formidable than all the rest. The pride of man is loth to be humbled. Forced to abandon the plea of innocence, and pressed so closely that he can no longer escape from the conclusion to which we would drive him, some more bold objector faces about and stands at bay, endeavouring to justify what he cannot deny. "Whatever I am," he contends, "I am what my Creator made me. I inherited a nature, you yourself confess, depraved and prone to evil: how then can I withstand the temptations to sin, by which I am environed? If this plea cannot establish my innocence, it must excuse or at least extenuate my guilt. Frail and weak as I am, a Being of infinite justice and goodness will never try me by a rule which, however equitable in the case of creatures of a higher nature, is altogether disproportionate to mine."

Let not my readers be alarmed! The writer is not going to enter into the discussion of the grand question concerning the origin of moral evil, or to attempt at large to reconcile its existence and consequent punishment with the acknowledged attributes and perfections of God. These are questions, of which, if one may judge from the little success with which the acutest and profoundest reasoners have been ever labouring to solve the difficulties they contain, the full and clear comprehension is above the intellect of man. Yet, as such an objection as that which has been stated is sometimes heard from the mouths of professed Christians, it must not be passed by without a few short observations.

Were the language in question to be addressed to us by an avowed sceptic, though it might not be very difficult to expose to him the futility of *his* reasonings, we should almost despair of satisfying him of the soundness of our own. We should perhaps suggest impossibilities, which might stand in the way of such a system as he would establish: we might indeed point out wherein (arguing from concessions which he would freely make) his pre-conceptions concerning the conduct of the Supreme Being had been in fact already contradicted, particularly by the existence at all of natural or moral evil: and if thus proved erroneous in one instance, why might they not be so likewise in another? But though by these and similar arguments we might at length silence our objector, we could not much expect to bring him over to our opinions. We should probably do better, if we were to endeavour rather to draw him off from these dark and slippery regions, (slippery in truth they are to every human foot) and to contend with him, where we might tread with firmness and freedom, on sure ground, and in the light of day. Then we might fairly lay before him all the various arguments for the truth of our holy religion; arguments which have been sufficient to satisfy the wisest, and the best, and the ablest of men. We should afterwards perhaps insist on the abundant confirmation Christianity receives from its being exactly suited to the nature and wants of man; and we might conclude, with fairly putting it to him, whether all this weight of evidence were to be overbalanced by this one difficulty, on a subject so confessedly high and mysterious, considering too that he must allow, we see but a part (O how small a part!) of the universal creation of God, and that our faculties are wholly incompetent to judge of the schemes of his infinite wisdom. This, if the writer may be permitted to offer his own judgment, is (at least in general) the best mode, in the case of the objection now in question, of dealing with unbelievers; and to adopt the contrary plan, seems somewhat like that of any one, who having to convince some untutored Indian of the truth of the Copernican system,[12] instead of beginning with plain and simple propositions, and leading him on to what is more abstruse and remote, should state to him, at the outset, some astonishing problems, to which the understanding can only yield its slow assent, when constrained by the decisive force of demonstration. The novice, instead of lending himself to such a mistaken method of instruction, would turn away in disgust, and be only hardened against his preceptor. But, it must be remembered, that the present work is addressed to those who acknowledge the authority of the holy Scriptures. And in order to convince all such that there is, somewhere or other, a fallacy in our objector's reasoning, it will be sufficient to establish that though the word of God clearly asserts the justice and goodness of the Supreme Being, and also the natural depravity of man, yet it no less clearly lays down that this natural depravity shall never be admitted as an excuse for sin, but that "they which have done evil, shall rise to the resurrection of damnation" [John 5:29], —"That the wicked shall be turned into hell, and all the people that forget God" [Psalm 9:17]. And it is worthy of remark, that as if for the very purpose of more effectually silencing those unbelieving doubts which are ever springing up in the human heart, our blessed Saviour, though messenger of peace and good will to man, has again and again repeated these awful denunciations.

Nor (it must also be remarked) are the holy Scriptures less clear and full in guarding us against supposing our sins, or the dreadful consequences of them, to be chargeable on God.— "Let no man say when he is tempted, I am tempted of God: for

God cannot be tempted with evil, neither tempteth he any man" [James 1:13]. "The Lord is not willing that any should perish" [2 Peter 3:9]. And again, where the idea is repelled as injurious to his character,—"Have I any pleasure at all that the wicked should die? saith the Lord God; and not that he should return from his ways, and live?" [Ezekiel 18:23]. "For I have no pleasure in the death of him that dieth, saith the Lord God" [Ezekiel 18:32]. Indeed, almost every page of the word of God contains some warning or invitation to sinners; and all these, to a considerate mind, must unquestionably be proofs of present position.

It has been the more necessary not to leave unnoticed the objection which we have been now refuting, because, where not admitted to such an unqualified extent as altogether to take away the moral responsibility of man, and when not avowed in the daring language in which it has been above stated, it may frequently be observed to exist in an inferior degree: and often, when not distinctly formed into shape, it lurks in secret, diffusing a general cloud of doubt or unbelief, or lowering our standard of right, or whispering fallacious comfort, and producing a ruinous tranquillity. Not to anticipate what will more properly come under discussion, when we consider the nature and strictness of practical Christianity; let us here, however, remark, that though the holy Scriptures so clearly state the natural corruption and weakness of man, yet they never, in the most minute degree, countenance, but throughout directly oppose, the supposition to which we are often too forward to listen, that this corruption and weakness will be admitted as lowering the demands of divine justice, and in some sort palliating [making less severe] our transgressions of the laws of God. It would not be too difficult to shew that such a notion is at war with the whole scheme of redemption by the atonement of Christ. But perhaps it may be enough when any such suggestions as those which we are condemning force themselves into the imagination of a Christian, to recommend it to him to silence them by what is their best practical answer: that if our natural condition be depraved and weak, our temptations numerous, and our Almighty Judge infinitely holy; yet that the offers to penitent sinners of pardon, and grace, and strength, are universal and unlimited. Let it not however surprise us, if in all this, there seem to be involved difficulties which we cannot fully comprehend. How many such every where present themselves! Scarcely is there an object around us, that does not afford endless matter of doubt and argument. The meanest reptile which crawls on the earth, nay, every herb and flower which we behold, baffles the imbecility of our limited inquiries. All nature calls upon us to be humble. Can it then be surprising if we are at a loss on this question, which respects, not the properties of matter, or of numbers, but the counsels and ways of him whose "Understanding is infinite" [Psalm 147:5], "whose judgments are declared to be unsearchable, and his ways past finding out?" [Romans 11:33]. In this our ignorance however, we may calmly repose ourselves on his own declaration, "That though clouds and darkness are round about him, yet right-eousness and judgment are the habitation of his throne" [Psalm 97:2]. Let it also be remembered, that if in Christianity some things are difficult, that which it most concerns us to know, is plain and obvious. To this it is true wisdom to attach ourselves, assenting to what is revealed where above our faculties, we do not say contradictory to them, on the credit of what is clearly discerned, and satisfactorily established. In truth, we are all perhaps too apt to plunge into depths, which it is beyond our power to fathom; and it was to warn us against this very error, that the inspired writer [Moses], when he has been threatening the people, whom God had selected as the objects of his special favour with the most dreadful punishments, if they should forsake the law of the Lord, and has introduced surrounding nations as asking the meaning of the severe infliction, winds up the whole with this instructive admonition: "Secret things be-long unto the Lord our God: but those which are revealed belong unto us, and to our children for ever, that we may *do* all the words of this law" [Deuteronomy 29:29].

To any one who is seriously impressed with a sense of the critical state in which we are here placed, a short and uncertain space in which to make our peace with God, and then the last judgment, and an eternity of unspeakable happiness or misery, it is indeed an awful and an affecting spectacle, to see men thus busying themselves in these vain speculations of arrogant curiosity, and trifling with their dearest, their everlast-ing interests. It is but a feeble illustration of this exquisite folly, to compare it to the conduct of some convicted rebel, who, when brought into the presence of his Sovereign, instead of seizing the occasion to sue for mercy, should even neglect and trifle with the pardon which should be offered to him, and insolently employ himself in prying into his Sovereign's designs and criticising his counsels. Our case indeed is, in another point of comparison, but too much like that of the convicted rebel. But there is this grand difference—that at the best, his success must be uncertain, ours, if it be not our own fault is sure; and while, on the other hand, our guilt is unspeakably greater than that of any rebel against an earthly monarch; so, on the other, we know that our Sovereign is "Long-suffering, and easy to be intreated" [James 3:17]; more ready to grant, than we to ask, forgiveness. Well then may we adopt the language of the poet:

> What better can we do, than. . .prostrate fall
> Before him reverent; and there confess
> Humbly our faults, and pardon beg; with tears
> Watering the ground, and with our sighs the air
> Frequenting, sent from hearts contrite, in sign
> Of sorrow unfeign'd, and humiliation meek?

> [—John Milton][13]

Notes ⤻

1. This Latin citation used by Wilberforce is taken from Book IV, line 287 of *Metamorphoses,* a work by the poet Ovid (43 B.C.– A.D.18?). I have inserted Frank Justus Miller's English translation, which appears in the Loeb Classical Library's edition of Ovid's *Metamorphoses* Vol. I (Cambridge: Mass.: Harvard University Press, 1984), p. 199. I have corrected the Latin citation by inserting the word "fontis." It appears that Wilberforce either inaccurately cited this passage from memory or that the printer failed to detect this slight mistake.

2. See John Milton's *Paradise Lost,* Book 2, line 432.

3. See William Shakespeare's *The Tempest,* act 5, scene 1. Here Wilberforce appears to have paraphrased the character Miranda's line "O brave new world, that has such people in't!"

4. Following the citation of Romans 1:28 Wilberforce continues in Latin:

> Exempla duo, quae pravitatis humanae vim animo meo luculenter exhibent, non proferre non possum. Alterum decens ille Virgilius, alterum Cicero, probus idem verique studiosus, suppeditat. Virgilius innocuam certe pastorum vitam depicturus, ita incipit[:]

Translated this passage reads:

I can't help to not provide two examples, which brilliantly exhibit the force of human perversity to my mind. The one, the proper Virgil, the other Cicero, upright and also devoted to the truth, provides. Virgil, about to describe the truly harmless life of shepherds, begins thus:

Formosum pastor Corydon ardebat Alexim.

[A shepherd, Corydon, burned with love for his master's favourite, handsome Alexis.

—*Eclogue* II, line 1]

See *The Eclogues of Virgil*, translated by C. Day Lewis (London: Jonathan Cape, 1963), p. 13. Wilberforce goes on to state:

Cicero in libro *de Officiis* primo, ubi de actionibus prout inter se apte & convenientes sint, loci, temporis, & agentis ratione habita, disserit, argumentum sic illustrat:

Translated, this passage reads:

Cicero, in his first book *On Duties*, when he speaks about actions as they are closely among themselves and coming together, considering the matter of time, place & action, illustrates his argument thus:

Turpe est enim, valdeque vitiosum, in re severa, convivio dignum, aut delicatum aliquem inserre sermonem. Bene Pericles, quum haberet collegam in praetura Sophoclem poëtam, hique de communi officio convenissent, & casu formosus puer praeteriret, dixissetque Sophocles, O puerum pulchrum Pericle! At enim, inquit Pericles, praetorem Sophoclem decet non solum manus, sed etiam oculos abstinentes habere. Atiqui hoc idem Sophocles, si in athletarum probatione dixisset, *justa reprehensione caruisset, tanta vis est, & loci & temporis.*

Translated, this reads:

For it is unbecoming and highly censurable, when upon a serious theme, to introduce such jests as are proper at a dinner, or any sort of loose talk. When Pericles was associated with the poet Sophocles as his colleague in command and they had met to confer about official business that concerned them both, a handsome boy chanced to pass and Sophocles said: "Look, Pericles; what a pretty boy!" How pertinent was Pericles reply: "Hush, Sophocles, a general should keep not only his hands but his eyes under control." And yet, if Sophocles had made this same remark at a trial of athletes, he would have incurred no just reprimand, *so great is the significance of both place and circumstance.*

These texts come from Marcus Tullius Cicero, *De Officiis* (Loeb Classical Library; English translation by Walter Miller; Cambridge, Mass.: Harvard University Press, 1913). Wilberforce concludes by asserting:

Quomodo sese res habuisse necesse est, cum vir antiquorum pr[a]estantissimis adscribendus, philosophiam, immo mores & officia tranctans, talia doceret! Qualem sibi ipse virtutis normam proposuerat, satis liquet. Vide inter alia, *justa reprehensione, &c. &c; & tanta vis est, &c. &c.*

Translated, this passage reads:

Just as matters must have stood, when a man of ancient times must be added to a list of the most eminent, dealing with philosophy, yes indeed customs and duties taught such things. Of what set of sort of standard of virtue he had set forth for himself is clear enough. See among other things, *'just reprimand,' &c &c;* 'So great is . . .,' *&c. &c.*

5. William Robertson (1721–93). Scottish historian and minister. His historical works include a *History of Scotland* and a *History of America.* During his lifetime, Robertson enjoyed fame throughout Europe, and it is said that he had no rival in historical composition except for Edward Gibbon.

6. Wilberforce writes, "Robertson, Vol. 2, p. 130."

7. Wilberforce writes, "Robertson, Book 4, Sect. 2., Head[ing], 'Condition of Women,' vol. 2, 8vo. pp. 90–91."

8. Richard Hooker (1554–1600) was an Anglican apologist, political theorist, and theologian. He was a major figure of the Elizabethan Settlement of 1559. His works include the *Treatise on the Laws of Ecclesiastical Polity.* Today Hooker is generally regarded as one of the greatest theologians that the English church has ever produced and as a writer of masterly prose.

9. This Latin citation is taken from Book IX, line 580 of *Pharsalia,* a work by Lucan (A.D. 39–65). I have inserted an English translation by J. D. Duff. Duff's translation appears in the Loeb Classical Library's edition of *Pharsalia* (Cambridge, Mass.: Harvard University Press, 1969), p. 549.

10. Sir Isaac Newton (1642–1727) was a philosopher, scientist, and theologian.

11. Wilberforce writes, "Vide [See] Butler's *Analogy.*" Joseph Butler (1692–1752), the Bishop of Durham, is commonly ranked among the greatest exponents of natural theology and ethics in England since the Reformation. Prime Minister William Pitt recommended that Wilberforce read his *Analogy of Religion* after Wilberforce shared the news of his "great change" or conversion with him.

12. Wilberforce is referring to the astronomer Nicolaus Copernicus (1473–1543). The Copernican system is the model of the solar system centered on the Sun, with the Earth and other planets moving around it. This system was formulated and published in 1543.

13. See John Carey and Alastair Fowler, eds., *The Poems of John Milton* (London: Longmans, Green, & Co. Ltd., 1968), p. 980. Wilberforce has cited lines 1086–92 of Book Ten of Milton's "Paradise

Lost." The edition that Wilberforce cited appears to be slightly different from the more authoritative text used by Carey and Fowler. The text they have used, including the part Wilberforce omitted using ellipsis, reads:

> What better can we do, than to the place
> Repairing where he judged us, prostrate fall
> Before him reverent, and there confess
> Humbly our faults, and pardon beg, with tears
> Watering the ground, and with our sighs the air
> Frequenting, sent from hearts contrite, in sign
> Of sorrow unfeigned, and humiliation meek.

⌐Chapter Three

Chief Defects of the Religious System of the
Bulk of Professed Christians, in What Regards
Our Lord Jesus Christ, and the Holy Spirit—
With a Dissertation Concerning the Use
of the Passions in Religion

SECTION ONE ⌐

Scripture Doctrines

THAT "GOD SO LOVED THE WORLD, AS OF HIS TENDER mercy to give his only Son Jesus Christ for our redemption" [John 3:16]; That our blessed Lord willingly left the glory of the Father, and was made man: That "he was despised and rejected of men; a man of sorrows, and acquainted with grief" [Isaiah 53:3]: That "he was wounded for our transgressions;" that "he was bruised for our iniquities" [Isaiah 53:5]: That "the Lord laid on him the iniquity of us all" [Isaiah 53:6]: That at length "he humbled himself even to the death of the Cross, for us miserable sinners; to the end that all who with hearty repentance and true faith, should come to him, might not perish, but have everlasting life" [John 3:16]: That he "is now at the right hand of God, making intercession" for his people [Romans 8:34]: That, "being reconciled to God by the death of his Son, we may come boldly unto the throne of grace, to obtain mercy and find grace to help in time of need:" That our heavenly Father "will surely give his Holy Spirit to them that ask him" [Luke 11:13]: That "the Spirit of God must dwell in us;" and that "if any man hath not the Spirit of Christ, he is none of his" [Romans 8:9]: That by this divine influence "we are to be renewed in knowledge after the image of him who created us" [Colossians 3:10], and "to be filled with the fruits of righteousness, to the praise of the glory of his grace" [Ephesians 1:6]; that, "being thus made meet for the inheritance of the saints in light" [Colossians 1:12], we shall sleep in the Lord [cf. 1 Corinthians 15:51]; and that when the last trumpet shall sound [1 Corinthians 15:52], this corruption shall put on incorruption [1 Corinthians 15:53]; —and that, being at length perfected after his likeness [cf. Romans 6:5], we shall be admitted into his heavenly kingdom.

These are the leading Doctrines concerning our Saviour, and the Holy Spirit, which are taught in the Holy Scriptures, and held by the Church of England. The truth of them, agreeably to our general plan, will be taken for granted. Few of those, who have been used to join in the established form of worship, can have been, it is hoped, so inattentive, as to be ignorant of these grand truths, which are to be found every where dispersed throughout our excellent Liturgy. Would to God it could be presumed, with equal confidence, that all who assent to them in terms, discern their force and excellency in the understanding, and feel their power in the affections, and their transforming influence in the heart. What lively emotions are they calculated to excite in us of self-abasement, and abhorrence of our sins; and of humble hope, and firm faith, and heavenly joy, and ardent love, and active unceasing gratitude!

But here, it is to be feared, will be found the grand defect of the religion of the bulk of professed Christians; a defect, like the palsy [a kind of paralysis, often accompanied by involuntary tremors] at the heart, which, while in its first attack, it changes but little the exterior appearance of the body, extinguishes the internal principle of heat and motion, and soon extends its benumbing influence to the remotest fibres of the frame. This defect is closely connected with that which was the chief subject of the last chapter: "they that are whole need not a physician, but they that are sick" [Matthew 9:12]. Had we duly felt the burthen of our sins, that they are a load which our own strength is wholly unable to support, and that the weight of them must finally sink us into perdition, our hearts would have danced at the sound of the gracious invitation, "Come unto me, all ye that labour and are heavy laden, and I will give you rest" [Matthew 11:28]. But in those who have scarcely felt their sins as any incumbrance, it would be mere affectation to pretend to very exalted conceptions of the value and acceptableness of the proffered deliverance. This pretence accordingly, is seldom now kept up; and the most superficial observer, comparing the sentiments and views of the bulk of the Christian world, with the articles still retained in their creed, and with the strong language of Scripture, must be struck with the amazing disproportion.

To pass over the throng from whose minds Religion is altogether excluded by the business or the vanities of life, how is it with the more decent and moral? To what criterion shall we appeal? Are their hearts really filled with these things, and warmed by the love which they are adapted to inspire? Then surely their minds are apt to stray to them almost unseasonably; or at least to hasten back to them with eagerness, when escaped from the estrangement imposed by the necessary cares and business of life. He was a masterly describer of human nature, who thus pourtrayed the characters of an undissembled affection:

> Unstaid and fickle in all other things,
> Save in the constant image of the object,
> That is beloved.

> [—William Shakespeare][1]

"And how," it may be perhaps replied, "do you know, but that the minds of these people are thus occupied? Can you look into the bosoms of men?" Let us appeal to a test to which we resorted in a former instance. "Out of the abundance of the heart," it has been pronounced, "the mouth speaketh" [Matthew 12:34]. Take these persons then in some well selected hour, and lead the conversation to the subject of Religion. The utmost which can be effected is, to bring them to talk of things in the gross. They appear lost in generalities; there is nothing precise and determinate, nothing which implies a mind used to the contemplation of its object. In vain you strive to bring them to speak on that topic, which one might expect to be ever uppermost in the hearts of redeemed sinners. They elude all your endeavours; and if you mention of it yourself, it is received with no very cordial welcome at least, if not with unequivocal disgust; it is at the best a forced and formal discussion. The excellence of our Saviour's moral precepts, the kindness and simplicity, and self-denial and unblemished purity of his life, his patience and meekness in the hour of death, cannot indeed be spoken of but with admiration, when spoken of at all, as they have often extorted unwilling praise from the most daring and malignant infidels. But are not these mentioned as qualities in the abstract, rather than as the perfections and lineaments of our patron and benefactor and friend, "who loved us, and gave himself for us [Galatians 2:20]; of him "who died for *our* offences, and rose again for *our* justification" [Romans 4:25]; "who is even now at the right hand of God, making intercession for *us?* " [Romans 8:34]. Who would think that the kindness and humanity, and self-denial, and patience in suffering, which we so drily commend, had been exerted towards *ourselves,* in acts of more than finite benevolence of which *we* were to derive the benefit, in condescensions and labours submitted to for *our* sakes, in pain and ignominy endured for *our* deliverance?

But these grand truths are not suffered to vanish altogether from our remembrance. Thanks to the compilers of our Liturgy, more than to too many of the occupiers of our pulpits, they are forced upon our notice in their just bearings and connections, as often as we attend the service of the church. Yet is it too much to affirm, that though there entertained with decorum, as what belong to the day and place, and occupation, they are yet too generally heard of with little interest; like the legendary tales of some venerable historian, or other transactions of great antiquity, if not of doubtful credit, which, thought important to our ancestors, relate to times and circumstances so different from our own, that we cannot be expected to take any great concern in them? We hear of them therefore with apparent indifference; we repeat them almost as it were by rote, assuming by turns the language of the deepest humiliation and of the warmest thankfulness, with a calm and unaltered composure; and when the service of the day is ended, they are dismissed altogether from our thoughts, till, on the return of another Sunday, a fresh attendance on public worship gives occasion for the renewed expressions of our periodical gratitude. In noticing such lukewarmness as this, surely the writer were to be pardoned, if he were to be betrayed into some warmth of condemnation. The Unitarian and Socinian[2] indeed, who deny, or explain away the peculiar doctrines of the Gospel, may be allowed to feel, and talk of these grand truths with little emotion. But in those who profess a sincere belief in them, this coldness is insupportable. The greatest possible services of man to man must appear contemptible, when compared with "the unspeakable mercies of Christ" [1 Peter 1:3]: mercies so dearly bought, so freely bestowed—A deliverance from eternal misery—The gift of "a crown of glory, that fadeth not away" [1 Peter 5:4]. Yet, what judgment should we form of such conduct, as is here censured, in the case of any one who had received some signal services from a fellow creature? True love is an ardent, and an active principle—a cold, a dormant, a phlegmatic gratitude, are contradictions in terms. When these generous affections really exist in vigour, are we not ever fond of dwelling on the value, and enumerating the merits of our benefactor? How are we moved when any thing is asserted to his disparagement! How do we delight to tell of his kindness! With what pious care do we preserve any memorial of him, which we may happen to possess! How gladly do we seize any opportunity of rendering to him, or to those who are dear to him, any little good offices, which, though in themselves of small intrinsic worth, may testify the sincerity of our thankfulness! The very mention of his name will cheer the heart, and light up the countenance! And if he be now no more, and if he had made it his dying request that, in a way of his own appointment, we would occasionally meet to keep the memory of his person, and of his services in lively exercise; how would we resent the idea of failing in the performance of so sacred an obligation!

Such are the genuine characters, such the natural workings of a lively gratitude. And can we believe, without doing violence to the most established principles of human nature, that where the *effects* are so different, the *internal principle* is in truth the same?

If the love of Christ be thus languid in the bulk of nominal Christians, their joy and trust in him cannot be expected to be very vigorous. Here again we find reason to remark, that there is nothing distinct, nothing specific, nothing which implies a mind acquainted with the nature and familiarized with the use of the Christian's privileges, habitually solacing itself with the hopes held out by the Gospel, animated by the sense of its high relations and its glorious reversion.

The doctrine of the sanctifying operations of the Holy Spirit, appears to have met with still worse treatment. It would be to convey a very inadequate idea of the scantiness of the conceptions on this head, of the bulk of the Christian world, to affirm merely, that they are too little conscious of the inefficacy of their own unassisted endeavours after holiness of heart and life, and that they are not daily employed in humbly and diligently using the appointed means for the reception and cultivation of the divine assistance. It would hardly be to go beyond the truth to assert, that for the most part their notions on this subject are so confused and faint, that they can scarcely be said in any fair sense to believe the doctrine at all.

The writer of these sheets is by no means unapprized of the objections which he may expect from those, whose opinions he has been so freely condemning. He is prepared to hear it urged, that often where there have been the strongest pretences to religious affections, of which the want has now been censured, there has been little or nothing of the reality of them; and that even omitting the instances (which however have been but too frequent) of studied hypocrisy, what have assumed to themselves the name of religious affections have been merely the flights of a lively imagination, or the working of a heated brain; in particular, that this love of our Saviour, which has been so warmly recommended, is no better than a vain fervor, which dwells only in the disordered mind of the enthusiast [one considered to be driven by uncontrollable religious passions]. That Religion is of a more steady nature; of a more sober and manly quality; and that she rejects with scorn, the support of a mere feeling, so volatile and indeterminate, so trivial and useless; as that with which we would associate her; a feeling varying in different men, and even in the same man at different times, according to the accidental flow of the animal spirits; a feeling, lastly, of which it may perhaps be said, we are from our very nature, hardly susceptible towards an invisible Being.

"As to the operations of the Holy Spirit," it may probably be further urged, that "it is perhaps scarcely worth while to spend much time in inquiring into the theory, when, in practice at least, it is manifest, that there is no sure criterion whereby any one can ascertain the reality of them, even in his own case, much less in that of another. All we know is, that pretenders to these extraordinary assistances have never been wanting to abuse the credulity of the vulgar, and to try the patience of the wise. From the canting hypocrites and wild fanatics of the last century, to their less dangerous, chiefly because less successful, descendents of the present day, we hear the same unwarranted claims, the same idle tales, the same low cant [insincere use of religious language]; and we may discern not seldom the same mean artifices and mercenary ends. The doctrine, to say the best of it, can only serve to favour the indolence of man, while professing to furnish him with a compendious method of becoming wise and good, it supersedes the necessity of his own personal labours. Quitting therefore all these slothful and chimerical [the product of unrestrained imagination] speculations, it is true wisdom to attach ourselves to what is more solid and practical; to the work which you will not yourself deny to be sufficiently difficult to find us of itself full employment: the work of rectifying the disorders of the passions, and of implanting and cultivating the virtues of the moral character." "It is the service of the understanding which God requires of us, which you would degrade into a mere matter of bodily temperament, and imaginary impulses. You are contending for that which not only is altogether unworthy of our Divine Master, but which, with considerate men, has ever brought his religion into suspicion and disrepute, and under a shew of honouring him, serves only to injure and discredit his cause." Our Objector, warming as he proceeds, will perhaps assume a more impatient tone. "Have not these doctrines," he may exclaim, "been ever perverted to the purposes of the most disgraceful to the religion of Jesus? If you want an instance, look to the standard of the inquisition, and behold the Dominicans[3] torturing their miserable victims for the Love of Christ.[4] Or would you rather see the effects of your principles on a larger scale, and *by wholesale* (if the phrase may be pardoned;) cast your eyes across the Atlantic, and let your zeal be edified by the holy activity of Cortez and Pizarro,[5] and their apostles of the western hemisphere. To what else have been owing the extensive ravages of national persecutions, and religious wars and crusades; whereby rapacity, and pride, and cruelty, sheltering themselves (sometimes from the furious bigots themselves) under the mask of this specious principle, have so often afflicted the world? The prince of peace has been made to assume the post of a ferocious conqueror, and forgetting the message of good will toward men [Luke 2:14], has issued forth like a second 'Scourge of the Earth,'[6] to plague and desolate the human species."

Objection Discussed

That the sacred name of Religion has been too often prostituted to the most detestable purposes; that furious bigots and bloody persecutors, and self-interested hypocrites of all qualities and dimensions, from the rapacious leader of an army, to the canting oracle of a congregation, have falsely called themselves Christians, are melancholy and humiliating truths, which (as none so deeply lament them) none will more readily admit, than they who best understand the nature, and are most concerned for the honour of Christianity. We are ready to acknowledge also without dispute, that the religious affections, and the doctrine of divine assistances, have almost at all times been more or less disgraced by the false pretences and extravagant conduct of wild fanatics and brain-sick enthusiasts. All this, however, is only as it happens in other instances, wherein the depravity of man perverts the bounty of God. Why is it here only to be made an argument, that there is danger of abuse? So is there also in the case of all the potent and operative principles, whether in the natural or moral world. Take for an instance the powers and properties of matter. These were doubtless designed by Providence for our comfort and well-being; yet they are often misapplied to trifling purposes, and still more frequently turned into so many agents of misery and death. On this fact indeed is well founded the well-known maxim, not more trite than just, that "the best things when corrupted become the worst;"[7] a maxim which is especially just in the instance of Religion. For in this case it is not merely, as in some others, that a great power, when mischievously applied, must be hurtful in proportion to its strength; but that the very principle on which in general we depend for restraining and retarding the progress of evil, not only ceases to interpose any kindly check, but is actively operative in the opposite direction. But will you therefore discard Religion altogether? The experiment was lately tried in a neighboring country [France], and professedly on this very ground. The effects however with which it was attended, do not much encourage its repetition. But suppose Religion were discarded, then Liberty remains to plague the world; a power which though when well employed, the dispenser of light and happiness, has been often proved, and eminently in this very instance, to be capable when abused, of becoming infinitely mischievous. Well then, extinguish Liberty. Then what more abused by false pretenders, than Patriotism? well, extinguish Patriotism. But the the wicked career to which we have adverted, must be checked but for Courage. Blot out Courage—and so might you proceed to extinguish one by one, Reason, and Speech, and Memory, and all the discriminating prerogatives of man. But perhaps more than enough has already been urged, in reply to an objection, which bottoms on ground so indefensible as that which would equally warrant our condemning any physical or moral faculty altogether, on account of its being occasionally abused.

As to the position of our Opponent, that there is no way whereby the validity of any pretensions to the religious affections be ascertained, it must partly be admitted. Doubtless we are not able always to read the hearts of men, and to discover their real characters; and hence it is, that we in some measure lie open to the false and hypocritical pretences which are brought forward against us so triumphantly. But then these pretences no more prove all similar claims to be founded in falsehood and hypocrisy, than there having been many false and interested pretenders to wisdom and honesty, would prove that there can be no such thing as a wise or an honest man. We do not argue thus but where our reason is under a corrupt bias. Why should we be so much surprized and scandalized, when these impostors are detected in the church of Christ? It is no more than our blessed Master himself taught us to expect; and when the old difficulty is stated, "didst thou not sow good seed in thy field, whence then hath it tares?" [Matthew 13:27] his own answer furnishes the best solution, "—An enemy hath done this" [Luke 13:28]. Hypocrisy is indeed *detestable,* and enthusiasm sufficiently mischievous to justify our guarding against its approaches with jealous care. Yet it may not be improper to take this occasion for observing, that we are now and then apt to draw too unfavourable conclusions from unpleasant appearances which may perhaps be chiefly or altogether owing to gross or confused conceptions, or to a disgusting formality of demeanor, or to indeterminate, low, or improperly familiar expressions. The mode and language in which a vulgar man will express himself on the subject of Religion, will probably be vulgar, and it is difficult for people of literature and refinement not to be unreasonably shocked by such vulgarities. But we should at least endeavour to correct the rash judgments which we may be disposed to form on these occasions, and should learn to recognize and to prize a sound texture and just configuration, though disguised beneath a homely or uncouth drapery. It was an Apostle [Paul] who declared that he had come (to the learned and accomplished Grecians too) "not with excellency of speech, or the wisdom of words" [1 Corinthians 2:1; see also Acts 17]. From these he had studiously abstained, lest he should have seemed to owe his success rather to the graces of oratory, than to the efficacy of his doctrines, and to the divine power with which they were accompanied. Even in our own times, when, the extraordinary operations and miraculous gifts of the Holy Spirit having ceased, the necessity of study and preparation, and of attention to manner as well as matter, in order to qualify men to become teachers of religion, are no longer superseded, yet it is no more than an act of justice explicitly to remark, that a body of Christians, which from the peculiarly offensive grossnesses of language in use among them, had, not without reason, excited suspicions of the very worst nature, have since reclaimed their character,[8] and have perhaps excelled all mankind in solid and unequivocal proofs of the love of Christ, and of the most ardent, and active, and patient zeal in his service. It is a zeal tempered with prudence, softened with meekness, soberly aiming at great ends by the gradual operation of well adapted means, supported by a courage which no danger can intimidate, and a quiet constancy which no hardships can exhaust.

SECTION TWO

On the Admission of the Passions into Religion

The objection of our Opponent, that by insisting on the obligation of making our blessed Saviour the object of our religious affections, we are degrading the worship of the understanding, and are substituting and raising up a set of mere feelings in its stead, is one which deserves most serious consideration. If it be just, it is decisive; for ours must be unquestionably "a reasonable service" [Romans 12:1]. The Objector must mean, either, that these affections are unreasonable in themselves, or that they are misplaced in religion. He can scarcely however intend that the affections are in their own nature unreasonable. To suppose him to maintain this position, were to suppose him ignorant of what every schoolboy knows of the mechanism of the human mind. We shall therefore take it for granted that this cannot be his meaning, and proceed to examine the latter part of the alternative. Here also it may either be intended, that the affections are misplaced in Religion, *generally,* or that our blessed Saviour is not the blessed object of them. The strain of our Objector's language, no less than the objections themselves which he has urged, render it evident that (perhaps without excluding the latter position) the former is in full possession of his mind.

This notion of the affections being out of place in Religion, is indeed an opinion which appears to be generally prevalent. The affections are regarded as the strong-holds of enthusiasm. It is therefore judged most expedient to act, as prudent generals are used to do, when they raze the fortress, or spike up the cannon, which are likely to fall into the hands of an enemy. Mankind are apt to be the dupes of misapplied terms; and the progress of the persuasion now in question, has been considerably aided by an abuse of language, not sufficiently checked in its first advances, whereby that species of religion which is opposite to the warm and affectionate kind, has been suffered almost without disturbance, to usurp to itself the epithet of *rational*. But let not this claim be too hastily admitted. Let the position in question be thoroughly and impartially discussed, and it will appear, if I mistake not, to be a gross and pernicious error. If amputation be indeed indispensable, we must submit to it; but we may surely expect to be heard with patience, or rather with favour and indulgence, while we proceed to shew that there is no need to have recourse to so desperate a remedy. The discussion will necessarily draw us into length. But our prolixity [lengthy writing] will not be greater than may well be claimed by the importance of the subject, especially as it scarcely seems to have hitherto sufficiently engaged the attention of writers on the subject of Religion.

It cannot methinks but afford a considerable presumption against the doctrine which we are about to combat, that it proposes to exclude at once from the service of Religion so grand a part of the composition of man; that in this our noblest employment it condemns as worse than useless, all the most active and operative principles of our nature. One cannot but suppose that like the organs of the body, so the elementary qualities and original passions of the mind were all given us for valuable purposes by our allwise Creator. It is indeed one of the sad evidences of our fallen condition, that they are now perpetually tumultuating and rebelling against the powers of reason and conscience, to which they should be subject. But even if Revelation had been silent, natural reason might have in some degree presumed, that it would be the effect of a Religion which should come from God, completely to repair the consequences of our superinduced [abnormally brought about] depravity. The schemes of mere wisdom had indeed tacitly confessed, that this was a task beyond their strength. Of the two most celebrated systems of philosophy, the one expressly confirmed the usurpation of the passions; while the other, despairing of being able to regulate, saw nothing left but to extinguish them. The former acted like a weak government, which give independence to a rebellious province, which it cannot reduce. The latter formed its bloated scheme merely upon the plan of that barbarous policy, which composes the troubles of a turbulent land by the extermination of its inhabitants. This the calm, not of order, but of inaction; it is not tranquillity, but the stillness of death:

> [Auferre] Trucidare rapere falsis nominibus imperium,
> atque ubi solitudinem faciunt, pacem appellant.

> [To plunder, butcher, steal, these things they
> misname empire:
> they make a desolation and they call it peace.

> —Tacitus][9]

Christianity, we might hope, would not be driven to any such wretched expedients; nor in fact does she condescend to them. They only thus undervalue her strength, who mistake her character, and are ignorant of her powers. It is her peculiar glory, and her main office, to bring all the faculties of our nature into their just subordination and dependence; that so the whole man, complete in all his functions, may be restored to the true ends his being, and be devoted, entire and harmonious, to the service and glory of God. "My son, give me thine *heart*." [Proverbs 23:26]—"Thou shalt love the Lord thy God with all thy *heart*" [Deuteronomy 6:5]. Such are the direct and comprehensive claims which are made on us in the holy Scriptures. We can scarcely indeed look into any part of the sacred volume without meeting abundant proofs, that it is the religion of the Affections which God particularly requires. Love, Zeal, Gratitude, Joy, Hope, Trust: are each of them specified; and are not allowed to us as weaknesses, but enjoined on us as our bounden duty, and commended to us as our acceptable worship. Where passages are so numerous, there would be no end of particular citations. Let it be sufficient therefore, to refer the reader to the word of God. There let him observe too, that as the lively exercise of the passions towards their legitimate object, is always spoken of with praise, so a cold, hard, unfeeling heart, is represented as highly criminal. Lukewarmness is stated to be the object of God's disgust and aversion; zeal and love, of his favour and delight; and the taking away of the heart of stone and the implanting of a warmer and more tender nature in its stead, is specifically promised as the effect of his returning favour, and the work of his renewing grace. It is the prayer of an inspired teacher [Paul], in behalf of those for whom he was most interested, "that their love" (already acknowledged to be great) might abound "yet more and more" [1 Thessalonians 4:1]. Those modes of worship are set forth and prescribed, which are best calculated to excite the dormant affections, and to maintain them in lively exercise; and the aids of music and singing are expressly superadded to increase their effect. If we look to the most eminent of the Scripture Characters, we shall find them warm, zealous, and affectionate. When engaged in their favourite work of celebrating the goodness of their Supreme Benefactor, their souls appear to burn within them, their hearts kindle into rapture; the powers of language are made inadequate to the expression of their transports; and they call on all nature to swell the chorus, and to unite with them in hallelujahs of gratitude, and joy, and praise. The man after God's own heart [King David] most of all abounds in these glowing effusions; and his compositions [the Book of Psalms] appear to have been given us in order to set the tone, as it were, to all succeeding generations. Accordingly, (to quote the words of a late excellent prelate,[10] who was himself warmed with the same heavenly flame) "in the language of this divine book, the praises of the church have been offered up to the Throne of Grace from age to age." Again, when it pleased God to check the future apostle of the Gentiles [Paul of Tarsus] in his wild career, and to make him a monument of transforming grace; was the force of his affections diminished, or was it not only that their direction was changed? He brought his affections entire and unabated into the service of his blessed Master. His zeal now burned even with an increase of brightness; and no intenseness, no continuance of suffering could allay its ardor or damp the fervors of his triumphant exaltations. Finally—The worship and service of the glorified spirits in Heaven is not represented to us as a cold intellectual investigation, but as the worship and service of gratitude and love. And surely it will not be disputed, that it should be even here the humble endeavour of those, who are promised while here on earth "to be made

meet to be partakers of the inheritance of the saints in light"
[Colossians 1:12], to bring their hearts into capacity for joining
in those everlasting praises.

But it may not be unadvisable for the writer here to
guard against a mistaken supposition, from which the mind of
our Objector by no means appears exempt, that the force of the
religious affections is to be mainly estimated (I had almost said
by the thermometer) by the degree of mere animal fervor, by
ardors, and transports, and raptures, of which, from constitutional temperament, a person may be easily susceptible; or into
which daily experience must convince us, that people of strong
conceptions and of warm passions may work themselves without much difficulty, where their hearts are by no means truly or
deeply interested. Every tolerable actor can attest the truth of
this remark. These high degrees of the passions bad men may
experience, good men may want. They may be affected; they
may be genuine; but whether genuine or affected, they form
not the true standard by which the real nature or strength of
the religious affections is to be determined. To ascertain these
points, we must examine, whether they appear to be grounded
in knowledge, to have their root in strong and just conceptions
of the great and manifold excellences of their object, or to be
ignorant, unmeaning, or vague; whether they are natural and
easy, or constrained and forced; wakeful and apt to fix on their
great objects, delighting in their proper nutriment (if the expression may be allowed) the exercises of prayer and praise,
and religious contemplation; or voluntarily omitting offered
occasions of receiving it, looking forward to them with little
expectation, looking back on them with little complacency, and
being disappointed of them with little regret: by observing
whether these religious affections are merely occasional visi-
tants, or the abiding inmates of the soul: whether they have got
the mastery over the vicious passions and propensities, with
which their origin and nature, and tendency, they are at open
variance; or whether if the victory be not yet complete, the war
is at least constant, and the breach irreconcilable: whether they
moderate and regulate all the inferior appetites and desires
which are culpable only in their excess, thus striving to reign in
the bosom with a settled undisputed predominance: by examining, whether above all they manifest themselves by prompting
to the active discharge of the duties of life, the personal, and
domestic, and relative, and professional, and social, and civil
duties. Here the wideness of their range and the universality of

their influence, will generally serve to distinguish them from those partial efforts of diligence and self-denial, to which mankind are prompted by subordinate motives. All proofs other than this deduced from conduct, are in some degree ambiguous. This, this only, whether we argue from Reason or from Scripture, is a sure infallible criterion. From the daily incidents of conjugal and domestic life, we learn that a heat of affection occasionally vehement, but superficial and transitory, may consist too well with a course of conduct, exhibiting incontestable proofs of neglect and unkindness. But the passion which alone the Holy Scriptures dignify with the name of Love, is a deep, not a superficial feeling; a fixed and permanent, not an occasional emotion. It proves the validity of its title, by actions corresponding with its nature, by practical endeavours to gratify the wishes and to promote the interests of the object of affection. "If a man love me, he will keep my sayings" [John 14:24]. "This is the love of God, that we keep his commandments" [2 John 1:6]. This therefore is the best standard by which to try the quality, or, the quality being ascertained, to estimate the strength of the religious affections. Without suffering ourselves to derive too much complacency from transient fervors of devotion, we should carefully and frequently prove ourselves by this less dubitable test; impartially examining our daily conduct; and often comparing our actual, with our possible services, the fair amount of our exertions with our natural or acquired means and opportunities of usefulness. After this large explanation, the prolixity [lengthy discussion] of which will we trust be pardoned on account of the importance of the subject, and the danger of mistakes both on the right hand and on the left, we are perfectly ready to concede to the Objector, whose arguments we have been so long considering, that the religious affections must be expected to be more or less lively in different men, and in the same man at different times, in proportion to natural tempers, ages, situations, and habits of life. But, to found an objection on this ground, would be as unreasonable as it were altogether to deny the obligation of the precepts which command us to relieve the necessities of the indigent, because the infinitely varying circumstances of mankind must render it impossible to specify beforehand the sum which each individual ought on the whole to allot to this purpose, or to fix in every particular instance, on any determinate measure, and mode of contribution. To the one case no less than to the other, we may apply the maxim of an eminent writer; "An honest heart is the best casuist" [a casuist is one who engages in reasoning (usually theological in nature) in order to settle questions of conscience or conduct]. He who every where but in Religion is warm and animated, there only phlegmatic [apathetic] and cold, can hardly expect (especially if this coldness be not the subject of unfeigned humiliation and sorrow) that his plea on the ground of natural temper should be admitted; any more than that of a person who should urge his poverty as a justification of his not relieving the wants of the necessitous, at the very time that he should be launching out into expense without restraint, on occasions in which he should be really prompted by his inclinations. In both cases, "it is the *willing* mind which is required." Where that is found "every man will be judged according to what he hath, and not according to what he hath not" [2 Corinthians 8:12].

After the decisive proofs already adduced from the word of God, of the unreasonableness of the objection to the admission of the passions into Religion, all further arguments may appear superfluous to any one who is disposed to bow to scriptural authority. Yet, the point is of so much importance, and it is to be feared, so little regarded, that it may not be amiss to continue the discussion. The best results of our understanding will be shewn to fall in with what clearly appears to be the authoritative language of revelation; and to call in the aid of the affections to the service of Religion, will prove to be not only what sober reason may permit, as in some sort allowable; but to be that which she clearly and strongly dictates to our deliberate judgments, as being what the circumstances of our natural condition indispensably require. We have every one of us a work to accomplish, wherein our eternal interests are at stake; a work to which we are naturally indisposed. We live in a world abounding with objects which distract our attention and divert our endeavours; and a deadly enemy is ever at hand to seduce and beguile us. If we persevere indeed, success is certain; but our efforts must know no remission. There is a call on us for vigorous and continual resolution, self-denial, and activity. Now, man is not a being of mere intellect.

> Video meliora proboque, deteriora sequor,
>
> [I see the better and approve it, but I follow the worse.][11]

is a complaint which, alas! we all of us might daily utter. The slightest solicitation of appetite is often able to draw us to act in opposition to our clearest judgment, our highest interests, and most resolute determinations. Sickness, poverty, disgrace, and even eternal misery itself, sometimes in vain solicit our regards; they are all excluded from the view, and thrust as it were beyond the sphere of vision, by some poor unsubstantial transient object, so minute and contemptible as almost to escape the notice of eye of reason.

These observations are more strikingly confirmed in our religious concerns than in any other; because in them the interests at stake are of transcendent importance: but they hold equally in every instance according to its measure, wherein there is a call for laborious, painful, and continued exertions, from which any one is likely to be deterred by obstacles, or seduced by the solicitations of pleasure. What then is to be done in the case of any such arduous and necessary undertaking? The answer is obvious—You should endeavour not only to convince the understanding, but also to affect the heart; and for this end, you must secure the reinforcement of the passions. This is indeed the course which would be naturally followed by every man of common understanding, who should know that some one for whom he was deeply interested, a child, for instance, or a brother, were about to enter on a long, difficult, perilous, and critical adventure, wherein success was to be honour and affluence; defeat was to be contempt and ruin. And still more, if the parent were convinced that his child possessed faculties which, strenuously and unremittingly exerted, would prove equal to all the exigencies of the enterprize, but knew him also to be volatile and inconstant, and had reason to doubt his resolution and his vigilance; how would the friendly monitor's endeavour be redoubled, so as to possess his pupil's mind with the worth and dignity of the undertaking that there should be no opening for the entrance of any inferior consideration! "Weigh well (he would say) the value of the object for which you are about to contend, and contemplate and study its various excellences, till your whole soul be on fire for its acquisition. Consider too, that, if you fail, misery and infamy are united in the alternative which awaits you. Let not the mistaken notion of its being a safe and easy service, for a moment beguile you into the discontinuance or remission of your efforts. Be aware of your imminent danger, and at the same time know your true security. It is a service of labour and peril; but one wherein the powers which you possess, strenuously and perseveringly exerted, cannot but crown you with victory. Accustom yourself to look first to the dreadful consequences of failure; then fix your eye on the glorious prize which is before you [Philippians 3:13–14]; and when your strength begins to fail, and your spirits are well nigh exhausted, let the animating view rekindle your resolution, and call forth in renewed vigour the fainting energies of your soul."

It was the remark of an unerring observer [Jesus], "the children of this world are wiser in their generation than the children of light" [Luke 16:8]. And it is indisputably true, that in religion we have to argue and plea with men for principles of action, the wisdom and expediency of which are universally acknowledged in matters of worldly concern. So it is in the instance before us. The case which has been just described, is an exact, but a faint representation of our condition in this life. Frail and "infirm of purpose," we have a business to execute of supreme and indispensable necessity. Solicitations to neglect it every where abound; the difficulties and dangers are numerous and urgent; and the night of death cometh, how soon we know not, "when no man can work" [John 9:4]. All this is granted. It seems to be a state of things wherein one should look out with solicitude for some powerful stimulants. Mere knowledge is confessedly too weak. The affections alone remain to supply the deficiency. They precisely meet the occasion, and suit the purposes intended. Yet, when we propose to fit ourselves for our great undertaking, by calling them in to our help, we are to be told that we are acting contrary to reason. Is this reasonable, to strip us first of our armour of proof, and then to send us to the sharpest of encounters? To summon us to the severest labours, but first to rob us of the precious cordials which should brace our sinews and recruit our strength?

Let these pretended advocates for reason at length then confess their folly, and do justice to the superior wisdom as well as goodness of our heavenly Instructor, who better understanding our true condition, and knowing our frowardness and inadvertency, has most reasonably as well as kindly pointed out and enjoined on us the use of those aids which may counteract our infirmities; who commanding the effect, has commanded also the means whereby it may be accomplished.

And now, if the use of the affections in religion, in *general*, be at length shewn to be conformable to reason, it will not require many words to prove that our blessed Saviour is the proper object of them. We know that love, gratitude, joy, hope, trust, (the affections in question) all have their appropriate objects. Now it must be at once conceded, that if these appropriate objects be not exhibited, it is perfectly unreasonable to expect that the correspondent passions should be excited. If we ask for love, in the case of an object which has no excellence or desirableness; for gratitude, where no obligation has been conferred; for joy, where there is no just cause of self-congratulation; for hope, where nothing is expected: for trust, where there exists no ground of reliance; then indeed, we must kiss the rod, and patiently submit to correction. This would be indeed Egyptian bondage, to demand the effects without the means of producing them.[12] Is the case then so? Are we ready to adopt the language of the avowed enemies of our adorable Saviour; and again to say of him "in whom dwelleth all the fulness of the Godhead bodily," that, "he hath no form nor comeliness; and when we shall see him, there is no beauty that we should desire him?" [Isaiah 53:2]. Is it no obligation, that he who "thought it not robbery to be equal with God," should yet, for our sakes, "make himself of no reputation, and take upon him the form of a servant, and be made in the likeness of men; and humble himself, and become obedient unto death, even the death of the cross!" [Philippians 2:6–8]. Is it no cause of *joy*, "that to us is born a Saviour" [Luke 2:10–11], by whom we may "be delivered from the power of darkness; and be made meet to be partakers of the inheritance of the saints in light?" [Colossians 1:12–13]. Can there be a "*hope* comparable to that of our calling" [Ephesians 1:18], "which is Christ in us, the hope of glory?" [Colossians 1:27]. Can there be a *trust* to be preferred to the reliance on "Christ Jesus; who is the same yesterday, to-day, and for ever?" [Hebrews 13:8]. Surely, if our Opponent be not dead to every generous emotion, he cannot look his own objection in the face without a blush of shame and indignation.

SECTION THREE ⌁

*Consideration of the Reasonableness of Affections
towards an Invisible Being*

But forced at last to retreat from his favourite position, and compelled to acknowledge that the religious affections towards our blessed Saviour are not unreasonable; he still however, maintains the combat, suggesting that by the very constitution of our nature, we are not susceptible of them towards an invisible Being; in whose case, it will be added, we are shut out from all those means of communication and intercourse, which knit and cement the union between man and man.

We mean not to deny that there is something in this objection. It might even seem to plead the authority of Scripture in its favour—"He that loveth not his brother whom he hath seen, how can he love God whom he hath not seen?" [1 John 4:20]. And it was indeed no new remark in Horace's days,

> Segnius irratant animos demissa per aures
> quam quae sunt oculis subjecta fidelibus.
>
> [Less vividly is the mind stirred by what finds entrance through
> the ears than by what is brought before the
> trusty eyes. . . .
>
> —Horace][13]

We receive impressions more readily from visible objects, we feel them more strongly, and retain them more durably. But though it must be granted that this circumstance makes it a more difficult task to preserve the affections in question in a healthful and vigorous state; is it thereby rendered impossible? This were indeed a most precipitate conclusion; and any one who should be disposed to admit the truth of it, might be at least induced to hesitate, when he should reflect that the argument applies equally against the possibility of the love of God, a duty of which the most cursory reader of Scripture, if he admit divine authority, cannot but acknowledge the indispensable obligation. But we need only look back to the Scripture proofs which have been lately adduced, to be convinced that the religious affections are therein inculcated on us, as a matter of high and serious obligation. Hence we may be assured that the impossibility stated by our Opponent does not exist.

Let us scrutinize this matter, however, a little more minutely, and we shall be compelled to acknowledge, that though the conclusion may make against ourselves, that the objection vanishes when we fairly and accurately investigate the circumstances of the case. With this view, let us look a little into the nature of the affections of the human mind, and endeavour to ascertain whence it is that they derive their nutriment, and are found from experience to increase in strength.

The state of man is such, that his feelings are not the obedient servants of his reason, prompt at once to follow his dictates, as to their direction, and their measure. Excellence is the just object of love; good in expectancy, of hope; evil to be apprehended, of fear; our fellow creatures' misfortunes, and sufferings, constitute the just objects of pity. Each of these passions, it might be thought, would be excited, in proportion to what our reason should inform us were the magnitude and consequent claims of its corresponding object. But this is by no means the case. Take first for a proof the instance of pity. We read of slaughtered thousands with less emotion, than we hear the particulars of a shocking accident which has happened in the next street; the distresses of a novel, which at the same time we know to be fictitious affect us more than the dry narrative of a battle. We become so much interested by these incidents of the imagination (aware all the while that they are merely such) that we cannot speedily banish them from our thoughts, nor recover the tone of our minds; and often, we scarcely bring ourselves to lay down our book at the call of real misfortune, of which we go perhaps to the relief on a principle of duty, but with little sense of interest or emotion of tenderness. It were easy to shew that it is as much the same in the case of the other affections. Whatever be the cause of this disproportion, which (as metaphysics [the nature of existence, truth, and knowledge] fall not within our province) we shall not stop to examine, this fact is undeniable. There appears naturally, to be a certain strangeness between the passion and its object, which familiarity and the power of habit must gradually overcome.

You must contrive to bring them into *close contact;* they must be jointed and glued together by the particularities of little incidents. Thus in the production of heat in the physical world; the flint and the steel produce not the effect without collision; the rudest Barbarian will tell us the necessity of attrition, and the chemist of mixture. Now, an object, it is admitted, is brought into *closer contact* with this corresponding passion, by its being seen and conversed with. This we grant is one way; but does it follow that there is no other? To assert this, would be something like maintaining, in contradiction to universal experience, that objects of vision alone are capable of attracting our regard. But nothing can be more unfounded than such a supposition. It might appear to be too nearly approaching to the ludicrous, to suggest as an example to the contrary, the metaphysician's attachment to his insubstantial speculations, or the zeal displayed in the pursuit,

Extra flammantia moenia mundi,

[Beyond the blazing ramparts of the earth,]

of abstract sciences, where there is no idea of bringing them "within the visible diurnal sphere" to the vulgarity of practical application. The instance of the novel before mentioned, proves, that we may be extremely affected by what we know to be merely ideal incidents and beings. By much thinking or talking of any one; by using our minds to dwell on his excellences; by placing him in imaginary situations which interest and affect us; we find ourselves becoming insensibly more and more attached to him: whereas it is the surest expedient for extinguishing an attachment which already exists, to engage in such occupations or society as may cause our casual thoughts and more fixed mediations to be diverted from the object of it. Ask a mother who has been long separated from her child, specially if he has been in circumstances of honour, or of danger, to draw her attention to him, and to keep it in wakefulness and exercise, and she will tell you, that so far from becoming less dear, he appears to have grown more the object of her affections. She seems to herself to love him even better than the child who has been living under her roof, and has been daily in her view. How does she rejoice in his good fortune, and weep over his distresses! With what impatience does she anticipate the time of his return!

We find therefore that sight and personal intercourse do not seem necessary to the production or increase of attachment, where the means of *close contact* have been afforded; but on the other hand, if an object had been prevented from coming *into close contact*, sight and personal intercourse are not sufficient to give it the power of exciting the affections in proportion to its real magnitude. Suppose the case of a person whom we have often seen, and may have occasionally conversed with, and of whom we have been told in the general, that he possesses extraordinary merits. We assent to the assertion. But if we have no knowledge of particulars, no close acquaintance with him, nothing in short which brings his merits home to us, they interest us less than what we know to be a far inferior

degree of the very same qualities in one of our common associates. A parent has several children, all constantly under his eye,
and equally dear to him. Yet if any one of them be taken ill, it is
brought into such *closer contact* than before, that it seems to
absorb and engross the parent's whole affection. Thus then,
though it will not be denied that an object by being visible may
thereby excite its corresponding affection with more facility; yet
this is manifestly far from being the prime consideration. And
so far are we from being the slaves of the sense of vision, that a
familiar acquaintance with the intrinsic excellences of an object, aided, it must be admitted by the power of habit, will
render us almost insensible to the impressions which its out-
ward form conveys, and able entirely to lose the consciousness
of an unsightly exterior.

We may be permitted to remark, that the foregoing
observations furnish an explanation less discreditable than that
which has been sometimes given of an undoubted phaenomenon in the human mind, but the greatest public misfortunes,
however the understanding may lecture, are apt really to affect
our feelings less than the most trivial disaster which happens to
ourselves. An eminent writer[14] scarcely overstated the point
when he observed. "That it would occasion a man of humanity
more real disturbance to know that he was the next morning to
lose his little finger, than to hear that the great empire of
China had been suddenly swallowed up by an earthquake. The
thoughts of the former, would keep him awake all night: in the
latter case, after making many melancholy reflections on the
precariousness of human life, and the vanity of all the labours
of man which could be thus annihilated in a moment; after a
little speculation too perhaps on the causes of the disaster, and
its effect in the political and commercial world; he would
pursue his business or his pleasure with the same ease and
tranquility as if no such accident had happened; and snore at
night with the most profound serenity over the ruin of hundred
million of his fellow creatures. Selfishness is not the cause of
this, for the most unfeeling brute of earth would surely think
nothing of the loss of a finger, if he could thereby prevent so
dreadful a calamity." This doctrine of *contact* which has been
opened above, affords a satisfactory solution; and from all
which has been said (the writer has reason perhaps to apologize
for the length of the discussion) the circumstances by which the
affections of the mind towards any particular object are gener-
ated and strengthened, may be easily collected. The chief of

these appear to be, whatever tends to give a distinct and lively impression of the object, by setting before us its minute parts, and by often drawing towards it the thoughts and affections, so as to invest it by degrees with a confirmed ascendency: whatever tends to excite and to keep in exercise a lively interest in its behalf: in other words, full knowledge, distinct and frequent mental entertainment, and pathetic contemplations. Supposing these means to have been used in any given degree, it may be expected, that they will be more or less efficacious, in proportion as the intrinsic qualities of the object afford greater or less scope for their operation, and more or fewer materials with which to work. Can it then be conceived, that they will be of no avail when steadily practiced in the case of our Redeemer! If the principles of love, and gratitude, and joy, and hope, and trust, are not utterly extinct within us, they cannot but be called forth by the various corresponding objects which that blessed contemplation would gradually bring forth to our view. Well might the language of the apostle [Simon Peter] be addressed to Christians, "Whom having *not seen* ye love; in whom, though now ye *see him not*, yet believing, ye *rejoice* with joy unspeakable and full of glory" [1 Peter 1:8].

But fresh considerations pour in to render in this instance, the plea of its being impossible to love an invisible being, still more invalid. Our blessed Saviour, if we may be permitted so to say, is not removed far from us; and the various relations in which we stand towards him, seem purposely made known to us, in order to furnish so many different bonds of connection with him, and consequent occasions of continual intercourse. He exhibits not himself to us "dark with excessive brightness," but is let down as it were to the possibilities of human converse. We may not think that he is incapable of entering into our little concerns, and sympathizing with them; for we are graciously assured that he is not one "who cannot be touched with the feeling of our infirmities, having been in all points tempted like as we are" [Hebrews 4:15]. The figures under which he is represented, are such as convey ideas of the utmost tenderness. "He shall feed his flock like a shepherd; he shall gather the lambs in his arm, and carry them in his bosom, and shall gently lead those that are with young" [Isaiah 40:11]. "They shall not hunger nor thirst, neither shall the heat nor sun smite them; for he that hath mercy on them, shall lead them, even by the springs of water shall he guide them" [Isaiah 49:10]. "I will not leave you orphans" [John 14:18],[15] was one of his last consolatory declarations. The children of Christ are here separated indeed from the personal view of him; but not from his paternal affection and paternal care. Meanwhile let them quicken their regards by the animating anticipation of that blessed day, when he "who is gone to prepare a place for them, will come again to receive them unto himself" [John 14:3]. Then shall they be admitted to his more immediate presence: "Now we see through a glass, darkly; but then face to face: now I know in part; but then shall I know even as also I am known" [1 Corinthians 13:12].

Surely more than enough has been now said to prove that this particular case, from its very nature furnishes the most abundant and powerful considerations and means for exciting the feelings; and it might be contended, without fear of refutation, that by the diligent and habitual use of those considerations and means, we might, with confident expectation of success, engage in the work of raising our affections towards our blessed Saviour to a state of due force and activity. But, blessed be God, we have a still better reliance; for the grand circumstance of all yet remains behind, which the writer has been led to defer, from his wish to contend with his opponents on their own ground. This circumstance is, that here, no less than in other particulars, the Christian's hope is founded, not on the speculations or the strength of man, but on the declaration of Him who cannot lie, on the power of Omnipotence.

We learn from the Scriptures that it is one main part of the operations of the Holy Spirit, to implant these heavenly principles in the human mind, and to cherish their growth. We are encouraged to believe that in answer to our prayers, this aid from above will give efficacy to our earnest endeavours, if used in humble dependence on divine grace. We may therefore with confidence take the means which have been suggested. But let us, in our turn, be permitted to ask our opponents, have *they* humbly and perseveringly applied for this divine strength? or disclaiming that assistance, perhaps as tempting them to indolence, have they been so much the more strenuous and unwearied in the use of their own unaided endeavours? or rather have they not been equally negligent of both? Renouncing the one, they have wholly omitted the other. But this is far from being all. They even reserve all the methods which we have recommended as being calculated to increase regard, and exactly follow that course which would be pursued by any one who should wish to reduce an excessive affection. Yet thus leaving untried all the means which, whether from Reason or Scripture, we maintain to be necessary to the production of the end, nay using such as are of a directly opposite nature, these men presume to talk to us of impossibilities! We may rather contend that they furnish a fresh proof of the soundness of our reasonings. We lay it down as a fundamental position, that speculative knowledge alone, that mere superficial cursory considerations, will be of no avail. Nothing is to be done without the diligent continued use of the appointed method. They themselves afford an instance of the truth of our assertions; and while they supply no argument against the efficacy of the mode prescribed, they acknowledge at least that they are wholly ignorant of any other.

But let us now turn our eyes to Christians of a higher order, to those who actually proved the truth of our reasonings; who have not only assumed the name, but who have possessed the substance, and felt the power of Christianity; who though often foiled by their remaining corruptions, and shamed and cast down under a sense of their many imperfections, have known in their better seasons, what it was to experience its firm hope, its dignified joy, its unshaken trust, its more than human consolations. In their hearts, love also towards their Redeemer has glowed; a love not *superficial* and unmeaning (think not that this would be the subject of our praise) but constant and rational, resulting from a strong impression of the worth of its object, and heightened by an abiding sense of great, unmerited, and continually accumulating obligations; ever manifesting itself in acts of diligent obedience, or of patient suffering. Such was the religion of the holy martyrs of the 16th century, the illustrious ornaments of the English church. They realized the theory which we have now been faintly tracing. Look to their writings, and you will find that their thoughts and affections had been much exercised in habitual views of the blessed Jesus. Thus they used the required *means.* What were the *effects?* Persecution and distress, degradation and contempt, in vain assailed them—all these evils served but to bring their affections into *closer contact* with their object; and not only did their love feel no diminution or abatement, but it rose to all the exigencies of the occasion, and burned with an increase of ardor;[16] and when brought forth at last to a cruel and ignominious death, they repined not at their fate; but rather rejoiced that they were counted worthy to suffer for the name of Christ. By the blessing of God the writer might refer to still more recent times. But lest his authorities should be disputed, let us go to the Apostles of our Lord; and while, on a very cursory perusal of their writings, we must acknowledge that they commend and even prescribe to us the love of Christ, as one of the chief of the Christian graces; so on a more attentive inspection of those writings, we shall discover abundant proofs that they were themselves bright examples of their own precept; that our blessed Saviour was really the object of their warmest affection, and what he had done and suffered for them the continual matter of their grateful remembrance.

The disposition so prevalent in the bulk of nominal Christians, to form a religious system for themselves, instead of taking it from the word of God, is strikingly observable in their scarcely admitting, except in the most vague and general sense, the doctrine of the influence of the Holy Spirit. If we look into the Scriptures for information on this particular, we learn a very different lesson. We are in them distinctly taught, that "of ourselves we can do nothing" [cf. Philemon 1:14]; that "we are by nature children of wrath" [Ephesians 2:3], and under the power of the evil spirit, our understandings being naturally dark, and our hearts averse from spiritual things; and we are directed to pray for the influence of the Holy Spirit to enlighten our understandings, to dissipate our prejudices, to purify our corrupt minds, and renew us after the image of our heavenly Father. It is this influence which is represented as originally awakening us from slumber, as enlightening us in darkness, as "quickening us when dead" [Ephesians 2:1, 5], as "delivering us from the power of the devil" [cf. Hebrews 2:14–15], as drawing us to God, as "translating us into the kingdom of his dear Son" [Colossians 1:13], as "creating us anew in Christ Jesus" [Ephesians 2:10], as "dwelling in us, and walking in us" [2 Corinthians 6:16]; so that "putting off the old man with his deeds" [Ephesians 4:22], we are to consider ourselves as "having put on the new man, which is renewed in knowledge after the image of Him that created him" [Colossians 3:9–10]; and as those who are to be "an habitation of God through the Spirit" [Ephesians 2:22]. It is by this Divine assistance only that we grow in Grace, and improve in all Holiness. So expressly, particularly, and repeatedly does the word of God inculcate these lessons, that one would think there were scarcely room for any difference of opinion among those who admit its authority. Sometimes[17] the whole of a Christian's repentance and faith, and consequent holiness, are ascribed *generally* to the Divine influence; sometimes these are spoken of separately, and ascribed to the same Almighty power. Sometimes different particular graces of the Christian character, those which respect our duties and tempers towards our fellow-creatures, no less than those which have reference to the Supreme Being, are particularly traced to this source. Sometimes they are all referred collectively to this common root, being comprehended under the compendious denomination of "the Fruits of the Spirit" [Galatians 5:22–23; cf. Ephesians 5:9]. In exact correspondence with these representations, this aid from above is promised in other parts of Scripture for the production of those effects; and the withholding or withdrawing of it is occasionally threatened as a punishment for the sins of men, and as one of the most fatal consequences of the Divine displeasure.

The Liturgy of the Church of England strictly agrees with the representation, which has here been given of the instructions of the word of God.

SECTION FOUR ◞

Inadequate Conceptions Entertained by Nominal Christians of the Terms of Acceptance with God

If then it be indeed so as has been now stated; that, in contradiction to the plainest dictates of Scripture, and to the ritual of our established Church, the sanctifying operations of the Holy Spirit, the first fruits of our reconciliation to God, the purchase of our Redeemer's death, and his best gift to his true disciples, are too generally undervalued and slighted; if it be also true, as was formerly proved, that our thoughts of the blessed Saviour are confused and faint, our affections towards him languid and lukewarm, little proportioned to what they, who at such a price have been rescued from ruin, and endowed with a title to eternal glory, might be justly expected to feel towards the Author of their deliverance; little proportioned to what has been felt by others, ransomed from the same ruin, and partakers of the same inheritance: if this, let it be repeated, be indeed so, let us not shut our eyes against the perception of our real state; but rather endeavour to trace the evil to its source. We are loudly called on to *examine well our foundations*. If any thing be *there* unsound or hollow, the superstructure could not be safe, though its exterior were less suspicious. Let the question then be asked, and let the answer be returned with all the consideration and solemnity which a question so important may justly demand, whether, in the grand concern of all, *the means of a sinner's acceptance with God,* there be not reason to apprehend, that the nominal Christians whom we have been addressing, too generally entertain very superficial, and confused, and (to speak in the softest terms) highly dangerous notions? Is there not cause to fear, that with little more than an indistinct and nominal reference to Him who "bore our sins in his own body on the tree" [1 Peter 2:24], they really rest their eternal hopes on a vague, general persuasion of the unqualified mercy of the supreme Being; or that, still more erroneously, they rely in the main, on their own negative or positive merits? "They can look upon their lives with an impartial eye, and congratulate themselves on their inoffensiveness in society; on their having been exempt, at least, from gross vice, or if sometimes accidently betrayed into it, on its never having been indulged habitually; or if not even so (for there are but few who can say this, if the term vice be explained according to the strict requisitions of the Gospel) yet on the balance being in their favour, or on the whole not much against them, when their good and bad actions are fairly weighed, and due allowance is made for human frailty." These considerations are sufficient for the most part to compose their apprehensions; these are the cordials which they find most at hand in the moments of serious thought, or of occasional dejection; and sometimes perhaps in seasons of less than ordinary self-complacency, they call in also to their aid the general persuasion of the unbounded mercy and pity of God. Yet persons of this description by no means disclaim a Saviour, or avowedly relinquish their title to a share in the benefits of his death. They close their petitions with the name of Christ; but if not chiefly from the effect of habit, or out of decent conformity to the established faith, yet surely with something of the same ambiguity of principle which influenced the expiring philosopher, when he ordered the customary mark of homage to be paid to the god of medicine [this is a reference to Socrates, a philosopher of ancient Greece who lived during the fourth century B.C.].

   Others go farther than this; for there are many shades of difference between those who flatly renounce, and those who cordially embrace the doctrine of Redemption by Christ. This class has a sort of general, indeterminate, and ill understood dependence on our blessed Saviour. But their hopes, so far as they can be distinctly made out (for their views also are very obscure) appear ultimately to bottom on the persuasion that they are now, through Christ, become members of a new dispensation, wherein they will be tried by a more lenient rule than that to which they must have been otherwise subject. "God will not now be extreme to mark what is done amiss: but will dispense with the rigorous exactions of his law, too strict indeed for such frail creatures as we are to hope that we can fulfill it. Christianity has moderated the requisitions of Divine Justice; and all which is now required of us, is thankfully to trust to the merits of Christ for the pardon of our sins, and the acceptance of our sincere though imperfect obedience. The frailties and infirmities to which our nature is liable, or to which our situation in life exposes us, will not be severely judged: as it is the practice that really determines the character, we may rest satisfied, that if on this whole our lives be tolerably good, we shall escape with little or no punishment, and through Jesus Christ our Lord, shall be finally partakers of heavenly felicity."

We cannot dive into the human heart, and therefore should always speak with caution and diffidence, when from external appearances or declarations we are affirming the existence of any internal principles and feelings; especially as we are liable to be misled by the ambiguities of language, or by the inaccuracy with which others may express themselves. But is sometimes not difficult to any one who is accustomed, if the phrase may be allowed, to the anatomy of the human mind, to discern, that generally speaking, the persons who use the above language, rely not so much on the merits of Christ, and on the agency of Divine Grace, as on their own power of fulfilling the moderated requisitions of Divine Justice. He will hence therefore discover in them a disposition rather to extenuate the malignity of their disease, than to magnify the excellence of the proffered remedy. He will find them apt to palliate in themselves what they cannot fully justify, to enhance the merit of what they believe to be their good qualities and commendable actions, to set as it were in an account the good against the bad; and if the result be not very unfavourable, they conceive that they shall be entitled to claim the benefits of our Saviour's sufferings as a thing of course. They have little idea, so little, that it might almost be affirmed that they have no idea at all, of the importance or difficulty of the duty of what the Scripture calls "submitting ourselves to the righteousness of God" [Romans 10:3]; or of our proneness rather to justify ourselves in his sight, than in the language of imploring penitents to acknowledge ourselves guilty and helpless sinners. They have never summoned themselves to this entire and unqualified renunciation of their own merits, and their own strength; and therefore they remain strangers to the natural lostness of the human heart, which such a call would have awakened into action, and roused to resistance. ALL THESE THEIR SEVERAL ERRORS NATURALLY RESULT FROM THE MISTAKEN CONCEPTION ENTERTAINED OF THE FUNDAMENTAL PRINCIPLES OF CHRISTIANITY. They consider not that Christianity is a scheme "for justifying *the ungodly*" [Romans 4:5], by Christ's dying for them "*when yet sinners* " [Romans 5:6–8],[18] a scheme "for reconciling us to God—*when enemies*" [Romans 5:10]; and for making the fruits of holiness *the effects,*[19] *not the cause,* of our being justified and reconciled: that, in short, it opens freely the door of mercy, to the greatest and vilest of penitent sinners; that obeying the blessed impulse of the grace of God, whereby they had been awakened from the sleep of death, and moved to seek for pardon, they might enter in, and through the regenerating influence of the Holy Spirit might be enabled to bring forth the fruits of Righteousness. But they rather conceive of Christianity as opening the door of mercy, that those who on the ground of their own merits could not have hoped to justify themselves before God, may yet be admitted for Christ's sake, on condition of their having previously satisfied the moderated requisitions of Divine Justice. In speaking to others also of the Gospel scheme, they are apt to talk too much of terms and performances on our part, on which we become entitled to an interest in the sufferings of Christ; instead of stating the benefits of Christ's satisfaction as extended to us freely, "without money and without price" [Isaiah 55:1].

The *practical* consequences of these errors are such as might be expected. They tend to prevent that sense which we ought to entertain of our own natural misery and helplessness; and that deep feeling of gratitude for the merits and intercession of Christ, to which we are wholly indebted for our reconciliation to God, and for the will and the power, from first to last, to work out our own salvation. They consider it too much in the light of a contract between two parties, wherein each, independently of the other, has his own distinct condition to perform; man—to do his duty; God—to justify and accept for

Christ's sake: If they fail not in the discharge of their condition, assuredly the condition on God's part will be faithfully fulfilled. Accordingly, we find in fact, that any who represent the Gospel scheme in the manner above described, give evidence of the subject with which their hearts are most filled, by their proneness to run into merely moral disquisitions, either not mentioning at all, or at least but cursorily touching on the sufferings and love of their Redeemer; and are little apt to kindle at their Saviour's name, and like the apostles to be betrayed by their fervor into what may be almost an untimely descant on the riches of his unutterable mercy. In addressing others also whom they conceive to be living in habits of sin, and under the wrath of God, they rather advise them to amend their ways as a preparation for their coming to Christ, than exhort them to throw themselves with deep prostration at the foot of the cross, there to obtain pardon and find grace in time of need.

The great importance of the subject in question will justify our having been thus particular. It has arisen from a wish that on a question of such magnitude, to mistake our meaning should be impossible. But after all which has been said, let it also be remembered, that except so far as the instruction of others is concerned, the point of importance is, the internal disposition of the mind; *where* the dependence for pardon, and for holiness, is really placed; not what the language is, in which men express themselves. And it is to be hoped that he who searches the heart, sees the right dispositions in many who use the mistaken and dangerous language to which we have objected.

If this so generally prevailing error concerning the nature of the Gospel offer be in any considerable degree just; it will then explain that so generally prevailing languor in which the affections towards our blessed Saviour which was formerly remarked, and that inadequate impression of the necessity and value of the assistance of the divine Spirit. According to the soundest principles of reasoning, it may be also adduced as an additional proof of the correctness of our present statement, that it so exactly falls in with those phaenomena, and so naturally accounts for them. For even admitting that the persons above spoken of, particularly the last class, do at the bottom mainly rely on the atonement of Christ; yet on their scheme, it must necessarily happen, that the object to which they are most accustomed to look, with which their thoughts are chiefly conversant, from which they most habitually derive complacency, is rather their own qualified merit and services, though confessed to be inadequate, than the sufferings and atoning death of a crucified Saviour. The affections towards our blessed Lord therefore (according to the theory of the passions formerly laid down) cannot be expected to flourish, because they receive not that which was shewn to be necessary to their nutriment and growth. If we would love him affectionately, and rejoice in him as triumphantly as the first Christians did; we must learn like them to repose our entire trust in him and to adopt the language of the apostle [Paul], "God forbid that I should glory, save in the cross of Jesus Christ" [Galatians 6:14]. "Who of God is made unto us wisdom and righteousness, and sanctification, and redemption" [1 Corinthians 1:30].

Doubtless, there have been too many who, to the manifest danger of eternal ruin, have abused the doctrine of Salvation by Grace; and vainly trusted in Christ for pardon and acceptance, when by their vicious lives they have plainly proved the groundlessness of their pretensions. The tree is to be known by its fruits; and there is too much reason to fear that there is no principle of faith, when it does not decidedly evince itself by the fruits of holiness. Dreadful indeed will be the doom, above that of all others, of those loose professors of Christianity, to whom at the last day our blessed Saviour will address those words, "I never knew you: depart from me, all ye that work iniquity" [Matthew 7:23]. But the danger of error on this side ought not to render us insensible to the opposite error; an error against which in these days it seems particularly necessary to guard. It is far from the intention of the writer of this work to enter into the niceties of controversy. But surely without danger of being thought to violate this design, he may be permitted to contend, that they who in the main believe the doctrines of the church of England, are bound to allow that our dependence on our blessed Saviour, as alone the meritorious cause of our acceptance with God, and as the means of all its blessed fruits and glorious consequences, must not be merely formal and nominal, but real and substantial; not vague, qualified, and partial, but direct, cordial and entire. "Repentance towards God, and faith towards our Lord Jesus Christ" [Acts 20:21], was the sum of the apostolical instructions. It is not an occasional invocation of the name, or a transient recognition of the authority of Christ, that fills up the measure of the terms, *believing in Jesus*. This we shall find no such easy task; and if we trust that we do believe, we should all perhaps do well to cry out in the words of an imploring supplicant (he supplicated not in vain) "Lord, help thou our unbelief" [Mark 9:24]. We must be deeply conscious of our guilt and misery, heartily repenting of our sins, and firmly resolving to forsake them: and thus penitently "fleeing for refuge to the hope set before us" [Hebrews 6:18], we must found altogether on the merit of the crucified Redeemer our hopes of escape from their deserved punishment, and of deliverance from their enslaving power. This must be our first, our last, our only plea. We are to surrender ourselves up to him to "be washed in his blood" [Revelation 1:5], to be sanctified by his Spirit, resolving to receive him for our Lord and Master, to learn in his school, to obey all his commandments.

It may perhaps be not unnecessary, after having treated so largely on this important topic, to add a few words in order to obviate a charge which may be urged against us, that we are insisting on nice and abstruse distinctions in what is a matter of general concern; and this too, in a system which on its original promulgation was declared to be particularly intended for the simple and poor. It will be abundantly evident however on a little reflection, and experience fully proves the position, that what has been required is not the perception of a subtle distinction, but a state and condition of heart. To the former, the poor and ignorant must be indeed confessed unequal; but they are far less indisposed than the great and learned, to bow down to that "preaching of the cross which is to them that perish foolishness, but unto them that are saved the power of God, and the wisdom of God" [1 Corinthians 1:18]. The poor are not liable to be puffed up by the intoxicating fumes of ambition and worldly grandeur. They are less likely to be kept from entering into the straight and narrow way, and when they have entered to be drawn back again or to be retarded in their progress, by the cares of pleasure of life. They may express themselves ill; but their views may be simple, and their hearts humble, penitent, and sincere. It is as in other cases; the vulgar are the subjects of phaenomena, the learned explain them: the former know nothing of the theory of vision or of sentiment but this ignorance hinders not that they see and think, and though unable to discourse elaborately on the passions, they can feel warmly for their children, their friends, their country.

After this digression, if that be indeed a digression which by removing a formidable objection renders the truth of the position we wish to establish more clear and less questionable, we may now resume the thread of our argument. Still entreating therefore the attention of those, who have not been used to think much of the necessity of this undivided, and if it may be so termed, unadulterated reliance, for which we have been contending; we would still more particularly address ourselves to others who are disposed to believe that though, in some obscure and vague sense, the death of Christ as the satisfaction for our sins, and for the purchase of our future happiness, and the sanctifying influence of the Holy Spirit, are to be be admitted as fundamental articles of our creed, yet that these are doctrines so much above us, that they are not objects suited to our capacities; and that, turning our eyes therefore from these difficult speculations, we should fix them on the practical and moral precepts of the Gospel. "These it most concerns us to know; these therefore let us study. Such is the frailty of our nature, such the strength and number of our temptations to evil, that in reducing the Gospel morality to practice we shall find full employment: and by attending to these moral precepts, rather than to those high mysterious doctrines which you are pressing on us, we shall best prepare to appear before God on that tremendous day, when "He shall judge every man according to his WORKS" [Matthew 16:27].

> Vain wisdom all, and false philosophy!
>
> [—John Milton][20]

It will at once destroy this flimsy web, to reply in the words of our blessed Saviour, and of his beloved Disciple— "This is the *work* of God, that ye *believe* in him whom he hath sent" [John 6:29]. "This is his *commandment,* that we should *believe* on the name of his Son Jesus Christ" [1 John 3:23]. In truth, if we consider but for a moment the opinions (they scarcely deserve the name of system) of men who argue thus, we must be conscious of their absurdity. This may be not inconsistently the language of the modern of the modern Unitarian; but surely it is in the highest degree unreasonable to admit into our scheme all the grand peculiarities of Christianity, and having admitted, to neglect and think no more of them. "Wherefore" (might the Socinian say) "Wherefore all this costly and complicated machinery? It is like the Tychonic astronomy,[21] encumbered and self-convicted by its own complicated relations and useless perplexities. It is so little like the simplicity of nature, it is so unworthy of the divine hand, that it even offends against those rules of propriety which we require to be observed in the imperfect composition of the "human intellect."[22]

Well may the Socinian assume this lofty tone, with those whom we are now addressing. If these be indeed the doctrines of Revelation, common sense suggests to us that from their nature and their magnitude, they deserve our most serious regard. It is the very theology of Epicurus to allow the existence of these "heavenly things,"[23] but to deny their connection with human concerns, and their influence on human actions. Besides the unreasonableness of this conduct, we might strongly urge also in this connection the profaneness of thus treating as matters of subordinate consideration those parts of the system of Christianity, which are so strongly impressed on our reverence by the dignity of the person to whom they relate. This very argument is indeed repeatedly and pointedly pressed by the sacred writers.[24]

Nor is the profane irreverence of this conduct more striking than its ingratitude. When from reading that our Saviour was "the brightness of his Father's glory, and the express image of his person, upholding all things by the word of his power" [Hebrews 1:3], we go on to consider the purpose for which he came to earth, and all the he did and suffered for us; surely if we have a spark of ingenuousness left within us we shall condemn ourselves as guilty of the blackest ingratitude, in rarely noticing, or coldly turning away, on whatever shallow pretences, from the contemplation of these miracles of mercy. For those baser minds however on which fear can alone operate, that motive is superadded: and we are plainly forewarned, both directly and indirectly, by the example of the Jewish nation, that God will not hold them guiltless who are thus unmindful of his most signal acts of condescension and kindness. But as this is a question of pure Revelation, reasonings from probability may not be deemed decisive. To Revelation therefore we must appeal; and as it might be to trespass on the reader's patience fully to discuss this most important subject, we must refer him to the sacred Writings themselves for complete satisfaction. We would earnestly recommend it to him to weigh with the utmost seriousness those passages of Scripture wherein the peculiar doctrines of Christianity as expressly mentioned; and farther, to attend with due regard to illustration and confirmation which the conclusions resulting from those passages receive incidentally from the word of God. They who maintain the opinion which we are combating, will hereby

become convinced that their's is indeed an *unscriptural* Religion; and will learn instead of turning off their eyes from the
grand peculiarities of Christianity, to keep these ever in view, as
the pregnant principles whence all the rest must derive their
origin, and receive their best support.[25]

Let us then each for himself solemnly ask ourselves,
whether *we* have fled for refuge to the appointed hope? And
whether we are habitually looking to it, as to the only source of
consolation? "Other foundation can no man lay:" there is no
other ground of dependence, no other plea for pardon; but *here*
there *is* hope, even to the uttermost. Let us labour then to
affect our hearts with a deep conviction of our need of a
Redeemer, and of the value of his offered mediation. Let us fall
down humbly before the throne of God, imploring pity and
pardon in the name of the Son of his love. Let us beseech him
to give us a true spirit of repentance, and of hearty undivided
faith in the Lord Jesus. Let us not be satisfied till the cordiality
of our belief be confirmed to us by that character of the Apostle
[Peter], "that to as many as believe Christ is precious" [1 Peter
2:7]; and let us strive to increase daily in *love* towards our
blessed Saviour; and pray earnestly that "we may be filled with
Joy and *Peace* in believing, that we may abound in *Hope* through
the power of the Holy Ghost" [Romans 15:13]. Let us diligently
put in practice the directions formerly given for cherishing and
cultivating the principle of the Love of Christ. With this view let
us labour assiduously to increase in knowledge, that our's may
be a deeply rooted and rational affection. By frequent medita-
tion on the incidents of our Saviour's life, and still more on the
astonishing circumstances of his death; by often calling to mind
the state from which he proposes to rescue us, and the glories
of his heavenly kingdom; by continual intercourse with him of
prayer and praise, of dependence and confidence in dangers,
of hope and joy in our brighter hours, let us endeavour to keep
him constantly present in our minds, and to render all our
conceptions of him more distinct, lively, and intelligent. The
title of Christian is a reproach to us, if we estrange ourselves
from Him after whom we are denominated. The name of Jesus
is not to be to *us* like the Allah of the Mahometans [Allah, the
God of the Muslim faith], a talisman or an amulet to be worn
on the arm, as an external badge merely and symbol of our
profession, and to preserve us from evil by some mysterious
and unintelligible potency; but is is to be engraved deeply on
the heart, there written by the finger of God himself in everlast-

ing characters. It is our title known and understood to present peace and future glory. The assurance which it conveys of a bright reversion, will lighten the burthens, and alleviate the sorrows of life; and in some happier moments, it will impart to us somewhat of that fulness of joy which is at God's right hand, enabling us to join even here in the heavenly Hosannah, "Worthy is the lamb that was slain, to receive power, and riches, and wisdom, and strength, and honour, and glory, and blessing" [Revelation 5:12]. "Blessing, and honour, and glory, and power, be unto him that sitteth upon the throne, and unto the Lamb forever and ever." [Revelation 5:13].

Notes ✍

1. Here Wilberforce cites William Shakespeare's play *Twelfth Night* (act 2, scene 4, line 15). However, he appears to have paraphrased this portion of the play. It actually reads:

> If ever thou shalt love,
> In the sweet pangs of it remember me;
> For such as I am all true lovers are:
> Unstaid and skittish in all motions else,
> Save in the constant image of the creature
> That is beloved.

2. Socinianism was a belief system developed by Faustus and Laelius Socinus in the sixteenth century. Faustus Socinus wrote two important works which set forth Socinian teaching: *De Jesu Christo servatore* and *Christianae religionis brevissima institutio.* Socinianianism persists today in the Unitarian church. Prior to his acceptance of Evangelical Christianity in 1785, Wilberforce had a sitting in the Essex Street chapel established by Theolpilius Lindsey. Lindsey was an exponent of Socinian thought and today is generally regarded as a father of modern Unitarianism. Lindsey and his parishoners believed in a benign Providence that judged the actions of humanity. They rejected Christ's divinity, the Christian understanding of the Atonement, and the authority of Scripture. Bearing all of this in mind, it is not difficult to see why Wilberforce sought so vigorously to refute Socinian and Unitarian teaching in *A Practical View of Christianity:* he wanted to keep others from rejecting orthodox Christianity, as he himself had done for a time. See John Pollock's *Wilberforce* (Tring, Herts, England: Lion, 1982), pp. 33–34. Here, Pollock presents an excellent overview of Wilberforce's pre-1785 religious views. For further information about Socinianism, see theologian Millard Erickson's summary of Socinian teaching in his *Christian Theology* (Grand Rapids, Mich.: Baker, 1992), pp. 783–85.

3. Dominicans are members of the mendicant order of friars founded by St. Dominic in 1215. During the Spanish Inquisition, members of this order were known to have tortured people in their efforts either to force conversions or to destroy perceived enemies of the Catholic Church.

4. Wilberforce writes, "This was the motto on their banner," meaning that "for the love of Christ," was the motto that the Dominicans placed on the banner of the Spanish Inquisition.

5. These men are Hernando Cortes (c. 1485–1547), the Spanish conqueror of Mexico, and Francisco Pizarro (1471–1541), the Spanish conqueror of Peru.

6. Wilberforce notes that the title "Scourge of the Earth," was the one given to Attila, the warrior king of the Huns [who reigned from A.D. 433–453?].

7. This is an English translation of a Latin proverb. In Latin this phrase is rendered "Optima corrupta pessima."

8. Wilberforce writes, "Vide [See] the testimony of the West India merchants to the Moravians, in the *Report of the Privy Council on the Slave Trade.*" The Moravians or Moravian Brethren is a name which refers to the settlement of Protestant Pietists at Herrnhut who were led by Count Zinzendorf in the early eighteenth century. The Moravians were pioneers in the modern missions movement, sending missionaries throughout much of the world—including the West Indies.

9. This Latin passage cited by Wilberforce is taken from Book XXX of *Agricola,* a work by Tacitus (c. A.D. 55–c. 117). I have inserted an English translation by M. Hutton, which appears in the Loeb Classical Library's edition of *Agricola* (Cambridge, Mass.: Harvard University Press, 1980), p. 81. I have corrected Wilberforce's slightly inaccurate citation of this Latin passage by inserting the word "Auferre" and correcting the spelling of some Latin words. I have used the Latin in the Loeb edition as the authoritative text.

10. Wilberforce attributes this quote to "Dr. Horne." This "late excellent prelate" was Bishop George Horne (1730–92) of Norwich. His wrote many works of a scholarly and devotional nature. He is best remembered for his *Commentary on the Psalms,* published in 1771. Horne was a great friend of Hannah More, who was, in turn, a great friend of William Wilberforce.

11. This Latin citation used by Wilberforce is taken from Book VII, lines 20–21 of *Metamorphoses,* a work by the poet Ovid (43 B.C.–A.D. 18?). I have inserted an English translation by Frank Justus Miller. Miller's translation appears in the Loeb Classical Library's edition of Ovid's *Metamorphoses* Vol. I (Cambridge: Mass.: Harvard University Press, 1984), p. 343.

12. See Exodus 5:7–19. The "Egyptian bondage" to which Wilberforce is referring is a reference to Pharaoh's command that the Israelite slaves produce without straw the same number of bricks as they had previously produced with straw.

13. The Latin citation used here by Wilberforce is taken from lines 180–81 of *Ars Poetica,* a work by the poet Horace (65–8 B.C.). I have inserted H. Rushton Fairclough's English translation, which appears in the Loeb Classical Library's edition of Horace's *Satires, Epistles, Ars Poetica* (Cambridge, Mass.: Harvard University Press, 1970), p. 465. NOTE: I have corrected the capitalization and punctuation originally used in this Latin citation by Wilberforce to avoid any possible confusion on the part of the reader. Also, the word "aures" in the Latin citation above should have read "aurem." It appears that Wilberforce was either quoting this passage from memory (as Horace was one of his favorite Latin writers) or that this was a typographical error.

14. The "eminent writer" Wilberforce is referring to here is the political economist Adam Smith (1723–90). Wilberforce is quoting here from Smith's book, *Theory of Moral Sentiments.*

15. In this verse, Wilberforce notes that in the margin of his Bible the word "comfortless" was rendered "orphans."

16. Wilberforce writes, "Of true love it may be affirmed as of eloquence[:]

> Materia alitur, et motibus excitatur, et uresido[?] clarescit.

> [It is fed by tinder, and it is fed by movements, and it glows brightly by burning.]

17. Wilberforce writes "Vide [See] Mr. Doddridge's *Eight Sermons of Regeneration,* a most valuable compilation; and M'Laurin's *Essay on Divine Grace.*" Philip Doddridge (1702–51) was a nonconformist divine (clergyman or theologian). His best known work was *The Rise and Progress of Religion in the Soul,* published in 1745. This book played a major role in the conversion of William Wilberforce. John Maclaurin (1963–1754) was a Presbyterian divine and is generally regarded as one of the most famous preachers of his day. His works include a collection entitled *Sermons and Essays,* which was published in 1755.

18. Wilberforce writes,

> The writer trusts he cannot be misunderstood to mean that any, continuing sinners and ungodly, can, by believing, be accepted or finally saved. The following chapter, particularly the latter part of it, (Section 6) would abundantly vindicate him from such misconstruction. Meanwhile, he will only remark, that true faith (in which repentance is considered as involved) is in Scripture regarded as *the radical principle of holiness.* If the root exist, the proper fruits will be brought forth. An attention to this consideration would have easily explained and reconciled those passages of St. Paul's and St. James' Epistles, which have furnished so much matter of argument and criticism. St. James, it may be observed, all along speaks of a man, not who has faith, but who says that he has faith. Vide [See] James 2:14. &c. &c.

19. Wilberforce refers the reader to a note in chapter 4, section 6.

20. John Milton, *Paradise Lost*, Book 2, line 565.

21. Tychonic astronomy refers to the scheme for the structure of the solar system advanced in 1583 by the Danish astronomer Tycho Brahe (1546–1601). Brahe's work in developing astronomical devices and measuring as well as fixing the positions of stars helped to pave the way for future discoveries. His celestial observations were the most accurate ones produced prior to the invention of the telescope.

22. Wilberforce writes "Nec Deus intersit, &c." The citation used here by Wilberforce is taken from lines 191–92 of *Ars Poetica*, a work by the Latin poet Horace (65–8 B.C.). The definitive edition of this work is that contained in the Loeb Classical Library. See Horace's *Satires, Epistles, Ars Poetica* (Cambridge, Mass.: Harvard University Press, 1970), p. 467. In Latin, the lines to which Wilberforce is referring are: "nec deus intersit, nisi dignus vindice nodus inciderit, nec quarta loqui persona laboret." In English, the lines have been translated by H. Rushton Fairclough to read: "And let no god intervene, unless a knot come worthy of such a deliverer, nor let a fourth actor essay to speak."

23. The Greek philosopher Epicurus (341–270 B.C.) wrote a work entitled *To Menoeceus*, which concerned ethics and theology. Wilberforce may have had this work in mind when he made reference to Epicurus' ideas about "heavenly things."

24. Wilberforce states in the note here: "Vide [See] Hebrews 2:1. 'Therefore we ought to give the more earnest heed to the things which we have heard, lest at any time we should let them slip.' &c."

25. Wilberforce writes:

> Any one who wishes to investigate this subject, will do well to study attentively M'Laurin's *Essay on Prejudices against the Gospel.*—It may not be amiss here to direct the reader's attention to a few leading arguments, many of them those of the work just recommended. Let him maturely estimate the force of those terms, whereby the Apostle [Paul] in the following passages designates and characterizes the whole of the Christian system. "We preach Christ crucified"—"We determined to know nothing among you, save Jesus Christ and him crucified." The value of this argument will be acknowledged by all who consider that a system is never designated by an immaterial or an inferior part of it, but by that which constitutes its prime consideration and essential distinction. The conclusion suggested by this remark is confirmed by the Lord's Supper being the rite by which our Saviour himself commanded his Disciples to keep him in remembrance; and indeed a familiar lesson is taught by the Sacrament of Baptism, which shadows out our souls being washed and purified by the blood of Christ. Observe next the frequency with which our Saviour's death and sufferings are introduced, and how often they are urged as practical motives.

The minds of the Apostles seem full of this subject. Every thing put them in mind of it; they did not allow themselves to have it long out of their view, nor did any other branch of spiritual instruction make them lose sight of it." Consider next that part of the Epistle to the Romans, wherein St. Paul speaks of some who went about to establish their own righteousness, and had not submitted themselves to the righteousness of God. May not this charge in some degree be urged, and even more strongly than in the case of the Jews, against those who satisfy themselves with vague, general, occasional thoughts of our Saviour's mediation; and the source of whose habitual complacency, as we explained above, is rather their being tolerably well satisfied with their own characters and conduct? Yet St. Paul declares concerning those of whom he speaks, as concerning persons whose sad situation could not be too much lamented, that he had great heaviness and continual sorrow in his heart, adding still more emphatical expressions of deep and bitter regret.

Let the Epistle to the Galatians be also carefully examined and considered; and let it be fairly asked, what was the particular in which the Judaizing Christians were defective, and the want of which is spoken of in such strong terms as these; that it frustrates the grace of God, and must debar from all the benefits of the death of Jesus? The Judaizing converts were not immoral. They seem to have admitted the chief tenets concerning our Saviour. But they appear to have been disposed to trust *(not wholly, be it observed also, but only in part)* for their acceptance with God, to the Mosaic institutions, instead of reposing wholly on the merits of Christ. Here let it be remembered, that when a compliance with these institutions was not regarded as conveying this inference, the Apostle shewed by his own conduct, that he did not deem it criminal; whence, no less than from the words of the Epistle, it is clear that the offence of the Judaizing Christians whom he condemned, was what we have stated; not their obstinately continuing to adhere to a dispensation the ceremonial of which Christianity had abrogated, or their trusting to the sacrifices of the Levitical Law which were in their own nature inefficacious for the blotting out of sin. Vide [See] Heb[rews 7, 8, 9, 10].

$\curlywedge$Chapter Four

*On the Prevailing Inadequate Conceptions
Concerning the Nature and the Strictness of
Practical Christianity*

SECTION ONE $\backsim$

ONE PART OF THIS TITLE MAY PERHAPS ON THE FIRST
view excite some surprise in any one, who may have drawn a
hasty inference from the charges conveyed by the two preceding chapters. Such a one might be disposed to expect, that they
who have very low conceptions of the corruption of human
nature, would be proportionably less indulgent to human frailty;
and that they who lay little stress on Christ's satisfaction for sin,
or on the operations of the Holy Spirit, would be more high
and rigid in their demands of diligent endeavours after universal holiness; since their scheme implies that we must depend
chiefly on our own exertions and performances for our acceptance with God.

But any such expectations as these would be greatly
disappointed. There is in fact a region of truth, and a region of
errors. They who hold the fundamental doctrines of Scripture
in their due force, hold also in its due degree of purity the
practical system which Scripture inculcates. But they who explain away the former, soften down the latter also, and reduce it
to the level of their own defective scheme. It is not from any
confidence in the superior amount of their own performances,
or in the greater vigour of their own exertions, that they
reconcile themselves to their low views of the satisfaction of
Christ, and of the influence of the Spirit; but it should rather

seem their plan so to depress the required standard of practice, that no man need fall short of it, that no superior aid can be wanted for enabling us to attain to it. It happens however with respect to their simple method of morality, as in the case of the short ways to knowledge, of which some vain pretenders have vaunted themselves to be possessed: despising the beaten path in which more sober and humble spirits have been content to tread, they have indignantly struck into new and untried paths; but these have failed of conducting them to the right object, and have issued only in ignorance and conceit.

It seems in our days to be the commonly received opinion, that provided a man admit in general terms the truth of Christianity, though he know not or consider not much concerning the particulars of the system; and if he be not habitually guilty of any of the grosser vices against his fellow creatures, we have no great reason to be dissatisfied with him, or to question the validity of his claim to the name and consequent privileges of a Christian. The title implies no more than a sort of formal, general assent to Christianity in the gross, and a degree of morality in practice, but little if at all superior to that for which we look in a good Deist, Mussulman [Muslim], or Hindoo [Hindu].[1]

If any one be disposed to deny that this is a fair representation of the religion of the bulk of the Christian world, he might be asked, whether if it were proved to them beyond dispute that Christianity is a mere forgery, would this occasion any great change in their conduct or habits of mind? Would any alteration be made in consequence of this discovery, except in a few of their speculative opinions, which, when distinct from practice, it is a part of their own system, as has been before remarked, to think of little consequence, and in their attendance on public worship, which however (knowing the good effects of religion upon the lower orders of the people) they might still think it better to attend occasionally for example's sake? Would not their regard for their character, their health, their domestic and social comforts, still continue to restrain them from vicious excesses, and to prompt them to persist in the discharge, according to their present measure, of the various duties of their stations? Would they find themselves dispossessed of what had been to them hitherto the repository of counsel and instruction, the rule of their conduct, their habitual source of peace, and hope, and consolation?

It were needless to put these questions. They are answered in fact already by the lives of many known unbelievers, between whom and these professed Christians, even the familiar associates of both, though men of discernment and observation, would discover little difference either in conduct or temper of mind. How little then does Christianity deserve that title to novelty and superiority which has been almost universally admitted; that pre-eminence, as a practical code, over all other systems of ethics! How unmerited are the praises which have been lavished upon it by its friends; praises, in which even its enemies (not in general disposed to make concessions in its favour) have so often been unwarily drawn in to acquiesce!

Was it then for this, that the Son of God condescended to become our instructor and our pattern, leaving us an example that we might tread in his steps? Was it for this that the apostles of Christ voluntarily submitted to hunger and nakedness and pain, and ignominy and death, when forewarned too by their Master that such would be their treatment? That, after all, their disciples should attain to no higher a strain of virtue than those who rejecting the Divine authority, should still adhere to the old philosophy?

But it may perhaps be objected that we are forgetting an observation which we ourselves have made, that Christianity has raised the general standard of morals; to which therefore Infidelity herself now finds it prudent to conform, availing herself of the pure morality of Christianity, and sometimes wishing to usurp to herself the credit of it, while she stigmatizes the authors with the epithets of ignorant dupes or designing imposters.

But let it then be asked, are the motives of Christianity so little necessary to the practice of it, its principles to its conclusions, that the one may be spared and yet the other remain in undiminished force? Still, then, its *Doctrines* are no more than a barren and inapplicable or at least an unnecessary theory, the place of which, it may perhaps be added, would be well supplied by a more simple and less costly scheme.

But can it be? Is Christianity then reduced to a mere creed? Is its practical influence bounded within a few external plausibilities? Does its essence consist only in a few speculative opinions, and a few useless and unprofitable tenets? And can this be the ground of that portentous distinction, which is so unequivocally made by the Evangelist [John the Baptist] between those who accept and those who reject the gospel: "He that believeth on the Son hath everlasting life: and he that believeth not the Son, shall not see life: but the wrath of God abideth on him?" [John 3:36]. This were to run into the very error which the bulk of professed Christians would be most forward to condemn, of making an unproductive faith the rule of God's future judgment, and the ground of an eternal separation. Thus not unlike the rival circumnavigators from Spain and Portugal, who setting out in contrary directions, found themselves in company at the very time they thought themselves farthest from each other; so the bulk of professed Christians arrive, though by a different course, almost at the very same point, and occupy nearly the same station as a set of enthusiasts, who also rest upon a barren faith, to whom on the first view they might be thought the most nearly opposite, and whose tenets they with reason profess to hold in peculiar detestation. By what pernicious courtesy of language is it, that this wretched system has been flattered with the name of Christianity?

The morality of the Gospel is not so slight a fabric. Christianity throughout exhibits proofs of its Divine original, and its practical precepts are no less pure than its doctrines are sublime. Can the compass of language furnish injunctions stricter in their measure or larger in their comprehension, than those with which the word of God abounds? *"Whatsoever* ye do in *word* or *deed,* do *all* in the name of the Lord Jesus" [Colossians 3:17] —"Be *ye* holy, *for God is holy"* [1 Peter 1:16]: —"Be ye *perfect,* as your Father which is in heaven is *perfect"* [Matthew 5:48]? We are commanded to *perfect* holiness, to go on unto *perfection.*

Such are the Scripture admonitions; and surely they to whom such admonitions are addressed, may not safely acquiesce in low attainments: a conclusion to which also we are led by the force of the expressions by which Christians are characterized in Scripture, and by the radical and thorough change which is represented as taking place in any man on his becoming a real Christian. "Every one," it is said, "that has this hope, purifieth himself even as God is pure" [1 John 3:3]: true Christians are said to be "partakers of the Divine nature" [2 Peter 1:4]; —"to be created anew in the image of God" [cf. Colossians 3:10]; —"to be temples of the Holy Ghost" [1 Corinthians 6:19], the effects of which must appear "in *all* goodness and righteousness and truth."

Great as was the progress which the apostle Paul had made in all virtue, he declares of himself that *he* still presses forward, "forgetting the things which are behind, and reaching forth unto the things which are before" [Philippians 3:13]. He prays for his beloved disciples, "that they may be *filled* with *all* the fullness of God" [Ephesians 3:19]; "that they may be *filled* with the fruits of righteousness" [Philippians 1:11]; "that they might walk worthy of the Lord unto *all* pleasing, being fruitful in *every* good work" [Colossians 1:10]. Nor is it a less pregnant and comprehensive petition, which, from our blessed Saviour's inserting it in the form of prayer he has given as a model for our imitation, we may infer ought to be the habitual sentiment of our hearts; "Thy will be done on earth *as it is in Heaven*" [Matthew 6:10].

These few extracts from the word of God abundantly vindicate the *strictness* of the Christian morality: but this point will however be still more fully established, when we proceed to investigate the *nature, essence,* and *governing principles* of the Christian character.

It is the grand, essential, practical characteristic of true Christians, that relying on the promises to repenting sinners of acceptance through the Redeemer, they have renounced and abjured all other masters, and have cordially and unreservedly devoted themselves to God. This is indeed the very figure which baptism daily represents to us: like the father of Hannibal,[2] we there bring our infant to the altar, we consecrate him to the service of *his proper owner* and vow *in his name* eternal hostilities against all the enemies of his salvation. After the same manner Christians are become the sworn enemies of sin; they will henceforth hold no parley [a conference for discussion of points in dispute] with it, they will allow it in no shape, they will admit it to no composition; the war which they have denounced against it, is cordial, universal, irreconcilable.

But this is not all—It is now their determined purpose to yield themselves without reserve to the reasonable service of their rightful Sovereign. "They are not their own" [1 Corinthians 6:19]: —their bodily and mental faculties, their natural and acquired endowments, their substance, their authority, their time, their influence; all these, they consider as belonging to them, not for their own gratification, but as so many instruments to be consecrated to the honour and employed in the service of God. This must be the master principle to which every other must be subordinate. Whatever may have been

hitherto their ruling passion; whatever hitherto their leading
pursuit; whether sensual, or intellectual, of science, of taste, of
fancy, or of feeling, it must now possess but a secondary place;
or rather (to speak more correctly) it must exist only at the
pleasure, and be put altogether under the controul and direction, of its true and legitimate superior.

Thus it is the prerogative of Christianity "to bring into
captivity *every thought* to the obedience of Christ" [2 Corinthians 10:5]. They who really feel its power, are resolved (in the
language of Scripture) "to live no longer to themselves, but to
him that died for them" [2 Corinthians 5:15]: they know indeed their own infirmities; they know that the way on which
they have entered is strait and difficult, but they know too the
encouraging assurance, "They that wait on the Lord shall
renew their strength" [Isaiah 40:31]; and, relying on this animating declaration, they deliberately purpose that, so far as
they may be able, the grand governing maxim of their future
lives shall be, *"to do all to the glory of God"* [1 Corinthians 10:31].

Behold here the seminal principle, which contains within
it, as in an embryo state, the rudiments of all true virtue; which,
striking deep its roots, though feeble perhaps and lowly in its
beginnings, silently progressive, and almost insensibly matur-
ing, yet will shortly, even in the bleak and churlish temperature
of this world, lift up its head and spread abroad its branches,
bearing abundant fruits; precious fruits of refreshment and
consolation, of which the boasted products of philosophy are
but sickly imitations, void of fragrance and of flavour. But,

> Igneus est ollis vigor & coelestis origo
> seminibus . . .
>
> [Fiery is the vigour and divine the source of
> those life-seeds . . .
>
> —Virgil][3]

At length it shall transplanted into its native region,
and enjoy a more genial climate and a kindlier soil; and,
bursting forth into full luxuriance, with unfading beauty and
unexhausted odours, shall flourish for ever in the paradise
of God.

But while the servants of Christ continue in this life,
glorious as is the issue of their labours, they receive many
humiliating memorials of their remaining imperfections, and

daily find reason to confess that they cannot do the things that they would [cf. Romans 7:18–19]. Their *determination,* however, is still unshaken, and it is the fixed desire of their hearts to improve in *all holiness* —and this, let it be observed, on many accounts. Various passions concur to push them forward; they are urged on by the dread of failure, in this arduous but necessary work; they trust not, where their all is at stake, to lively emotions, or to internal impressions however warm; the example of Christ is their pattern, the word of God is their rule; there they read, that "without holiness no man shall see the Lord" [Hebrews 12:14]. It is the description of real Christians, that "they are gradually changed into the image of their Divine Master" [cf. 2 Corinthians 3:18]; and they dare not allow themselves to believe their title sure, except so far as they can discern in themselves the growing traces of this blessed resemblance.

It is not merely however the fear of misery, and the desire of happiness, by which they are actuated in their endeavours to excel in all holiness; they love it for its own sake: nor is it *solely* by the sense of self-interest (this, though often unreasonably condemned, is but a principle of an inferior order) that they are influenced in their determination to obey the will, and to cultivate the favour of God. This determination has its foundations indeed in a deep and humiliating sense of his exalted Majesty and infinite power, and of their own extreme inferiority and littleness, attended with a settled conviction of its being their duty as his creatures, to submit in all things to the will of their great Creator. But these awful impressions are relieved and ennobled by an admiring sense of the infinite perfections and infinite amiableness of the Divine Character; animated by a confiding though humble hope of his fatherly kindness and protection; and quickened by the grateful recollection of immense and continually increasing obligations. This is the Christian love of God! A love compounded of admiration, of preference, of hope, of trust, of joy; chastised by reverential awe, and wakeful with continual gratitude.

I would here express myself with caution, lest I should inadvertently wound the heart of some weak but sincere believer. The elementary principles which have been above enumerated may exist in various degrees and proportions. A difference in natural disposition, in the circumstances of the past life, and in numberless other particulars, may occasion a great difference in the predominant tempers of different

Christians. In one, the love, in another the fear of God may have the ascendancy; trust in one, and in another gratitude; but in greater or less degrees, a cordial complacency in the sovereignty, an exalted sense of the perfections, a grateful impression of the goodness, and a humble hope of the favour of the Divine Being, are common to them all—Common—the determination to devote themselves without exceptions, to the service and glory of God—Common—the desire of holiness and of continual progress towards perfection—Common—an abasing consciousness of their own unworthiness, and of their many remaining infirmities, which interpose so often to corrupt the simplicity of their intentions, thwart the execution of their purer purposes, and frustrate the resolutions of their better hours.

But some perhaps, who will not directly and in the gross oppose the conclusions for which we have been contending, may endeavour to elude them. It may be urged, that to represent them as of general application, is going much too far; and however true in the case of some individuals of a higher order, it may be asserted they are not applicable to ordinary Christians; from these so much will not surely be expected; and here perhaps there may be a secret reference to that supposed mitigation of the requisitions of the Divine Law under the Christian dispensation, which was formerly noticed. This is so important a point that it ought not to be passed over: let us call in the authority of Scripture; at the same time, not to tire the patience of our readers, but a few passages shall be cited, and we refer to the word of God itself those who wish for fuller satisfaction. The difficulty here is not to find proofs, but to select with discretion from the multitude which pour in upon us. Here also as in former instances, the positive injunctions of Scripture are confirmed and illustrated by various considerations and inferences suggested by other parts of the sacred Writings, all tending to the same infallible conclusion.

In the first place, the precepts are expressed in the broadest and most general terms; there is no hint given, that any persons are at liberty to conceive themselves exempted from the obligation of them; and in any who are disposed to urge such a plea of exemption, it may well excite the most serious apprehension to consider how the plea would be received by an earthly tribunal: no weak argument this to any who are acquainted the Scriptures, and who know how often God is there represented as reasoning with mankind on the principles which they have established for their dealings with each other.

But in the next place the precepts in question contain within themselves abundant proofs of their *universal* application, inasmuch as they are grounded on circumstances and relations common to *all* Christians, and of the benefits of which, even our Objectors themselves (though they would evade the practical deductions from them) would not be willing to relinquish their share. Christians "are not their own," because *"they are bought with a price"* [1 Corinthians 6:19–20]; they are not "to live unto themselves, but to *him that died for them;"* they are commanded to do the most difficult duties, "that they may be the children of their Father which is in heaven" [Matthew 5:45]; and "except a man *be born again of the Spirit"* [John 3:5] (thus again becoming one of the sons of God) *"he cannot enter into the kingdom of heaven"* [John 3:5]. It is *"because they are sons,"* that God has given them what in Scripture language is styled *"the spirit of adoption"* [Romans 8:14–15]. It is only of "as many *as are led by the Spirit of God,"* that it is declared "they are the sons of God" [again, Romans 8:14–15]; and we are expressly warned (in order as it were to prevent any such loose profession of Christianity as that which we are here combating) *"If any man* have not the Spirit of Christ, *he is none of his"* [Romans 8:9]. In short, Christians in general are every where denominated the *servants and the children* of God, and are required to serve him with that submissive obedience, and that affectionate promptitude of duty, which belong to those endearing relations.

Estimate next the force of that well known passage— "Thou shalt love the Lord thy God with *all* thy heart, and with *all* thy mind, and with *all* thy soul, and with *all* thy strength!" [Mark 12:30]. The injunction is multiplied on us, to silence the sophistry of the caviller [one who objects or criticizes adversely for trivial reasons], and to fix the most inconsiderate mind. And though, for the sake of argument, we should concede for the present, that, under *the qualifications formerly suggested,* an *ardent* and *vigorous* affection were not indispensably required of us; yet surely if the words have any meaning at all, the least can be intended by them is that settled, predominant esteem and cordial preference for which we are now contending. The conclusion which this passage forces on us, is strikingly confirmed by other parts of Scripture, wherein the love of God is positively commended to the *whole* of a Christian church [cf. 2 Corinthians 13:14]; or wherein the want of it [see 1 John 3:17;

Romans 16:18; cf. Philippians 3:19], or wherein its not being the chief and ruling affection [2 Timothy 3:14], is charged on persons professing themselves Christians, as being sufficient to disprove their claim to that appellation, or as being equivalent to denying it [cf. 2 Timothy 3:4]. Let not therefore any deceive themselves by imagining, that only an absolute unqualified renunciation of the desire of the favour of God is *here* condemned. God will not accept of a *divided* affection; a *single* heart, and a *single* eye are in express terms declared to be indispensably required of us. We are ordered, under the figure of amassing heavenly treasure, to make the favour and service of God our *chief* pursuit, for this very reason, because "*where our treasure is, there will our hearts be also*" [Matthew 6:21]. It is on this principle that, in speaking of particular vices, such phrases are used in Scripture, as suggest that their criminality mainly consists in drawing away the HEART from Him who is the just object of its preference; and that sins, which we might think very different in criminality, are classed together, because they all agree in this grand character. Nor is this preference asserted only over affections which are vicious in themselves, and to which therefore Christianity might well be supposed hostile; but over those also which in their just measure are not only lawful, but even most strongly enjoined on us. "He that loveth father and mother more than me," says our blessed Saviour, "is not worthy of me"; "and he that loveth son or daughter more than me, is not worthy of me" [Matthew 10:37]. The spirit of these injunctions harmonizes with many commendations in Scripture of zeal for the honour of God; as well as with that strong expression of disgust and abhorrence with which the lukewarm, those that are neither cold nor hot, are spoken of as being more loathsome and offensive than even open and avowed enemies.

Another class of instances tending to the same point is furnished by those many passages of Scripture, wherein promoting of *the glory* of God is commanded as our supreme and universal aim, wherein the honour due unto *Him* is declared to be that in which He will allow no competitor to participate. On this head indeed the Holy Scriptures are, if possible, more peremptory than on the former; and at the same time so full as to render particular citations unnecessary, in the case of any one who has ever so little acquaintance with the word of God.

To put the same thing therefore in another light. All who have read the Scriptures must confess that idolatry is the crime against which God's highest resentment is expressed, and his severest punishment denounced. But let us not deceive ourselves. It is not in bowing the knee to idols that idolatry consists, so much as in the internal homage of the heart; as in feeling towards them, any of that supreme love, or reverence, or gratitude, which God reserves to himself as his own exclusive prerogative. On the same principle, whatever else draws off the heart from him, engrosses our prime regard, and holds the chief place in our esteem and affections, *that,* in the estimation of reason, is no less an idol to us than an image of wood or stone would be; before which we should fall down and worship. Think not this a strained analogy; it is the very language and argument of inspiration. The servant of God is commanded not to set up his idol in his *Heart* [cf. Matthew 6:21]; and sensuality and covetousness are repeatedly termed *Idolatry.* The same God who declares—"My glory I will not give to another, neither my praise *to graven images*" [Isaiah 42:8], declares also—"Let not the wise man glory in his wisdom, neither let the mighty man *glory* in his might; let not the rich man *glory* in his riches" [Jeremiah 9:23]. "No flesh may *glory* in his presence" [1 Corinthians 1:29]; "he that *glorieth,* let him glory in the Lord" [1 Corinthians 1:31]. The sudden vengeance by which the vain glorious ostentation of Herod was punished, when, acquiescing in the servile adulation of an admiring multitude, "he gave not God the *glory*" [Acts 12:21–23], is a dreadful comment on these injunctions.

These aweful declarations, it is to be feared, are little regarded. Let the Great, and the Wise, and the Learned, and the Successful lay them seriously to heart, and labour habitually to consider their superiority, whether derived from nature, or study, or fortune, as the unmerited bounty of God. This reflection will naturally tend to produce a disposition, instead of that proud self complacency so apt to grow upon the human heart, in all respects opposite to it; a disposition honourable to God, and useful to man; a temper composed of reverence, humility, and gratitude, and delighting to be engaged in the praises, and employed in the benevolent service of the universal Benefactor.

But, to return to our subject, it only remains to be remarked, that here as in the former instances, the characters of the righteous and of the wicked, as delineated in Scripture, exactly correspond with the representations which have been given of the Scripture injunctions.

The necessity of this cordial unreserved devotedness to the glory and service of God, as indispensable to the character of the true Christian, has been insisted on at the greater length, not only on account of its own extreme importance, but also because it appears a duty too generally overlooked. Once well established, it will serve as a fundamental principle both for the government of the heart and regulation of the conduct; and will prove eminently useful in the decision of many practical cases, which it might be difficult to bring under the undisputed operation of any subordinate or appropriate rule.

SECTION TWO ᜧ

And now, having endeavoured to establish the strictness, and to ascertain the essential character of true practical Christianity, let us investigate a little more in detail the practical system of the bulk of professed Christians among ourselves.[4]

It was formerly remarked, that the whole subject of Religion was often viewed from such a distance as to be seen only in the gross. We now, it is to be feared, shall find too much cause for believing that they who approach a little nearer, and do discover in Christianity somewhat of a distinct form, yet come not close enough to discern her peculiar lineaments and conformation. The writer must not be understood to mean that the several misconceptions which he shall have occasion to point out, will be generally found to exist with any thing like precision, much less that they are regularly digested into a system; nor will it be expected they all should meet in the same person, nor that they will not be found in different people, and under different circumstances, variously blended, combined, and modified. It will be enough if we succeed in tracing out great and general outlines. The human countenance may be well described by its general characters, though infinitely varied by the peculiarities which belong to different individuals, and often by such shades and minutenesses of difference, as though abundantly obvious to our perceptions, it would exceed the power of definition to discriminate or even of language to express.

A very erroneous notion prevails concerning the true nature of Religion. Religion, agreeably to what has been already stated (the importance of the subject will excuse repetition) may be considered as the implantation of a vigorous and active principle; it is seated in the heart, where its authority is recognized as supreme, whence by degrees it expels whatever is opposed to it, and where it gradually brings all the affections and desires under its complete controul and regulation.

But though the heart be its special residence, it may be said to possess in a degree the ubiquity of its Divine Author. Every endeavour and pursuit must acknowledge its presence; and whatever does not, or will not, or cannot receive its sacred stamp, is to be condemned as inherently defective, and is to be at once abstained from or abandoned. It is like the principle of vitality, which animating and informing every part, lives throughout the whole of the human body, and communicates its kindly influence to the smallest and remotest fibres of the frame. But the notion of Religion entertained by many among us seems altogether different. They begin indeed, in submission to her clear prohibitions, by fencing off from the field of human action, a certain district, which, though it in many parts bear fruits on which they cast a longing eye, they cannot but confess to be forbidden ground. They next assign to Religion a portion, larger or smaller according to whatever may be their circumstances and views, in which however she is to possess merely a qualified jurisdiction, and having so done, they conceive that without let or hindrance they have a right to range at will over the spacious remainder. Religion can claim only a stated proportion of their thoughts, and time, and fortune, and influence; and of these, or perhaps of any of them, if they make her any thing of a liberal allowance, she may well be satisfied: the rest is now their own to do with what they will with; they have paid their tithes, say rather their composition, the demands of the Church are satisfied, and they may surely be permitted to enjoy what she has left without molestation or interference.

It is scarcely possible to state too strongly the mischief which results from this fundamental error. At the same time its consequences are so natural and obvious, that one would think it scarcely possible not to foresee that they must infallibly follow. The greatest part of human actions is considered as indifferent. If men are not chargeable with actual vices, and are decent in the discharge of their religious duties; if they do not stray into the forbidden ground, if they respect the rights of the conceded allotment, what more can be expected from them? Instead of keeping at a distance from *all sin,* in which alone consists our safety, they will be apt not to care how near they approach what they conceive to be the boundary line; if they have not actually passed it, there is no harm done, it is no trespass. Thus the free and active spirit of religion is "cribbed and hemmed in;" she is checked in her disposition to expand her territory, and enlarge the circle of her influence. She must keep to her prescribed confines, and every attempt to extend them will be resisted as an encroachment.

But this is not all. Since whatever can be gained from her allotment, or whatever can be taken in from the forbidden ground, will be so much of addition to that land of liberty, where men may roam at large, free from restraint or molestation, they will of course be constantly and almost insensibly straitening and pressing upon the limits of the religious allotment on the one hand, and on the other, will be removing back a little farther and farther the fence which abridges them on the side of the forbidden ground. If Religion attempt for a time to defend her frontier, she by degrees gives way. The space she occupies diminishes till it be scarcely discernible; whilst her spirit extinguished, and her force destroyed, she is little more than the nominal possessor even of the contracted limits to which she has been avowedly reduced.

This it is to be feared is but too faithful a representation of the general state of things among ourselves. The promotion of the glory of God, and the possession of his favour, are no longer recognized as the objects of our highest regard, and most strenuous endeavours; as furnishing to us, a vigorous, habitual, and universal principle of action. We set up for ourselves: we are become our own masters. The sense of constant homage and continual service is irksome and galling to us; and we rejoice in being emancipated from it as from a state of base and servile villainage. Thus the very tenure and condition by which life and all its possessions are held, undergo a total change: our faculties and powers are now our own: whatever we have is regarded rather as a property than as a trust; or if there still exist the remembrance of some paramount claim, we are satisfied with an occasional acknowledgment of a nominal right; we pay our pepper corn, and take our estates to ourselves in full and free enjoyment.

Hence it is that so little sense of responsibility seems attached to the possession of high rank, or splendid abilities, or affluent fortunes, or other means or instruments of usefulness. The instructive admonitions, "give an account of thy stewardship" [Luke 16:2], —"Occupy till I come" [Luke 19:13]; are forgotten. Or if it be acknowledged by some men of larger views than ordinary, that reference is to be had to some principle superior to that of our own gratification, it is, at best, to the good of society, or to the welfare of our families: and even then the obligations resulting from these relations, are seldom enforced on us by any higher sanctions than those of family comfort, and of worldly interest or estimation. Besides; what multitudes of persons are there, people without families, in private stations, or of a retired turn, to whom they are scarcely held to apply; and what multitudes of cases to which it would be thought unnecessary scrupulosity to extend them? Accordingly, we find *in fact*, that the generality of mankind among the higher order, in the formation of their schemes, in the selection of their studies, in the choice of their place of residence, in the employment and distribution of their time, in their thoughts, conversation and amusements, are considered as being at liberty, if there be no actual vice, to consult in the main their own gratification.

Thus the generous and wakeful spirit of Christian benevolence, seeking and finding, every where occasions for its exercise, is exploded, and a system of *decent selfishness* is avowedly established in its stead; a system scarcely more to be abjured for its impiety, than to be abhorred for its cold insensibility to the opportunities of diffusing happiness. "Have we no families, or are they provided for? Are we wealthy, and bred to no profession? Are we young and lively, and in the gaiety and vigour of youth? Surely we may be allowed to take our pleasure. We neglect no duty, we live in no vice, we do nobody any harm, and have a right to amuse ourselves. We have nothing better to do; we wish we had; our time hangs heavy on our hands for want of it."

I pity the man who can travel from Dan to Beer-sheba [tribal regions of ancient Israel] and cry "It is all barren." No man has a right to be idle—Not to speak of that great work which we all have to accomplish, and surely the *whole* attention of a short and precarious life is not more than an eternal interest may well require; where is it that in such a world as this, health, and leisure, and affluence may not find some ignorance to instruct, some wrong to redress, some want to supply, some misery to alleviate? Shall Ambition and Avarice never sleep? Shall they never want objects on which to fasten? Shall they be so observant to discover, so acute to discern, so eager, so patient to pursue, and shall the Benevolence of Christians want employment?

Yet thus life rolls away with too many of us in a course of "shapeless idleness." Its recreations constitute its chief business. Watering places—the sports of the field—cards! never-failing cards!—the assembly—the theatre—all contribute their aid—amusements are multiplied, and combined, and varied, "to fill up the void of a listless and languid life;" and by the judicious use of these different resources, there is often a kind of sober settled plan of domestic dissipation, in which with all imaginable decency year after year wears away in unprofitable vacancy. Even old age often finds us pacing in the same round of amusements which our early youth had tracked out. Meanwhile, being conscious that we are not giving into any flagrant vice, perhaps that we are guilty of no irregularity, and it may be, that we are not neglecting the offices of Religion, we persuade ourselves that we need not be uneasy. In the main we do not fall below the general standard of morals, of the class and station to which we belong, we may therefore allow ourselves to glide down the stream without apprehension of the consequences.

Some, of a character often hardly to be distinguished from the class we have been just describing, take up with *sensual* pleasures. The chief happiness of their lives consists in one species or another of animal gratification; and these persons perhaps will be found to compose a pretty large description. It will be remembered, that it belongs not to our purpose to speak of the grossly and scandalously profligate, who renounce all pretensions to the name of Christians; but of those who, maintaining a certain decency of character, and perhaps being tolerably observant of the forms of Religion, may yet be not improperly termed *sober sensualists*. These, though less impetuous and more measured, are not less staunch and steady, than the professed votaries of licentious pleasure, in the pursuit of their favourite objects. "Mortify the flesh, with its affections and lusts" [Galatians 5:24], is the Christian *precept;* but a soft luxurious course of habitual indulgence is the *practice* of the bulk of modern Christians: and that constant moderation, that wholesome discipline of restraint and self-denial, which are requisite to prevent the unperceived encroachments of the inferior appetites, seem altogether as disused as the exploded austerities of monkish superstition [this is an allusion to the ascetic religious lifestyles of some monastic orders].

Christianity calls her professors to a state of diligent watchfulness and active services. But the persons of whom we are now speaking, forgetting alike the duties they owe to themselves and to their fellow-creatures, often act as though their condition were meant to be a state of uniform indulgence, and vacant, unprofitable sloth. To multiply the comforts of affluence, to provide for the gratification of appetite, to be luxurious without diseases, and indolent without lassitude, seems the chief study of their lives. Nor can they be clearly exempted from this class, who, by a common error, substituting the means for the end, make the preservation of health and spirits, not as instruments of usefulness, but as sources of pleasure, their great business and continual care.

Others again seem more to attach themselves to what have been well termed the "pomps and vanities of this world." Magnificent houses, grand equipages, numerous retinues, splendid entertainments, high and fashionable connections, appear to constitute, in their estimation, the supreme happiness of life. This class too, if we mistake not, will be found numerous in our days; for it must be considered *that it is the heart, set on these things*, which constitutes the essential character. It often happens, that persons, to whose rank and station these indulgences most properly belong, often are the most indifferent to them. The undue solicitude about them is more visible in persons of inferior conditions and smaller fortunes, in whom it is not rarely detected by the studious contrivances of a misapplied ingenuity to reconcile parade with oeconomy, and glitter at a cheap rate. But this temper of display and competition is a direct contrast to the lowly, modest, unassuming carriage of the true Christian: and wherever there is an evident effort and struggle to excel in the particulars here in question, a manifest wish thus to rival superiors, to outstrip equals, to dazzle inferiors; it is manifest the great end of life, and of all its possessions, is too little kept in view, and it is to be feared that the gratification of a vain ostentatious humour is the predominant disposition of the heart.

As there is a sober sensuality, so is there also a sober avarice, and a sober ambition.

The commercial and the professional world compose the chief sphere of their influence. They are often recognized and openly avowed as just master principles of action. But where this is not the case, they assume such plausible shapes, are called by such specious names, and urge such powerful pleas, that they are received with cordiality, and suffered to gather strength without suspicion. The seducing considerations of diligence in our callings, of success in our profession, of making handsome provisions for our children, beguile our better judgments. "We rise early, and late take rest, and eat the bread of carefulness." In our few intervals of leisure, our exhausted spirits require refreshment; the serious concerns of our immortal souls, are matters of speculation too grave and gloomy to answer the purpose, and we fly to something that may better deserve the name of relaxation, till we are again summoned to the daily labours of our employment.

Meanwhile Religion seldom comes in our way, scarcely occurs to our thoughts; and when some secret misgivings begin to be felt on this head, company soon drowns, amusements dissipate, or habitual occupations insensibly displace or smother the rising apprehension. Professional and commercial men perhaps, especially when they happen to be persons of more than ordinary reflection, or of early habits of piety not quite worn away, easily quiet their consciences by the plea, that necessary attention to their business leaves them no time to think on these serious subjects at present. "Men of leisure they confess should consider them; they themselves will do it hereafter when they retire; meanwhile they are usefully or at least innocently employed." Thus business and pleasure fill up our time, and the "one thing needful" [Luke 10:42] is forgotten. Respected by others, and secretly applauding ourselves, (perhaps congratulating ourselves that we are not like such an one who is a spendthrift or a mere man of pleasure, or such another who is a notorious miser) the true principle of action is no less wanting in us, and personal advancement or the acquisition of wealth is the object of our supreme desires and predominant pursuit.

It would be to presume too much on the reader's patience to attempt a delineation of the characters of the politician, the metaphysician, the scholar, the poet, the virtuoso, the man of taste, in all their varieties. Of these and many other classes which might be enumerated, suffice it to remark, and to appeal to every man's own experience for the truth of the observation, that they in like manner are often completely engrossed by the objects of their several pursuits. In many of these cases indeed a generous spirit surrenders itself wholly up with the less reserve, and continues absorbed with the fuller confidence, from the consciousness of not being led to its object by self-interested motives. Here therefore these men are ardent, active, laborious, persevering, and they think, and speak, and act, as those, the whole happiness of whose life turns on the success or failure of their endeavours. When such as we have seen it, is the undisturbed composure of mere triflers, it is less wonderful that the votaries of learning and of taste, when absorbed in their several pursuits, should be able to check still more easily any growing apprehension, silencing it by the suggestion, that they are more than harmlessly, that they are meritoriously employed. "Surely the thanks of mankind are justly paid to those more refined spirits who, superior alike to the seductions of ease, and the temptations of avarice, devote their time and talents to the less gainful labours of increasing the stores of learning or enlarging the boundaries of science; who are engaged in raising the character and condition of society, by improving the liberal arts, and adding to the innocent pleasures or elegant accomplishments of life." Let not the writer be so far misunderstood, as to be supposed to insinuate that Religion is an enemy to the pursuits of taste, much less to those of learning and of science. Let these have their *due* place in the estimation of mankind; but this must not be the *highest* place. Let them know their just *subordination*. They deserve not to be the *primary* concern, for there is another, to which in importance they bear no more proportion than our span of existence to eternity.

Thus the supreme desires of the heart, the center to which they should tend, losing its attractive force, are permitted without controul to take that course, whatever it may be, which best suits our natural temper, or to which they are impelled by our various situations and circumstances. Sometimes they manifestly appear to be almost entirely confined to a single track; but perhaps more frequently the lines in which they move are so intermingled and diversified, that it becomes not a little difficult, even when we look into ourselves, to ascertain the object by which they are chiefly attracted, or to estimate with precision the amount of their several forces, in the different directions in which they move. "Know thyself," is in truth an injunction with which the careless and the indolent cannot comply. For this compliance, it is requisite, in obedience to the Scripture precept, "to keep the heart with all diligence" [Proverbs 4:23]. Mankind are in general deplorably ignorant of their true state; and there are few perhaps who have any adequate conception of the real strength of the ties, by which they are bound to the several objects of their attachment, or who are aware how small a share of their regard is possessed by those concerns on which it ought to be supremely fixed.

But if it be indeed true, that except the affections of the soul be supremely fixed on God; that unless it be *the leading and governing desire and primary pursuit* to possess his favour and promote his glory, we are considered as having transferred our fealty to an usurper, and as being in fact revolters from our lawful sovereign; if this be indeed the Scripture doctrine, all the several attachments which have been lately enumerated, of the different classes of society, wherever they interest the affections, and possess the soul in any such measure of strength as deserves to be called *predominance,* are but so many varied expressions of *disloyalty.* God requires to set up his throne in the heart, and to reign in it without a rival: if he be kept out of his right, it matters not by what competitor. The revolt may be more avowed or more secret; it may be the treason of deliberate preference, or of inconsiderate levity; we may be the subjects of a more or of a less creditable master; we may be employed in services more gross or more refined: but whether the slaves of avarice, of sensuality, of dissipation, of sloth, or the votaries of ambition, of taste, or of fashion; whether supremely governed by vanity and self-love, by the desire of literary fame or of military glory, we are alike estranged from the dominion our rightful sovereign. Let not this seem a harsh position; it can appear so only from not adverting to what was shewn to be the *essential nature* of true Religion. He who bowed the knee to the god of medicine or of eloquence, was no less an idolater than the worshipper of the deified patrons of lewdness or of theft. In the several cases which have been specified, the *external acts* indeed are different, but in *principle* the disaffection is the same; and unless we return to our allegiance, we must expect the title, and prepare to meet the punishment, of rebels on that tremendous day, when all false colours shall be done away and (there being no longer any room for the evasions of worldly sophistry [reasoning that is clever and subtle but perhaps misleading], or the smooth plausibilities of worldly language) "that which is often highly esteemed amongst men, shall appear to have been abomination in the sight of God" [Luke 16:15].

These fundamental truths seem vanished from the mind, and it follows of course, that every thing is viewed less and less through a religious medium. To speak no longer of instances wherein *we ourselves* are concerned, and wherein the unconquerable power of indulged appetite may be supposed to beguile our better judgment, or force us on in defiance of it; not to insist on the motives by which the conduct of men is determined, often avowedly, in what are to *themselves* the most important incidents of life; what are the judgements which men form in the case of *others?* Idleness, profusion, thoughtlessness and dissipation [the practice of habitually giving in to one's vices], the misapplication of time or of talents, the trifling away of life in frivolous occupations or unprofitable studies; all these things we may regret in those around us, in the view of their temporal effects; but they are not considered in a religious connection, or lamented as endangering everlasting happiness. Excessive vanity and inordinate ambition are spoken of as weaknesses rather than as sins; even covetousness itself, though a hateful passion, yet, if not extreme, scarcely presents the face of *Irreligion.* Is some friend, or even some common acquaintance sick, or has some accident befallen him? How solicitously do we inquire after him, how tenderly do we visit him, how much perhaps do we regret that he has not better advice, how apt are we to prescribe for him, and how should we reproach ourselves, if were to neglect any means in our power of contributing to his recovery! But "the mind diseased" is neglected and forgotten—"*that* is not our affair; we hope (we do not perhaps really believe) that here it is well with him." The truth is, we have no solicitude about his spiritual interest. Here he is treated like the unfortunate traveler in the Gospel; we look upon him we see but too well his sad condition, but (Priest and Levite alike) we pass by on the other side, and leave him to the officious tenderness of some poor despised Samaritan [see the parable of the Good Samaritan; Luke 10:30–37].

Nay, take the case of our very children, when out hearts being most interested to promote their happiness, we must be supposed most desirous of determining on right principles, and where therefore the real standard of our deliberate judgments may be indisputably ascertained: in their education and marriage, in the choice of their professions, in our comparative consideration and judgment of the different parts of their several characters, how little do we reflect that they are immortal beings? Health, learning, credit; the amiable and agreeable qualities; above all, fortune and success in life, are taken, and not unjustly taken, into the account; but how small a share in forming our opinions is allowed to the probable effect which may be produced on their eternal interests? Indeed the subjects of our mutual inquiries, and congratulations, and condolences, prove but too plainly what considerations are in these cases uppermost in our thoughts.

Such are the fatal and widely spreading effects, which but too naturally follow from the admission of the grand fundamental error before mentioned, that of not considering Religion as a principle of universal application and command. Robbed of its best energies, Religion now takes the form of a cold compilation of restraints and prohibitions. It is looked upon simply as a set of penal statutes; these, though wise and reasonable, are however so far as they extend, abridgements of our natural liberty, and nothing which comes to us in this shape is extremely acceptable:

> [Et]qui nolunt occidere quemquam posse volunt.

> [Even those who don't want to kill anybody
> would like to have the power to do it.

> —Juvenal][5]

Considering, moreover, that the matter of them is not in general very palatable, and that the partiality of every man, where his own cause is in question, will be likely to make him construe them liberally in his own favour, we might beforehand have formed a tolerable judgment of the manner in which they are actually treated. Sometimes we attend to the words rather than to the spirit of Scripture injunctions, overlooking the principle they involve, which a better acquaintance with the word of God would have clearly taught us to infer from them. At others, "the spirit of an injunction is all;" and this we contrive to collect so dexterously, as thereby to relax or annul the strictness of the terms. "Whatever is not expressly forbidden cannot be *very* criminal; whatever is not positively enjoined, cannot be indispensably necessary—If we do not offend against the laws, what more can be expected from us?—The persons to whom the strict precepts of the Gospel were given, were in very different circumstances from those in which we are placed. The injunctions were drawn rather tighter than is quite necessary, in order to allow for a little relaxation in practice. The expressions of the sacred Writers are figurative; the Eastern style is confessedly hyperbolical."

By these and other such dishonest shifts (by which however we seldom deceive ourselves, except it be in thinking that we deceive others) the pure but strong morality of the word of God is explained away, and its too rigid canons [rules or standards] are softened down, with as much dexterity as is exhibited by those who practice a logic of the same complexion, in order to escape from the obligations of human statutes. Life Swift's unfortunate Brothers, we are sometimes put to difficulties, but our ingenuity is little inferior to theirs. If totidem verbis will not serve our turn, try totidem syllabis; if totidem syllabis fail, try totidem literis: then there is in our case, as well as in theirs, "an allegorical sense" to be adverted to; and if every other resource fail us, we come at last to the same conclusion as the Brothers adopted, that after all, those rigorous clauses require some allowance, and a favourable interpretation, and ought to be understood "cum grano salis."[6]

But when the law both in its spirit and its letter is obstinate and incorrigible, what we cannot bend to our purpose we must break—"Our sins we hope are of the smaller order; a little harmless gallantry, a little innocent jollity, a few foolish expletives which we use from the mere force of habit, meaning nothing by them; a little warmth of colouring and license of expression; a few freedoms of speech in the gaiety of our hearts, which, though not perhaps strictly correct, none but the over-rigid would think of treating any otherwise than as venial [pardonable, or not serious] infirmities, and in which very grave and religious men will often take their share, when they may throw off their state, and relax without impropriety. We serve an all-merciful Being, who knows the frailty of our nature, the number and strength of our temptations, and will not be extreme to mark what is done amiss. Even the less lenient judicatures of human institution concede somewhat to the weakness of man. It is an established maxim—"De minimis non curat lex" ["The law does not regard trifles"]. We hope we are not worse than the generality. All men are imperfect. We own we have our infirmities; we confess it is so; we wish we were better, and trust as we grow older we shall become so; we are ready to acknowledge that we must be indebted for our admission into a future state of happiness, not to our own merit, but to the clemency of God, and the mercy of our Redeemer."

But let not this language be mistaken for that of true Christian humiliation, of which it is the very essence to feel the burden of sin, and to long to be released from it: nor let two things be confounded, than which none can be more fundamentally different, the allowed want of universality in our determination, and our endeavour to obey the will of God, and that defective accomplishment of our purposes, which even the best of men will too often find reason to deplore. In the persons of whom we now have been speaking, the unconcern with which they can amuse themselves upon the borders of sin, and the easy familiarity with which they can actually dally with it in its less offensive shapes, shew plainly that, distinctly from its consequences, it is by no means the object of their aversion; that there is no love of holiness as such; no endeavour to acquire it, no care to prepare the soul for the reception of this divine principle, and to expel or keep under whatever might be likely to obstruct its entrance, or dispute its sovereignty.

It is indeed a most lamentable consequence of the practice of regarding Religion as a compilation of statutes, and not as an internal principle, that it soon comes to be considered as being conversant about *external actions* rather than about *habits of mind.* This sentiment sometimes has indeed the hardiness to insinuate and maintain itself under the guise of extraordinary concern for *practical Religion;* but it soon discovers the falsehood of this pretension, and betrays its real nature. The expedient indeed of attaining to superiority in practice, by not wasting any of the attention on the internal principles, from which alone practice can flow, is about as reasonable, and will answer about as well, as the oeconomy of the architect, who should account it mere prodigality to expend any of his materials in laying foundations, from an idea that they might be more usefully applied to the raising of the superstructure. We know what would be the fate of such an edifice.

It is indeed true, and a truth never to be forgotten,that all pretensions to internal principles of holiness are vain when they are contradicted by the conduct; but it is no less true, that the only effectual way of improving the latter, is by a vigilant attention to the former. It was therefore our blessed Saviour's injunction, "Make the tree good" [Matthew 7:17–20] as the necessary means of obtaining good fruit; and the holy Scriptures abound in admonitions, to let it be our chief business to cultivate our hearts with all diligence, to examine into their state with impartiality, and watch over them with continual care. Indeed it is the *Heart* which constitutes the *Man;* and external actions derive their whole character and meaning from the motives and dispositions of which they are the indications. Human judicatures, it is true, are chiefly conversant about the former; but this is only because to our limited perceptions the latter can seldom be any otherwise clearly ascertained. The real object of inquiry to human judicatures is the *internal* disposition; it is to this that they adapt the nature, and proportion the degree, of their punishments.

Yet though this be a truth so obvious, so established, that to have insisted on it may seem almost needless; it is a truth of which we are apt to lose sight in the review of our religious Character, and with which the *habit*, of considering Religion as consisting rather in external actions, than internal principles, is at direct and open war. This mode of judging may well be termed *habitual*, for though by some persons it is advisedly adopted and openly avowed, yet in many cases for want of due watchfulness, it has stolen insensibly upon the mind; it exists unsuspected, and is practised, like other habits, without consciousness or observation.

In what degree soever this pernicious principle prevails, in that degree is the mischief it produces. The vicious affections, like noxious weeds, sprout up and increase of themselves but too naturally; while the graces of the Christian temper, exotics in the soil of the human heart, like the more tender productions of the vegetable world, though the light and breath of Heaven must quicken them, require on our part also, in order to their being preserved in health and vigour, constant superintendence and assiduous care. But so far from their being earnestly sought for, or watchfully reared, with unremitted prayers for that Divine Grace, without which all our labours must be ineffectual; such is the result of the principle we are here condemning, that no endeavours are used for their attainment, or they are suffered to droop and die, almost without an effort to preserve them. The culture of the mind is less and less attended to, and at length perhaps is almost wholly neglected. Way being thus made for the unobstructed growth of other tempers, the qualities of which are very different, and often directly opposite, these naturally overspread and quietly possess the mind; their contrariety to the Christian spirit not being discerned, and even perhaps their presence being scarcely acknowledged, except when their existence and their nature are manifested in the conduct by marks too plain to be overlooked or mistaken.

Some of the most important branches of the Christian temper, wherein the bulk of nominal Christians appear eminently and allowably defective, have been already noticed in this and in the preceding chapter. Many others still remain to be particularized.

First then, it is the comprehensive compendium of the character of true Christians, that "they are walking by faith, and not by sight" [2 Corinthians 5:7]. By this description is meant, not merely that they so firmly believe in the doctrine of future rewards and punishments, as to be influenced by that persuasion to adhere in the main to the path of duty, though tempted to forsake it by present interest, and present gratification; but farther, that the great truths revealed in Scripture concerning the unseen world, are the ideas for the most part uppermost in their thoughts, and about which, habitually, their hearts are most interested. This state of mind contributes, if the expression may be allowed, to rectify the illusions of vision, to bring forward into nearer view those eternal things which from their remoteness are apt to be either wholly overlooked, or to appear but faintly in the utmost bounds of the horizon; and to remove backward and reduce to their true comparative dimensions, the objects of the present life, which are apt to fill the human eye, assuming a false magnitude from their vicinity. The true Christian knows from experience however, that the former are apt to fade from the sight, and the latter again to swell on it. He makes it therefore his continual care to preserve those just and enlightened views which through Divine mercy he has obtained. Not that he will retire from that station in the world which Providence seems to have appointed him to fill; he will be active in the business of life, and enjoy its comforts with moderation and thankfulness; but he will not be "totus in illis" ["totally absorbed in those matters"], he will not give up his whole soul to them, they will be habitually subordinate in his estimation to objects of more importance. The aweful truth has sunk deep into his mind, "the things which are seen are temporal, but the things which are not seen are eternal" [2 Corinthians 4:18]; and in the tumult and bustle of life, he is sobered by the still small voice which whispers to him, "the fashion of this world passes away" [1 Corinthians 7:31; cf. Matthew 24:35]. This circumstance alone must, it is obvious, constitute a vast difference between the habitual temper of his mind, and that of the generality of nominal Christians, who are almost entirely taken up with the concerns of the present world. They *know* indeed that they are mortal, but they do not *feel* it. The truth rests in their understandings, and cannot gain admission into their hearts. This speculative persuasion is altogether different from that strong *practical* impression of the infinite importance of eternal things, which attended with a proportionate sense of the shortness and uncertainty of all below, while it prompts to activity from a conviction that "the night cometh when no man can work" [John 9:4], produces a certain firmness of texture, which hardens us against the buffets of fortune, and prevents our being very deeply penetrated by the cares and interests, the goods or evils, of this transitory state. Thus this just impression of the relative value of temporal and eternal things, maintains in the soul a dignified composure through all the vicissitudes of life. It quickens our diligence, yet moderates our ardour; urges us to just pursuits, yet checks any undue solicitude about the success of them, and thereby enables us, in the language of Scripture, "to use this world without abusing it" [1 Corinthians 7:31], rendering us at once beneficial to others and comfortable to ourselves.

But this is not all—besides the distinction between the nominal and the real Christian, which results from the impressions produced on them respectively by the *eternal duration* of heavenly things, there is another grounded on their *nature* no less marked, nor less important. They are stated in Scripture, not only as entitling themselves to the notice of the true Christian from considerations of interest, but as approving themselves to his judgement from a conviction of their excellence; and yet farther, as recommending themselves to his feelings by their being suited to the renewed dispositions of his heart. Indeed were the case otherwise, did not their qualities correspond with his inclinations, however he might endure them on principles of duty, and be coldly conscious of their superior worth, he could not lend himself to them with cordial complacency, much less look to them as the surest source of pleasure. But this is the light in which they are habitually regarded by the true Christian. He walks in the ways of Religion, not by constraint, but willingly; they are to him not only safe, but comfortable, "ways of pleasantness as well as of peace" [Proverbs 3:17]. Not but that here also he is from experience aware of the necessity of constant support, and continual watchfulness; without these, his old estimate of things is apt to return on him, and the former objects of his affections to resume their influence. With earnest prayers, therefore, for the Divine Help, with jealous circumspection and resolute self-denial, he guards against, and abstains from, whatever might be likely again to darken his *enlightened judgment*, or to vitiate his reformed taste;

thus making it his unwearied endeavour to grow in the knowledge and love of heavenly things, and to obtain a warmer admiration, and a more cordial relish of their excellence.

That this is a just representation of the habitual judgment, and of the leading disposition of true Christians, will be abundantly evident, if, endeavouring to form ourselves after our proper model, we consult the sacred Scripture. But in vain are Christians there represented as having set their *affections* on things above [cf. Colossians 3:2], as *cordially rejoicing* in the service, and delighting in the worship of God. Pleasure and Religion are contradictory terms with the bulk of nominal Christians. They may look back indeed on their religious offices with something of a secret satisfaction, and even feel it during the performance of them, from the idea of being engaged in the discharge of a duty; but this is altogether different from the pleasure which attends an employment in itself acceptable and grateful to us. The writer must here again guard against being understood to speak of a deficiency in the *warmth* and *vehemence* merely of Religious affections. Are the service and worship of God *pleasant* to these persons? it is not asked whether they are *delightful*. Do they diffuse over the soul any thing of that calm complacency, that mild and grateful composure, which bespeaks a mind in good humour with itself and all around it, and engaged in service suited to its taste, and congenial with its feelings?

Let us appeal to the Day which is especially devoted to the offices of Religion: Do they joyfully avail themselves of this blessed opportunity of withdrawing from the business and cares of life; when, without being disquieted by any doubt whether they are not neglecting the duties of their proper callings, they may be allowed to detach their minds from earthly things, that by a fuller knowledge of heavenly objects, and a more habitual acquaintance with them, their hope may grow more "full of immortality?" Is the day cheerfully devoted to those holy exercises for which it was appointed? Do they indeed "come into the courts of God with gladness?" [cf. Psalm 100:2; see also the rest of Psalm 100]. And how are they employed when not engaged in the public services of the day? Are they busied in studying the word of God, in mediating on his perfections, in tracing his providential dispensations, in admiring his works, in revolving his mercies, (above all, the transcendent mercies of redeeming love) in singing his praises, "and speaking good of his name?" [cf. Psalms 54:6; 92:1; 135:3]. Do their secret retirements witness the earnestness of their prayers and the warmth of their thanksgivings, their diligence and impartiality in the necessary work of self-examination, their mindfulness of the benevolent duty of intercession? Is the kind purpose of the institution of a Sabbath answered by them, in its being made to their servants and dependents a season of rest and comfort? Does the instruction of their families, or of the more poor and ignorant of their neighbours, possess its due share of their time? If blessed with talents or with affluence, are they sedulously employing a part of this interval of leisure in relieving the indigent and visiting the sick, and comforting the sorrowful, in forming plans for the good of their fellow creatures, in considering how they may promote both the temporal and spiritual benefit of their friends and acquaintance[s]; or if theirs be a larger sphere, in devising measures whereby through the Divine blessing, they may become the honoured instruments of the more extended diffusion of religious truth? In the hours of domestic or social intercourse, does their conversation manifest the subject of which their hearts are full? Do their language and demeanour shew them to be more than commonly gentle, and kind, and friendly, free from rough and irritating passions?

Surely an entire day should not seem long amidst these various employments. It might be deemed a privilege thus to spend it, in the more immediate presence of our Heavenly Father, in the exercises of humble admiration and grateful homage; of the benevolent and domestic, and social feelings, and of all the best affections of our nature, prompted by their true motives, conversant about their proper objects, and directed to their noblest end; all sorrows mitigated, all cares suspended, all fears repressed, every angry emotion softened, every envious or revengeful, or malignant passion expelled; and the bosom, thus quieted, purified, enlarged, ennobled, partaking almost of a measure of the Heavenly happiness, and become for a while the seat of love, and joy, and confidence, and harmony.

The nature, and uses, and proper employments of a Christian Sabbath, have been pointed out more particularly, not only because the day will be found when thus employed, eminently conducive, through the Divine Blessing, to the maintenance of the Religious principle in activity and vigour; but also because we must all have had occasion often to remark, that many persons of the graver and more decent sort, seem not seldom to be nearly destitute of religious resources. The Sunday is with them, to say the best of it, a *heavy* day; and that larger part of it which is not claimed by the public offices of the church, dully drawls on in comfortless vacuity, or without improvements, is trifled away in vain and unprofitable discourse. Not to speak of those who by their more daring profanation of this sacred season, openly violate the laws and insult the religion of their country, how little do many seem to enter into the *spirit* of the institution, who are not wholly inattentive to its exterior decorums! How glad are they to qualify the rigor of their religious labours. How hardly do they plead against being compelled to devote the *whole* of the day to Religion, claiming to themselves no small merit for giving up to it a part, and purchasing therefore, as they hope, a right to spend the remainder more agreeably! How dexterously do they avail themselves of any plausible plea for introducing some week-day employment into the Sunday, whilst they have not the same propensity to introduce any of the Sunday's peculiar employment into the rest of the week! How often do they find excuses for taking journeys, writing letters, balancing accounts; or in short doing something, which by a little management might probably have been anticipated, or which, without any material inconvenience, might be postponed. Even business itself is recreation, compared with Religion, and from the drudgery of this day of Sacred Rest, they fly for relief to their ordinary occupations.

Others again who would consider business as a prophanation, and who still hold out against the encroachments of the card table, get over much of the day and gladly seek for an innocent resource in the social circle or in family visits, where it is not even pretended that the conversation turns on such topics as might render it in any way conducive to religious instruction, or improvements. Their families meanwhile are neglected, their servants robbed of Christian privileges, and their example quoted by others who cannot see that they are themselves less religiously employed, while playing an innocent game at cards, or relaxing in the concert room.

But all these several artifices, *whatever they may be, to unhallow* the Sunday, and to change its character (it might almost be said "to relax its horrors,") prove but too plainly, however we may be glad to take refuge in Religion, when driven to it by the loss of every other comfort, and to retain as it were a reversionary interest in an asylum, which may receive us when we are forced from the transitory enjoyments of our present state, that *in itself* it wears to us a gloomy and forbidding aspect, and not a face of consolation and joy: that the worship of God is with us a *constrained* and not a *willing* service, which we are glad therefore to abridge though we dare not omit it.

Some indeed there are who with concern and grief will confess this to be their uncomfortable and melancholy state; who humbly pray, and diligently endeavour for an imagination less distracted at devotional seasons, for a heart more capable relishing the excellence of divine things; and who carefully guard against whatever has a tendency to chain down their affections to earthly enjoyments. Let not such be discouraged. It is not they whom we are condemning; but such as knowing and even acknowledging this to be their case, yet proceed in a way directly contrary: who scarcely seeming to suspect that any thing is wrong with them, voluntarily acquiesce in a state of mind which is directly contrary to the positive commands of God, which forms a perfect contrast to the representations given us in Scripture of the Christian character, and accords but too faithfully in one leading feature with the character of those, who are stated to be the objects of Divine displeasure in this life, and of Divine punishment in the next.

It is not however only in these essential constituents of a devotional frame that the bulk of nominal Christians are defective. This they freely declare (secretly feeling perhaps some complacency from the frankness of the avowal) to be a higher strain of piety than that to which they aspire. Their forgetfulness also of some of the leading dispositions of Christianity, is undeniably apparent in their allowed want of the spirit of kindness and meekness, and patience and long suffering; and above all, of that which is the stock on which alone these dispositions can grow and flourish, that *humility* and *lowliness of mind*, in which perhaps more than in any other quality may be said to consist the true essence and vital principle of the Christian temper. These dispositions are not only neglected, but even disavowed and exploded, and their opposites if not rising to any great height, are acknowledged and applauded. A just pride, a proper and becoming pride, are terms we daily hear from Christian lips. To possess *a high spirit,* to behave with *a proper spirit* when used ill,—by which is meant a quick feeling of injuries, and a promptness in resenting them,—entitles to commendation; and a meek-spirited disposition, the highest Scripture eulogium, expresses ideas of disapprobation and contempt. Vanity and vain glory are suffered without interruption to retain their natural possession of the heart. But here a topic opens upon us of such importance, and a which so many mistakes are to be found both in the writings of respectable authors, and in the commonly prevailing opinions of the world, that it may be allowed us to discuss it more at large, and for this purpose to treat of it in a separate section.

SECTION THREE ᠕

*On the Desire of Human Estimation and
Applause—The Generally Prevailing Opinions
Contrasted with Those of the True Christian*

The desire of human estimation and distinction, and honour, of the admiration and applause of our fellow creatures, if we take it in its full comprehension, and in all its various modifications, from the thirst of glory to the dread of shame, is the passion of which the empire is by far the most general, and perhaps the authority the most commanding. Though its power be most conspicuous and least controulable in the higher classes of society, it seems, like some resistless conqueror, to spare neither age, nor sex, nor condition; and taking ten thousand shapes, insinuating itself under the most specious pretexts, and sheltering itself necessary under the most artful disguises, it wins its way in secret, when it dares not openly avow itself, and mixes in all we think, and speak, and do. It is in some instances the determined and declared pursuit, and confessedly the main practical principle; but where this is not the case, it is not seldom the grand spring of action, and in the Beauty and the Author, no less than in the Soldier, it is often the master passion of the soul.

This is the principle which parents recognize with joy in their infant offspring, which is diligently instilled and nurtured in advancing years, which, under the names of honourable ambition and of laudable emulation, it is the professed aim of schools and colleges to excite and cherish. The writer is well aware that it will be thought he is pushing his opinions much too far when he ventures to assail this great principle of human action; a principle, its advocates might perhaps exclaim, "the extinction of which, if you could succeed in your rash attempt, would be like the annihilation in the material world of the principle of motion; without it all were and cold, and comfortless. We grant," they might go on to observe, "that we never ought to deviate from the paths of duty in order to procure the applause or to avoid the reproaches of men, and we allow that this is a rule too little attended to in practice. We grant that the love of praise is in some instances a ridiculous, and in others a mischievous passion; that to it we owe coquettes and coxcombs, and, a more serious evil, the noxious race of heroes and conquerors. We too are ready, when it appears in the shape of vanity, to smile at it as a foible, or in that of false glory, to condemn it as a crime. But all these are only its perversions; and on account of them to contend against its true forms, and its legitimate exercise, were to give into the very error which you formerly yourself condemned, of arguing against the use of a salutary principle altogether, on account of its being liable to occasional abuse. When turned into the right direction, and applied to its true purposes, it prompts to every dignified and generous enterprise. It is erudition in the portico [a place from which lectures or public discussions might be given], skill in the lyceum [a place for holding lectures or public discussions], eloquence in the senate, victory in the field. It forces indolence into activity, and extorts from vice itself the deeds of generosity and virtue. When once the soul is warmed by its generous ardor, no difficulties deter, no dangers terrify, no labours tire. It is this which giving by its stamp to what is virtuous and honourable its just superiority over the gifts of birth and fortune, rescues the rich from base subjection to the pleasures of sense, and makes them prefer a course of toil and hardship to a life of indulgence and ease. It prevents the man of rank from acquiescing in his hereditary greatness, and spurs him forward in pursuit of *personal* distinction, and of a nobility which he may justly term his own. It moderates and qualities the over-great inequalities of human conditions; and reaching to those who are above the sphere of laws, and extending to cases which fall not within their province, it limits and circumscribes the power of the tyrant on his throne, and gives gentleness to war, and to pride, humility.

Nor is its influence confined to public life, nor is it known only in the great and the splendid[.] To it is to be ascribed a large portion of that courtesy and disposition to please, which naturally producing a mutual appearance of good will, and a reciprocation of good offices, constitute much of the comfort of private life, and give their choicest sweets to social and domestic intercourse. Nay, from the force of habit, it follows us even into solitude, and in our most secret retirements we often act as if our conduct were subject to human observation, and we derive no small complacency from the imaginary applauses of an ideal spectator."

So far of the *effects* of the love of praise and distinction; and if after enumerating some of these, you should proceed to investigate its *nature*, "We admit[,"] it might be added, "that a hasty and misjudging world often misapplies commendations and censures: and whilst we therefore confess, that the praises of the discerning few are alone truly valuable; we acknowledge that it were better if mankind were always to act from the sense of right and the love of virtue, without reference to the opinions of their fellow-creatures. We even allow, that independently of consequences, this were perhaps in itself a higher strain of virtue; but it is a degree of purity which it would be vain to expect from the bulk of mankind. When the *intrinsic excellence* of this principle however is called in question, let it be remember'd, that in its higher degrees it was styled by one who meant rather to detract from its merits than to aggravate them, 'the infirmity of *noble* minds;' and surely, that in such a soil it most naturally springs up, and flourishes, is no mean proof of its exalted origin and generous nature.

But were these more dubious, and were it no more than a splendid error; yet considering that it works so often in the right direction, it were enough to urge in its behalf, that it is a principle of real *action,* and approved energy. That, as much as practice is better than theory, and solid realities than empty speculation, so much is it to be preferred for general use before those higher principles of morals, which however just and excellent in themselves, you would in vain attempt to bring home to the 'business and bosoms of mankind,' at large. Reject not then a principle thus universal in its influence, thus valuable in its effects; a principle, which, by whatever name you may please to call it, acts by motives and considerations suited to our condition; and which, putting it at the very lowest, must be confessed, in our present infirm state, to be an habitual aid and an ever present support to the feebleness of virtue! In a selfish world it produces the effects of disinterestedness; and when public spirit is extinct, it supplies the want of patriotism. Let us therefore with gratitude avail ourselves of its help, and not relinquish the good which

it freely offers, from we know not what vain dreams of imprac-
ticable purity and unattainable perfection."

All this and much more might be urged by the advocates of this favourite principle. It would be however, no difficult task to shew that it by no means merits this high eulogium.
To say nothing of that larger part of the argument of our
opponents, which betrays and even proceeds upon that mischievous notion of the innocence of error, against which we
have already entered our formal protest, the principle in question is manifestly of a most inconstant and variable nature; as
inconstant and variable as the innumerably diversified modes
of fashions, habits, and opinions in different periods and societies. What it tolerates in one age, it forbids in another; what in
one country it prescribes and applauds, in another it condemns
and stigmatizes! Obviously and openly, it often takes vice into
its patronage, and sets itself in direct opposition to virtue. It is
calculated to produce rather the *appearance* than the *reality* of
excellence; and at best not to check the *love* but only the
commission of vice. Much of this indeed was seen and acknowledged by the philosophers, and even by the poets, of the Pagan
world. They declaimed against it as a mutable and inconsistent
principle; they lamented the fatal effects which, under the
name of false glory, it had produced on the peace and happiness of mankind. They condemned the pursuit of it when it led
its followers out of the path of virtue, and taught that the praise
of the wise and of the good only was to be desired.

But it was reserved for the page of Scripture to point
out to us distinctly, wherein it is apt to be essentially defective
and vicious, and to discover to us more fully its encroaching
nature and dangerous tendencies; teaching us at the same time,
how, being purified from its corrupt qualities, and reduced
under just subordination, it may be brought into legitimate
exercise, and be directed to its true end.

In the sacred volume we are throughout reminded, that
we are originally the creatures of God's formation, and continual dependents on his bounty. There too we learn the painful
lesson of man's degradation and unworthiness. We learn that
humiliation and contrition are the tempers of mind best suited
to our fallen condition, and most acceptable in the sight of our
Creator. We learn that these (to the repression and extinction of
that spirit of arrogance and self-importance, so natural to the
heart of man) it should be our habitual care to cherish and
cultivate; studiously maintaining a continual sense, that, not

only for all the *natural* advantages over others which we may possess, but that for all our *moral* superiority also, we are altogether indebted to the unmerited goodness of God. It might perhaps be said to be the great end and purpose of all revelation, and especially to be the design of the Gospel, to reclaim us from our natural pride and selfishness, and their fatal consequences; to bring us to a just sense of our weakness and *depravity;* and to dispose us, with unfeigned humiliation, to abase ourselves, and give glory to God. "No flesh may glory in his presence [1 Corinthians 1:29]; he that glorieth, let him glory in the Lord" [1 Corinthians 1:31]. —"The lofty looks of man shall be humbled, and the haughtiness of men shall be bowed down, and the Lord alone shall be exalted" [Isaiah 2:11].

These solemn admonitions are too generally overlooked, their intimate connection with the subject we are now considering, appears to have been often entirely overlooked, even by Christian moralists. These authors, without reference to the main spring, and internal principle of conduct, are apt to speak of the love of human applause, as being meritorious or culpable [deserving blame], as being the desire of true or of false glory, accordingly as the external actions it produces and the pursuits to which it prompts, are beneficial or mischievous to mankind. But it is undeniably manifest, that in the judgment of the word of God, the love of worldly admiration and applause is in its *nature* essentially and radically corrupt, so far as it partakes of a disposition to exalt and aggrandize ourselves, to pride ourselves on our natural or acquired endowments, or to assume to ourselves the merit and credit of our good qualities, instead of ascribing all the honour and glory where only they are due.

Its *guilt* therefore in these cases, is not to be measured by its effects on the happiness of mankind; nor is it to be denominated *true or false* glory, accordingly as the ends to which it is directed are beneficial or mischievous, just or unjust objects of pursuit; but it is *false,* because it exalts that which ought to be abased, and *criminal,* because it encroaches on the prerogative of God.

The Scriptures further instruct us, not merely that mankind are liable to error, and therefore that the world's commendations *may be* sometimes mistaken; but that their judgment being darkened and their hearts depraved, its applauses and contempt will for the most part be systematically misplaced; that though the beneficent and disinterested spirit of Christianity, and her obvious tendency to promote domestic comfort and general happiness, cannot but extort applause; yet that her aspiring after more than ordinary excellence, by exciting secret misgivings in others, or a painful sense of inferiority not unmixed with envy, cannot fail often to disgust and offend. The word of God teaches us, that though such of the doctrines and precepts of Christianity as are coincident with worldly interests and pursuits, and with worldly principles and systems, may be professed without offence; yet, that what is opposite to these, or even different from them, will be deemed needlessly precise and strict, the indulgence of a morose and gloomy humour, the symptoms of a contracted and superstitious spirit, the marks of a mean, enslaved, or distorted understanding. That for these and other reasons the follower of Christ must not only make up his mind to the *occasional relinquishment* of worldly favour, but that it should even afford him matter of holy jealousy and suspicion of himself, when it is very lavishly and very generally bestowed.

But though the standard of worldly estimation differed less from that of the Gospel; yet since our affections ought to be set on heavenly things [Colossians 3:2], and conversant about heavenly objects; and since in particular the love and favour of God ought to be the matter of our supreme and habitual desire, to which every other should be subordinated; it follows, that the love of human applause must be manifestly injurious so far as it tends to draw down our regards to earthly concerns, and to bound and circumscribe our desires within the narrow limits of this world.

Particularly, that it is *impure,* so far as it is tinctured with a disposition to estimate too highly, and love too well the good opinion and commendations of man.

But though, by these and other instructions and considerations the Holy Scripture warns us against the inordinate desire or earnest pursuit of worldly estimation and honour; though it so greatly reduces their value, and prepares us for losing them without surprise, and for relinquishing them with little reluctance: yet it teaches us, that Christians in general, are not only not called upon absolutely and voluntarily to renounce or forego them; but that when, without our having solicitously sought them, they are bestowed on us for actions intrinsically good, we are to accept them as being intended by Providence, to be sometimes, even in this disorderly state of things, a present solace, and a reward to virtue. Nay more, we are instructed, that in our general deportment, that in little particulars of conduct otherwise indifferent, that in the *circum-stances* and *manner* of performing actions in themselves of a determined character and indispensable obligation, (guarding however against the smallest degree of artifice or deceit) that by watching for opportunities of doing little kindnesses, that by avoiding singularities, and even humouring prejudices where it may be done without the slightest infringement on truth or duty, we ought to have a due respect and regard to the approbation and favour of men. These however we should not value, chiefly as they administer to our own gratification, but as furnishing means and instruments of influence, which we may turn to good account, by making them subservient to the improvement and happiness of our fellow creatures, and thus conducive to the *glory of God.* The remark is almost superfluous, that on occasions like these we must even watch our hearts with the most jealous care, lest pride and self love insensibly infuse themselves, and corrupt the purity of principles so liable to contract a taint.

Credit and reputation, in the judgment of the true Christian, stand on ground not very different from riches; which he is not to prize highly, or to desire and pursue with solicitude; but which, when they are allotted to him by the hand of Providence, he is to accept with thankfulness, and to use with moderation; relinquishing them when it becomes necessary, without a murmur; guarding most circumspectly for so long as they remain with him, against that sensual and selfish temper, and no less against that pride and wantonness of heart, which they are too apt to produce and cherish; thus considering them as in themselves acceptable, but, from the infirmity of his nature, as highly dangerous possessions; and valuing them chiefly not as instruments of luxury or splendour, but as affording the means of honouring his heavenly Benefactor, and lessening the miseries of mankind.

Christianity however, as was formerly observed, proposes not to extinguish our natural desires, but to bring them under just controul, and direct them to their true objects. In the case of both riches and honour, she maintains the consistency of her character. While she commends us not to set our hearts on *earthly* treasures, she reminds us that we have in *Heaven* "a better and more enduring substance" [Matthew 6:19–21] than this world can bestow; and while she represses our solicitude respecting earthly credit, and moderate[s] our attachment to it, she holds forth to us, and bids us habitually to aspire after, the splendours of that better state, where is true glory, and honour, and immortality; thus exciting in us a just ambition, suited to our high origin and worthy of our large capacities, which the little, misplaced, and perishable distinctions of this life would in vain attempt to satisfy.

It would be a mere waste of time to enter into any laboured argument to prove at large that the light in which worldly credit and estimation are regarded by the bulk of professed Christians is extremely different from that in which they are placed by the page of Scripture. The *inordinate* love of *worldly glory* indeed, implies a passion, which from the nature of things cannot be called into exercise in the generality of mankind, because, being conversant about great objects, it can but rarely find that field which is requisite for its exertions. But we every where discover the same principle reduced to the dimensions of common life, and modified and directed according to every one's sphere of action. We may discover it in a supreme love of distinction, and admiration, and praise; in the universal acceptableness of flattery; and above all in the excessive valuation of our worldly character, in that watchfulness with which it is guarded, in that jealousy when it is questioned, in that solicitude when it is in danger, in that hot resentment when it is attacked, in that bitterness of suffering when it is impaired or lost. All these emotions, as they are too manifest to be disputed, so they are too reputable to be denied. Dishonour, disgrace, and shame present images of horror too dreadful to be faced; they are evils, which it is thought the mark of a generous spirit, to consider as excluding every idea of comfort and enjoyment, and to feel, in short, as too heavy to be borne.

The consequences of all this are natural and obvious. Though it be not openly avowed, that we are to follow after worldly estimation, or to escape from worldly disrepute, when they can only be pursued or avoided by declining from the path of duty; nay though the contrary be recognized as being the just opinion, yet all the effect of this speculative concession is soon done away *in fact*. Estimating worldly credit as of the highest intrinsic excellence, and worldly shame as the greatest of all possible evils, we sometimes shape and turn the path of duty itself from its true direction, so as it may favour our acquisition of the one, and avoidance of the other, or when this cannot be done, we boldly and openly turn aside from it, declaring the temptation is too strong to be resisted.

It were easy to adduce numerous proofs of the truth of these assertions. It is proved, indeed, by that general tendency in Religion to conceal herself from the view, for we might hope that in these cases she often is by no means altogether extinct; by her being apt to vanish from our conversations, and even to give place to a pretended licentiousness of sentiments and conduct, and a false shew of infidelity. It is proved, by that complying acquiescence and participation in the habits and manners of this dissipated age, which has almost confounded every external distinction between the Christian and the Infidel, and has made it so rare to find any one who dares incur the charge of Christian singularity, or who can say with the Apostle that "he is not ashamed of the gospel of Christ" [Romans 1:16]. It is proved (how can this proof be omitted by one to whose lot it has so often to witness and lament, sometimes he fears to afford an instance of it) by that quick resentment, those bitter contentions, those angry retorts, those malicious triumphs, that impatience of inferiority, that wakeful sense of past defeats, and promptness to revenge them, which too often change the character of a Christian deliberative Assembly, into that of a stage for prize fighters: violating at once the proprieties of public conduct, and the rules of social decorum, and renouncing and chasing away all the charities of the Religion of Jesus!

But from all lesser proofs, our attention is drawn to one of a still larger size, and more determined character. Surely the reader will here anticipate our mention of the practice of Duelling: a practice which, to the disgrace of a Christian society, has long been suffered to exist with little restraint or opposition.

This practice, whilst it powerfully supports, mainly rests on, that excessive over-valuation of character, which teaches, that wor[l]dly credit is to be preserved at *any* rate, and disgrace at *any* rate to be avoided. The *unreasonableness* of duelling has been often proved, and it has often been shewn to be criminal on various principles: sometimes it has been opposed on grounds hardly tenable; particularly when it has been considered as an indication of malice and revenge.[7] But it seems hardly to have been enough noticed in what chiefly consists its *essential* guilt; that it is a deliberate preference of the favour of man, before the favour and approbation of God, *in articulo mortis* ["at the point of death"], in an instance, wherein our own life, and that of a fellow creature are at stake, and wherein we run the risk of rushing into the presence of our Maker in the very act of offending him. It would detain us too long, and it were somewhat beside our present purpose, to enumerate the mischievous consequences which result from this practice. They are many and great; and if regard be had merely to the temporal interests of men, and to the well being of society, they are but poorly counterbalanced by the plea which must be admitted in its behalf by a candid observer of human nature, of a courtesy and refinement in our modern manners unknown to ancient times.

But there is one observation which must not be omitted, and which seems to have been too much overlooked: In the judgment of that Religion which requires purity of heart, and of that Being to whom, as was before remarked, "thought is action" [Matthew 5:28], he cannot be esteemed innocent of this crime, who lives in a settled habitual determination to commit it, when circumstances shall call upon him so to do.[8] This is a consideration which places the crime of duelling on a different footing from almost any other; indeed there is perhaps NO other, which mankind habitually and deliberately resolve to practice whenever the temptation shall occur. It shews also that the crime of duelling is far more general in the higher classes than is commonly supposed, and that the whole sum of the guilt which the practice produces is great, beyond what has perhaps been ever conceived: It will be the writer's comfort to have solemnly suggested this consideration, to the consciences of those by whom this impious practice might be suppressed: If such there be, which he is strongly inclined to believe, theirs is the crime, and theirs the responsibility of suffering it to continue.[9]

In the foregoing observations it has not been the writer's intention to discuss completely that copious subject, the love of worldly estimation. It would be to exceed the limits of a work like this, fully to investigate so large, and at the same time so important a topic. Enough however may have been said, to make it evident that this principle is of a character highly *questionable;* that it should be brought under absolute subjection, and watched with the most jealous care: That, notwithstanding its lofty pretensions, it often can by no means justly boast that high origin, and exalted nature, which its superficial admirers are disposed to concede to it. What real intrinsic essential value, it might be asked, does there appear to be in a virtue, which had wholly changed its nature and character, if public opinion had been different. But it is in truth of base

extraction, and ungenerous qualities, springing a from selfishness; and vanity, and low ambition; by these it subsists, and
thrives, and acts; and envy and jealousy, and detraction, and
hatred, and variance, are its faithful and natural associates. It
is, to say the best of it; a root which bears fruits of a poisonous
as well as of a beneficial quality. If it sometimes stimulates to
great and generous enterprises; if it urges to industry, and
sometimes to excellence, if in the more contracted sphere it
produces courtesy and kindness; yet to its account we must
place the ambition which desolates nations, and many of the
competitions and resentments which interrupt the harmony of
social life. The former indeed has been often laid to its charge,
but the latter have not been sufficiently attended to; and still
less has its *noxious* influence on the vital principle, and distinguishing graces of the Christian character, been duly pointed
out and enforced.

To read the writings of certain Christian moralists,[10]
and to observe how little they seem disposed to call it in
question, except where it raves in the conqueror, one should
be almost tempted to suspect; that, considering it as a principle of such potency and prevalence as that they must despair of bringing it into just subjection, they were intent only
on complimenting it into good humour (like those barbarous
nations which worship the evil Spirit through fear) or rather,
that they were making a sort of composition with an enemy
they could not master, and were willing, on condition of its
giving up the trade of war, to suffer it rule undisturbed, and
range at pleasure.

But the truth is, that the reasonings of Christian moralists too often exhibit but few traces of the genius of Christian
morality. Of this position, the case before us, is an instance.
This principle of the desire of worldly distinction and applause,
is often allowed, and even commended with too few qualifications, and too little reserve. To covet wealth is base and sordid,
but to covet honour is treated as the mark of a generous and
exalted nature. These writers scarcely seem to bear in mind,
that though the principle in question tends to prevent the
commission of those grosser acts of vice which would injure us
in the general estimation; yet that it not only stops there, but
that it there begins to exert almost an equal force in the
opposite direction. They do not consider how apt this principle
is, even in the case of those who move in a contracted sphere,
to fill us with vain conceits and vicious passions; and above all

how it tends to fix the affections on earthly things, and to steal away the heart from God. They acknowledge it to be criminal when it produces mischievous effects, but forget how apt it is by the substitution of a false and corrupt motive, to vitiate [to make imperfect or to spoil] the purity of our good actions, depriving them of all which rendered them truly and essentially valuable. That, not to be too hastily approved, because it takes the side of virtue, it often works her ruin, while it asserts her cause, and like some vile seducer, pretends affection only the more surely to betray.

It is the distinguishing glory of Christianity not to rest satisfied with superficial appearances, but to rectify the *motives*, and purify the *heart*. The true Christian, in obedience to the lessons of Scripture, no where keeps over himself a more resolute and jealous guard, than where the desire of human estimation and distinction is in question. No where does he more deeply feel the insufficiency of his unassisted strength, or more diligently and earnestly pray for divine assistance. He may well indeed watch and pray against the encroachments of a passion, which when suffered to transgress its just limits, discovers a peculiar hostility to the distinguishing graces of the Christian temper; a passion which must insensibly acquire force, because it is in continual exercise: To which almost every thing *without*, administers nutriment, and the growth of which *within* is favoured and cherished by such powerful auxiliaries as pride and selfishness, the natural and perhaps inexterminable inhabitants of the human heart; of which the predominance, if established, is thus so pernicious, and which possesses so many advantages for effecting its establishment.

Strongly impressed therefore with a sense of the indispensable necessity of guarding against the progress of this encroaching principle, in humble reliance on superior aid, the true Christian thankfully uses the means, and habitually exercises himself in the considerations and motives, suggested to him for that purpose by the word of God. He is much occupied in searching out, and contemplating his own infirmities. He endeavours to acquire and maintain a just conviction of his great unworthiness; and to keep in continual remembrance, that whatever distinguishes himself from others, is not properly his own, but that he is altogether indebted for it to the undeserved bounty of Heaven. He diligently endeavours also, habitually to preserve a *just* sense of the real worth of human distinction and applause, knowing that he shall covet them less when he has learned not to over-rate their value. He labours to bear in mind how undeservedly they are often bestowed, how precariously they are always possessed. The censures of good men justly render him suspicious of himself, and prompt him carefully and impartially to examine into those parts of his character, or those particulars of his conduct, which have drawn on him their animadversions [criticisms]. The favourable opinion and the praises of good men are justly acceptable to him, when they accord with the testimony of his own heart; that testimony being thereby confirmed and warranted. Those praises favour also and strengthen the growth of mutual confidence and affection, where it is his delight to form friendships, rich not less in use than comfort, and to establish connections which may last for ever. But even in the case of the commendations of good men, he suffers not himself to be beguiled into an over-valuation of them, lest he should be led to substitute them in the place of conscience. He guards against this by reflecting how indistinctly we can discern each other's motives, how little enter into each other's circumstances, how mistaken therefore may be the judgments formed of us, or of our actions, even by good men, and that it is far from improbable, that we may at some time be compelled to forfeit their esteem, by adhering to the dictates of our own consciences.

But if he endeavours thus to sit loose to the favour and applause even of good men, much more to those of the world at large: not but that he is so sensible of their worth as means and instruments of usefulness and influence; and under the limitations and for the ends allowed in Scripture (these it is needless to repeat) he is glad to possess, observant to acquire, and careful to retain them. He considers them however, if we may again introduce the metaphor, like the precious metals, as having rather an exchangeable than an intrinsic value, as desirable not simply in their possession, but in their use. In this view, he holds himself to be responsible for that share of them which he enjoys, and, to continue the figure, as bound not to let them lie by him unemployed, this were hoarding; not to lavish them prodigally, this would be waste; not imprudently to misapply them, this were folly and caprice; but as under an obligation to regard them as conferred on him that they might be brought into action, and as what therefore he may by no means throw away, though ready,

if it be required, to relinquish them with cheerfulness; and
never feeling himself at liberty, in consideration of the use he
intends to make of them to acquire or retain them unlawfully.
He holds it to be his bounden duty to seek diligently for
occasions of rendering them subservient to their true purposes; and when any such occasion is found, to expend them
cheerfully and liberally, but with discretion and frugality;
being no less prudent in determining the measure, than in
selecting the objects of their application, that they may go the
farther by being thus managed with oeconomy.

Acting therefore on these principles, he will studiously
and diligently use any degree of worldly credit he may enjoy, in
removing or lessening prejudices; in conciliating good-will, and
thereby making way for the less obstructed progress of truth;
and in providing for its being entertained with candour, or
even with favour, by those who would bar all access against it in
a rougher of more homely form. He will make it his business to
set on foot and forward benevolent and useful schemes; and
where they require united efforts, to obtain and preserve for
them this co-operation. He will endeavour to discountenance
vice, to bring modest merit into notice; to lend as it were his
light to men of real worth, but of less creditable name, and
perhaps of less conciliating qualities and manners; that they
may thus shine with a reflected lustre, and be useful in their
turn, when invested with their just estimation. But while by
these and various other means he strives to render his reputation so long as he possesses it, subservient to the great end of
advancing the cause of Religion and Virtue, and of promoting
the happiness and comfort of mankind, he will not transgress
the rule of the Scripture precepts in order to obtain, to cultivate, or to preserve it, resolutely disclaiming that dangerous
sophistry of doing evil that good may come [Romans 3:8].
Ready to relinquish his reputation when required so to do, he
will not throw it away; and so far as he allowably may, he will
cautiously avoid occasions of diminishing it, instead of studiously seeking, or needlessly multiplying them, as seems sometimes to have been the practice of worthy but imprudent men.
There will be no capricious humours, no selfish tempers, no
moroseness, no discourtesy, no affected severity of deportment,
no peculiarity of language, no indolent neglect, or wanton
breach of the ordinary forms, or fashions of society. His reputation is a possession capable of uses too important to be thus
sported away; if sacrificed at all, it shall be sacrificed at the call

of duty. The world shall be constrained to allow him to be
amiable, as well as respectable in other parts of his character;
though in what regards Religion, they may account him unreasonably precise and strict. In this no less than in other particulars he will endeavour to reduce the enemies of Religion to
adopt the confession of the accusers of the Jewish ruler, "we can
not find any fault or occasion against this Daniel—except concerning the law of his God" [Daniel 6:4]: and even there, if he
give offence, it will only be when he dares not do otherwise;
and if he fall into dis-esteem or disgrace it shall not be chargeable to any conduct which is justly dishonourable, or even to
any unnecessary singularities on his part, but to the false
standard of estimation of a misjudging world. When his character is thus mistaken, or his conduct thus misconstrued, he will
not wrap himself up in a mysterious sullenness; but will be
ready, where he thinks any one will be ready to listen to him
with patience and candour, to clear up what has been dubious,
to explain what has been imperfectly known, and "speaking the
truth in love" [Ephesians 4:15], to correct, if it may be, the
erroneous impressions have been conceived of him. He may
sometimes feel it his duty publicly to vindicate his character
from unjust reproach, and to repel false charges of his enemies;
but he will carefully watch against being led away by pride, or
being betrayed into some breach of truth or of Christian charity, when he is treading in a path so dangerous. At such a time
he will also guard with more than ordinary circumspection
against any undue solicitude about his worldly reputation for its
own sake, and when he has done what duty requires for its
vindication, he will sit down with a peaceable and quiet mind,
and it will be a matter of no very deep concern to him if his
endeavours should have been ineffectual. If good men in every
age and nation have been often unjustly calumniated [slan-
dered] and disgraced, and if in such circumstances, even the
darkness of paganism has been able contentedly to repose itself
on the consciousness of innocence, shall one who is cheered by
the Christian's hope, who is assured also, that a day will shortly
come in which whatever is secret shall be made manifest, and
the mistaken judgments of men, perhaps even of good men,
being corrected, that "he shall then have praise of God"
[1 Corinthians 4:5]; shall such a one, I say, sink; shall he even
bend or droop under such a trial? They might be more excusable in over-valuing human reputation to whom all beyond the
grave was dark and cheerless. They also might be more easily

pardoned for pursuing with some degree of eagerness and solicitude that glory which might survive them, thus seeking as it were to extend the narrow span of their earthly existence: but far different is our case, to whom these clouds are rolled away, and "life and immortality brought to light by the Gospel" [2 Timothy 1:10]. Not but that worldly favour and distinction are amongst the best things this world has to offer; but the Christian knows it is the very condition of his calling, *not* to have his portion here; and as in the case of any other earthly enjoyments, so in that also of worldly honour, he dreads, lest his supreme affections being thereby gratified, it should be hereafter said to him "remember that thou in thy life-time receivedst thy good things" [Luke 16:25].

He is required by his holy calling to be victorious over the world; and to this victory, the conquest of the dread of its dis-esteem and dishonour is essentially and indispensably required. He reflects on those holy men who "had trial of cruel mockings" [Hebrews 11:36]; he remembers that our blessed Saviour himself "was despised and rejected of men" [Isaiah 53:3]; and what is he that he should be exempted from the common lot, or think it much to bear the scandal of his profession. If therefore he is creditable and popular, he considers this, if the phrase may be pardoned, as something beyond his bargain, and he watches himself, with double care, lest he should grow over-fond of what he may be shortly called upon to relinquish. He meditates often on the probability of his being involved in such circumstances, as may render it necessary for him to subject himself to disgrace and obloquy [verbal abuse or censure]; thus familiarizing himself with them betimes, and preparing himself, that when the trying hour arrives they may not take him unawares.

But the cultivation of the desire of "that honour which cometh from God" [John 5:44], he finds the most effectual means of bringing his mind into a proper temper, in what regards the love of human approbation. Christian! wouldst thou indeed reduce this affection under just controul—*sursum corda!* ["Lift up your hearts!"]. Rise on the wings of contemplation, until the praises and censures of men die away upon the ear, and the still small voice of conscience is no longer drowned by the din of this nether [lower] world. Here the sight is apt to be occupied with earthly objects, and the hearing to be engrossed with earthly sounds; but there thou shalt come within the view of that resplendent and incorruptible crown, which is held forth to thy acceptance in the realms of light, and thine ear shall be regaled with Heavenly melody! Here we dwell in a variable atmosphere—the prospect is at one time darkened by the gloom of disgrace, and at another the eye is dazzled by the gleamings of glory: but thou hast now ascended above this inconstant region; no storms agitate, no clouds obscure the air, and the lightnings play, and the thunders roll beneath thee.

Thus, at chosen seasons, the Christian exercises himself; and when, from this elevated region he descends into the plain below, and mixes in the bustle of life, he still retains the impressions of his retired hours. By these he realizes to himself the unseen world: he accustoms himself to speak and act as in the presence of "an innumerable company of angels, and of the spirits of just men made perfect, and of God the Judge of all" [Hebrews 12:23]; the consciousness of *their* approbation cheers and gladdens his soul, under the scoffs and reproaches of an undiscerning world, and to his delighted ear, their united praises form a *harmony* which a few discordant earthly voices cannot interrupt.

But though the Christian is sometimes enabled thus to triumph over the inordinate love of human applause, he does not therefore deem himself secure from its encroachments. On the contrary, he is aware, so strong and active is its principle of vitality, that even where it seems extinct, let but circumstances favour its revival, and it will spring forth again in renewed vigour. And as his watch must thus during life know no termination, because the enemy will ever be at hand; so it must be the more close and vigilant, because he is no where free from danger, but is on every side open to attack. "*Sume superbiam quaesitam meritis*" ["Take on pride sought by deeds"], was the maxim of a worldly moralist: but the Christian is aware, that he is particularly assailable where he really excels; there he is in especial danger, lest his motives, originally pure, being insensibly corrupted, he should be betrayed into anxiety about worldly favour, false in principle or excessive in degree, when he is endeavouring to render his virtue amiable and respected in the eyes of others, and in obedience to the Scripture injunction, is willing to let his "light so shine before men, that they may see his good works, and glorify his Father which is in heaven" [Matthew 5:16; see also Matthew 7:17].

He watches himself also on small as well as on great occasions: the latter indeed, in the case of many persons, can hardly ever be expected to occur, whereas the former are continually presenting themselves; and thus, whilst on the one hand they may be rendered highly useful in forming and strengthening a just habit of mind in the particular in question; so, on the other, they are the means most at hand for enabling us to discover our own real character. Let not this be lightly passed over. If any one finds himself shrinking from disrepute or disesteem in little instances; but apt to solace himself with the persuasion, that his spirits being fully called forth to the encounter, he could boldly stand the brunt of sharper trials; let him be slow to give entertainment to so beguiling a suggestion; and let him not forget that these little instances, where no credit is to be got, and the vainest can find small room for self-complacency, furnish perhaps the truest test whether we are ashamed of the Gospel of Christ, and are willing, on principles really pure, to bear reproach for the name of Jesus.

The Christian too is well aware that the excessive desire of human approbation is a passion of so subtile a nature, that there is nothing into which it cannot penetrate; and from much experience, learning to discover it where it would lurk unseen, and to detect it under its most specious disguises, he finds, that elsewhere disallowed and excluded, it is apt to insinuate itself into his very religion, where it especially delights to dwell, and obstinately maintains its residence. Proud piety and ostentatious charity, and all the more open effects it there produces, have been often condemned, and we may discover the tendencies to them in ourselves, without difficulty. But where it appears not so large in bulk, and in shape so unambiguous, let its operation be still suspected. Let not the Christian suffer himself to be deceived by any external dissimilitudes between himself and the world around him, trusting perhaps to the sincerity of the principle to which they originally owed their rise; but let him beware lest through the insensible encroachments of the subtle usurper, his religion should at length have "only a name to live;" being gradually robbed of its vivifying [life-giving] principle; lest he should be mainly preserved in his religious course by the dread of incurring the charge of levity, for quitting a path on which he had deliberately entered. Or where, on a strict and impartial scrutiny of his governing motives, he may fairly conclude this not to be the case, let him beware lest he be influenced by this principle in particular parts of his charac-

ter, and especially where any external singularities are in question; closely scrutinizing his apparent motives, lest he should be
prompted to his more than ordinary religious observances,
and be kept from participating in the licentious pleasures of a
dissipated age, not so much by a vigorous principle of internal holiness, as by a fear of lessening himself in the good
opinion of the stricter circle of his associates, or of suffering
even in the estimation of the world at large, by violating the
proprieties of his assumed character.

To those who, in the important particular which we
have been so long discussing, wish to conform themselves to
the injunctions of the word of God, we must advise a laborious
watchfulness, a jealous guard, a close and frequent scrutiny of
their own hearts, that they may not mistake their real character,
and too late find themselves to have been mistaken, as to what
they had conceived to be their governing motives. Above all, let
them labour, with humble prayers for the Divine assistance, to
fix in themselves a deep, habitual, and practical sense of the
excellence of "that honour which cometh from God" [John
5:44], and of the comparative worthlessness of all earthly estimation and pre-eminence. In truth, unless the affections of the
soul be thus predominantly engaged on the side of heavenly in
preference to that of human honour, though we may have
relinquished the pursuit of fame, we shall not have acquired
that firm contexture of mind, which can bear disgrace and
shame without yielding to the pressure. Between these two
states, there is a wide interval, and he who, on a sober review of
his conduct and motives, finds reason to believe he has arrived
at the one, must not therefore conclude he has reached the
other. To the one, a little natural moderation and quietness of
temper may be sufficient to conduct us: but to the other, we can
only attain by much discipline and slow advances; and when we
think we have made great way, we shall often find reason to
confess in the hour of trial, that we had greatly, far too greatly,
over-rated our progress.

When engaged too in the prosecution of this course, we
must be aware of the snares which lie in our way, and of the
deceits to which we are liable: and we must be provided against
these impositions, by having obtained a full and distinct conception of the temper of mind with regard to human favour,
which is prescribed to us in Scripture; and by continually
examining our hearts and lives to ascertain how far they correspond with it. This will prevent our substituting contemplation

in the place of action, and giving ourselves too much up to those religious meditations which were formerly recommended, in which we must not indulge to the neglect of the common *duties* of life: this will prevent our mistaking the gratification of an indolent temper for the Christian's disregard of fame; for, never let it be forgotten, we must *deserve* estimation, though we may not *possess* it; forcing men of the *world* to acknowledge, that we do not want their boasted spring of action to set us in motion; but that its place is better supplied to us by another which produces all the good of theirs without its evil; thus demonstrating the superiority of the principle which animates us, by the superior utility and excellence of its effects. This principle, in order to be pure and genuine, though nerved with more than mortal firmness, must be sweetened by love, and tempered with humility. The former of these qualities will render us kind, friendly, and beneficent, preventing our being no longer on the watch to promote the happiness or comfort of others, than whilst we are stimulated by their applause; the produce of which passion, whatever may be vaunted of its effects on social intercourse, is often nothing better than selfishness, ill concealed under a superficial covering of exterior courtesy.

Humility, again, reducing us in our own value, will moderate our claims on worldly estimation. It will check our tendency to ostentation and display, prompting us rather to avoid, than to attract notice. It will dispose us to sit down in quiet obscurity, though, judging ourselves impartially, we believe ourselves better entitled to credit, than those on whom it is conferred; closing the entrance against a proud, painful, and malignant passion; from which, under such circumstances, we can otherwise be hardly free, the passion of "high disdain from sense of injured merit."

Love and humility will concur in producing a frame of mind, not more distinct from an ardent thirst of glory, than from that frigid disregard or insolent contempt, or ostentatious renunciation of human favour, and distinction, which we have sometimes seen opposed to it. These latter qualities may so infrequently be traced to a slothful, sensual, and selfish temper; to the consciousness of being unequal to any great and generous attempts; to the disappointment of schemes of ambition or of glory; to a little personal experience of the world's capricious and inconstant humour. The renunciation in these cases, however sententious [putting on an air of wisdom], is often far from sincere; and it is even made not infrequently, with a view to the attainment of that very distinction which it affects to disclaim. In some other of these instances, the over-valuation and inordinate desire of worldly credit, however disavowed, are abundantly evident, from the merit which is assumed for relinquishing them; or from that sour and surly humour, which betrays a gloomy and a corroded mind, galled and fretting under the irritating sense of the want of that which it most wishes to possess.

But the Christian's is a far different temper: not a temper of sordid sensuality, or lazy apathy, or dogmatizing pride, or disappointed ambition: more truly independent of worldly estimation than philosophy with all her boasts, it forms a perfect contrast to Epicurean [that which is overly sensuous or luxurious] selfishness, to Stoical [the ability to bear difficulties of discomfort without complaining] pride, and to Cynical [to believe that people's motives are bad or selfish and to show this by sneering at them][11] brutality. It is a temper compounded of firmness, and complacency, and peace, and love; and manifesting itself in acts of kindness and of courtesy; a kindness not pretended but genuine; a courtesy, not false and superficial, but cordial and sincere. In the hour of popularity it is not intoxicated, or insolent; in the hour of unpopularity, it is not desponding, or morose; unshaken in constancy, unwearied in benevolence, firm without roughness, and assiduous without servility.

Notwithstanding the great importance of the topic which we have been investigating, it will require much indulgence on the part of the reader, to excuse the disproportionate length into which the discussion has been almost insensibly drawn out: yet this, it is hoped, may not be without its uses, if the writer have in any degree succeeded in his endeavour to point out the dangerous qualities and unchristian tendencies of a principle, of such general predominance throughout the higher classes of society, and to suggest to the serious inquirer some practical hints for its regulation and controul. Since the principle too of which we have been treating is one of the most ordinary modifications of pride, the discussion may also serve in some degree to supply a manifest deficiency, a deficiency to be ascribed to the fear of trespassing too far on the reader's patience, in having but lightly touched on the allowed prevalence of that master passion, and on the allowed neglect of its opposite, humility.

SECTION FOUR ↣

The Generally Prevailing Error of Substituting
Amiable Tempers and Useful Lives in the Place
of Religion, Stated and Confuted; with Hints
to Real Christians

There is another practical error very generally prevalent, the effects of which are highly injurious to the cause of Religion; and which in particular is often brought forward when, upon Christian principles, any advocates for Christianity would press the practice of Christian virtues. Before we proceed, therefore, to comment upon what remains to be discussed, of the misconceptions and defects of the bulk of professed Christians, it may not be amiss to dispose of this objection to our whole scheme.

The error in question is that of exaggerating the the merit of certain amiable and useful qualities, and of considering them as of themselves sufficient to compensate for the want of the supreme love and fear of God.

It seems to be an opinion pretty generally prevalent, that kindness and sweetness of temper; sympathizing, and benevolent, and generous affections, attention to what in the world's estimation are the domestic, relative, and social duties, and above all, a life of general activity and usefulness, may well be allowed in our imperfect state, to make up for the deficit of what in strict propriety of speech is termed Religion.

Many indeed will unreservedly declare, and more will hint the opinion, that "the difference between the qualities above-mentioned and Religion, is rather a verbal or logical, than a real and essential difference; for in truth what are they but Religion in substance if not in name. Is it not the great end of Religion, and in particular the glory of Christianity, to extinguish the malignant passions; to curb the violence, to controul the appetites, and to smooth the asperities [mannerisms or kinds of conduct which are harsh or severe] of man; to make us compassionate and kind, and forgiving one to another; to make us good husbands, good fathers, good friends; and to render us active and useful in the discharge of the relative, social, and civil duties. We do not deny that in the general mass of society, and particularly in the lower orders, such conduct and tempers cannot be diffused and maintained by any other medium than that of Religion. But if the end be effected, surely it is only unnecessary refinement to dispute about the means. It is even to forget your own principles, and to refuse its just place to solid practical virtue, while you assign too high a value to speculative opinions."

Thus a fatal distinction is admitted between Morality and Religion: a great and desperate error, of which it is the more necessary to take notice, because many who would condemn, as too strong, the language in which this opinion is sometimes openly avowed, are yet more or less tinctured [tinged or colored by something] with the notion itself, and under the habitual and almost unperceived influence of this beguiling suggestion, are vainly solacing their imaginations, and repressing their well-grounded fears concerning *their own* state; and are also quieting their just solicitude concerning the spiritual condition of *others,* and soothing themselves in the neglect of friendly endeavours for their improvement.

There can hardly be a stronger proof of the cursory and superficial views, with which men are apt to satisfy themselves in religious concerns, than the prevalence of the opinion here in question, the falsehood and sophistry of which must be acknowledged by any one who, admitting the authority of Scripture, will examine it with ever so little seriousness and impartiality of mind.

Appealing indeed to a less strict standard, it would not be difficult to shew that the moral worth of these sweet and benevolent tempers, and of these useful lives, is apt to be greatly over-rated. The former involuntarily gain upon our affections and disarm our severer judgments, by their kindly, complying, and apparently disinterested nature; by their prompting men to flatter instead of mortifying our pride, to sympathize either with our joys or our sorrows, to abound in obliging attentions and offices of courtesy; by their obvious tendency to produce and maintain harmony and comfort in social and domestic life. It is not however unworthy of remark, that from the commendations which are so generally bestowed on these qualities, and their rendering men universally acceptable and popular, there is many a false pretender to them, who gains a credit for them which he by no means deserves; in whom they are no more than the properties of his assumed character, or even a mask which is worn in public, only the better to conceal an opposite temper. Would you see this man of courtesy and sweetness stripped of his false covering, follow him unobserved into his family; and you shall behold, too plain to be mistaken, selfishness and spleen [violent feelings of anger or spite] harassing and vexing the wretched subjects of their unmanly tyranny; as if being released at length from their confinement, they were making up to themselves for the restraint which had been imposed on them in the world.

But where the benevolent qualities are genuine, they often deserve the name rather of amiable instincts, than of moral virtues. In many cases, they imply no mental conflict, no previous discipline: they are apt to evaporate in barren sensibilities, and transitory sympathies, and indolent wishes, and unproductive declarations; they possess not that strength and energy of character, which, in contempt of difficulties and dangers, produce alacrity in service, vigour and perseverance in action. Destitute of proper firmness, they often encourage that vice and folly which it is their especial duty to repress; and it is well if, from their soft complying humour, they are not often drawn in to participate in what is wrong, as well as to connive [to conspire] at it. Thus their possessors are often, in the eye of truth and reason, bad magistrates, bad parents, bad friends; defective in those very qualities which give to each of those several relations its chief and appropriate value. And this, let it also be observed, is a defect which might well bring into question that freedom from selfishness which is so often claimed for them; inasmuch as there is too great reason to fear that it often arises in us chiefly from indisposition to submit to a painful effort, though real good-will commands the sacrifice, or from the fear of lessening the regard in which we are held, and the good opinion which is entertained of us.

It should farther also be observed concerning these qualities when they are not grounded and rooted in Religion, that they are of a sickly and short-lived nature, and want that hardy and vigorous temperament which is requisite for enabling them to bear without injury, or even to survive, the rude shocks and the variable and churlish seasons, to which in such a world as this they must ever be exposed. It is only a *Christian* love of which it is the character, that "it suffereth long, and yet is kind;" "that it is not easily provoked; that it beareth all things and endureth all things" [1 Corinthians 13:7]. In the spring of youth indeed, the blood flows freely through the veins; we are flushed with health and confidence; hope is young and ardent, our desires are unsated, and whatever we see, has the grace of novelty; we are the more disposed to be good-natured, because we are pleased; pleased because universally well received. Wherever we cast our eyes, we see some face of friendship, and love, and gratulation [congratulation]: All nature smiles around us. Now the amiable tempers of which we have been speaking naturally spring up. The soil suits, the climate favours them. They appear to shoot forth vigorously and blossom in gay luxuriance. To the superficial eye, all is fair and flourishing; we anticipate the fruits of Autumn, and promise ourselves an ample produce. But by and by the sun scorches, the frost nips, the winds rise, the rains descend; our golden dreams are blasted, all our fond expectations are no more. Our youthful efforts, let it be supposed have been successful; and we rise to wealth or eminence. A kind flexible temper and popular manners have produced in us, as they are too apt, a youth of easy social dissipation, and unproductive idleness; and we are overtaken too late by the consciousness of having wasted that time which cannot be recalled, and those opportunities which we cannot now recover. We sink into disregard and obscurity when, there being a call for qualities of more energy, indolent good nature must fall back. We are thrust out of notice by accident or misfortunes. We are left behind by those with whom we started on equal terms, and who, originally perhaps having less pretensions and fewer advantages, have greatly outstripped us in the race of honour; and their having got before us is often the more galling, because it appears to us, and perhaps with reason, to have been chiefly owing to a generous, easy, good-natured humour on our part, which disposed us to allow them first to pass by us without jealousy, and led us to give place without a struggle to their more lofty pretensions. Thus we suffered them quietly to occupy a station to which originally we had as fair a claim as they; but, this station being once tamely surrendered, we have forfeited it for ever. Our awkward and vain endeavours meanwhile to recover it, while they shew that we want self-knowledge and composure in our riper years, as much as in our younger we had been destitute of exertion, serve only to make our inferiority more manifest, and to bring our discontent into the fuller notice of an ill-natured world, which, however, not unjustly condemns and ridicules our misplaced ambition.

It may be sufficient to have hinted at a few of the vicissitudes and changes of advancing life; let the reader's own mind fill up the catalogue. Now the bosom is no longer cheerful and placid; and if the countenance preserve its exterior character, this is no longer the honest expression of the heart. Prosperity and luxury, gradually extinguishing sympathy, and puffing up with pride, harden and debase the soul. In other instances, shame secretly clouds, and remorse begins to sting, and suspicion to corrode, and jealousy and envy to embitter. Disappointed hopes, unsuccessful competitions, and frustrated pursuits, sour and irritate the temper. A little personal experience of the selfishness of mankind, damps our generous warmth and kind affections; reproving the prompt sensibility and unsuspecting simplicity of our earlier years. Above all, ingratitude sickens the heart, and chills and thickens the very life's-blood of benevolence; till at length our youthful Nero [a Roman emperor (A.D. 37–68) who was notable for his persecution of Christians],[12] soft and susceptible, becomes a hard and cruel tyrant; and our youthful Timon,[13] the gay, the generous, the beneficent, is changed into a cold, sour, sullen misanthrope.

And as in the case of amiable tempers, so in that also of what are called useful lives, it must be confessed that their intrinsic worth, arguing still merely on principles of reason, is apt to be greatly over-rated. They are often the result of a disposition naturally bustling and active, which delights in motion, and finds its labours more than repaid either by the very pleasure which it takes in its employments, or by the credit which it derives from them. More than this, if it be granted that Religion tends in general to produce usefulness, particularly in the lower orders who compose a vast majority of every society; and therefore that these irreligious men of useful lives are rather exceptions to the general rule; it must at least be confessed that they are so far useless, or even positively mischievous, as they either neglect to encourage or actually discourage that principle which is the great operative spring of usefulness in the bulk of mankind.

Thus it might well perhaps be questioned, estimating these men by their own standard, whether the *particular* good in this case, is not more than counterbalanced by the *general* evil; still more if their conduct being brought to a strict account, they should be charged, as they justly ought, with the loss of the good which if they had manifestly and avowedly acted from a higher principle, might have been produced, not only directly in themselves, but indirectly and remotely in others, from the extended efficacy of a religious example. They

may be compared, not unaptly, to persons whom some peculiarity of constitution enables to set at defiance those established
rules of living which must be observed by the world at large.
These healthy debauchees [those who indulge in harmful or
immoral pleasures], however they may plead in their defence
that they do themselves no injury, would probably, but for their
excesses, have both enjoyed their health better, and preserved
it longer, as well as have turned it to better account; and it may
at least be urged against them, that they disparage the laws of
temperance, and fatally betray others into the breach of them, by
affording an instance of their being transgressed with impunity.

But were the merit of the qualities in question greater
than it is, and though it were not liable to the exceptions which
have been alleged against it, yet could they be in no degree
admitted as a compensation for the want of the supreme love
and fear of God, and of a predominant desire to promote his
glory. The observance of one commandment, however clearly
and forcibly enjoined, cannot make up for the neglect of another which is enjoined with equal clearness and equal force.
To allow this plea in the present instance would be to permit
men to abrogate [to cancel or repeal] the first table of the law,
on condition of their obeying the second. But Religion suffers
not any such *composition* of duties. It is on the very self-same
miserable principle that some have thought to atone for a life
of injustice and rapine by the strictness of their religious observances. If the former class of men can plead the diligent
discharge of their duties to their fellow-creatures, the latter will
urge that of theirs to God. We easily see the falsehood of the
plea in the latter case; and it is only self-deceit and partiality
which prevent its being equally visible in the former. Yet so it is;
such is the unequal measure, if I may be allowed the expression, which we deal out to God, and to each other. It would
justly and universally be thought false confidence in the religious thief or the religious adulterer, (to admit for the sake of
argument such a solecism [a mistake in the use of language or
an offence against good manners] in terms) to solace himself
with the firm persuasion of the Divine favour; but it will, to
many, appear hard and precise, to deny this firm persuasion of
Divine approbation [a setting aside for a special purpose] to the
avowedly irreligious man of social and domestic usefulness.

Will it be urged here that the writer is not doing justice
to his opponent's argument: which is not that irreligious
men of useful lives may be excused for neglecting their duties

towards God, in consideration of their exemplary discharge of their duties towards their fellow-creatures; but that, in performing the latter, they perform the former *virtually* and *substantially,* if not in name?

Can then our opponent deny that the Holy Scriptures are in nothing more full, frequent, strong, and unequivocal, than in their injunctions on us supremely to love and fear God, and to worship and serve him continually with humble and grateful hearts, habitually regarding him as our benefactor, and sovereign, and father, and abounding in sentiments of gratitude, and loyalty, and respectful affection? Can he deny that these positive precepts are rendered if possible, still more clear, and their authority still more binding, by illustrations and indirect confirmations almost innumerable? And who then is that bold intruder into the council of infinite wisdom, who in palpable [obvious] contempt of these precise commands thus illustrated also and confirmed, will dare to maintain that, knowing the intention with which they were primarily given and the ends they were ultimately designed to produce, he may innocently neglect or violate their plain obligations, on the plea that he conforms himself though in a different manner, to this primary intention, and produces, though by different means, these real and ultimate ends?

This mode of arguing is one, with which, to say nothing of its insolent profaneness [irreverence], the heart of man, prone to deceive himself and partial in his own cause, is not fit to be trusted. Here again, more cautious and jealous in the case of our worldly, than of our religious interests, we readily discern the fallacy of this reasoning and protest against it, when it is attempted to be introduced into the commerce of life. We see clearly that it would afford the means of refining away by turns every moral obligation. The adulterer might allow himself with a good conscience, to violate the bed of his unsuspecting friend whenever he could assure himself that his crime would escape detection; for then, where would be the evil and misery, the prevention of which was the real ultimate object of the prohibition of adultery? The thief, in like manner, and even the murderer, might find abundant room for the *innocent* exercise of their respective occupations, arguing from the primary intention and real objects of the commands, by which theft and murder were forbidden. There perhaps exists not a crime to which this crooked morality would not furnish some convenient opening.

But this miserable sophistry deserves not that we should spend so much time in the refutation of it. To discern its fallaciousness [false reasoning], requires not acuteness of understanding, so much as a little common honesty. "There is indeed no surer mark of a false and hollow heart, than a disposition thus to quibble away the clear injunctions of duty and conscience."[14] It is the wretched resource of a disingenuous mind, endeavouring to escape from convictions, before which it cannot stand, and to evade obligations which it dares not disavow.

The arguments which have been adduced would surely be sufficient to disprove the extravagant pretensions of the qualities under consideration, though those qualities were *perfect* in their *nature*. But they are not perfect. On the contrary, they are radically defective and corrupt; they are without a soul; they want the vital actuating [motivating] principle, or rather they are animated and actuated by a false one. Christianity, let me avail myself of the very words of a friend[15] in maintaining her argument, is "a Religion of Motives." *That* only is Christian practice which flows from Christian principles; and none else will be admitted as such by Him who will be obeyed as well as worshiped "in spirit and in truth" [John 4:23].

This also is a position of which, in our intercourse with our fellow-creatures, we clearly discern the justice, and universally admit the force. Though we have received a benefit at the hands of any one, we scarcely feel grateful if we do not believe the intention towards us to have been friendly. Have we served any one from motives of kindness, and is a return of service made to us? We hardly feel ourselves worthily requited [repaid], except that return be dictated by gratitude. We should think ourselves rather injured than obliged by it, if it were merely prompted by a proud unwillingness to continue in our debt.[16] What husband, or what father, not absolutely dead to every generous feeling, would be satisfied with a wife or a child, who, though he could not charge them with any actual breach of their respective obligations, should yet confessedly perform them from a cold sense of duty, in place of the quickening energies of conjugal and filial affection? What an insult would it be to such a one, to tell him gravely that he had no reason to complain!

The unfairness with which we suffer ourselves to reason in matters of Religion, is no where more striking than in the instance before us. It were perhaps not unnatural to suppose that as we cannot see into each other's bosoms [hearts], and have no sure way of judging any one's internal principles, but by his external actions, it would have grown into an established rule, that when the latter were unobjectionable, the former were not to be questioned; and on the other hand, that in reference to a Being who searches the heart, our motives [cf. Psalm 139:1], rather than our external actions, would be granted to be the just objects of inquiry. But we exactly reverse these natural principles of reasoning. In the case of our fellow-creatures, the motive is that which we principally inquire after and regard. But in the case of our Supreme Judge, from whom no secrets are hid, we suffer ourselves to believe that internal principles may be dispensed with, if the external action be performed.

Let us not however be supposed ready to concede, in contradiction to what has been formerly contended, that where the true motive is wanting, the external actions themselves will not generally betray the defect. Who is there that will not confess in the instance so lately put, of a wife and a child who should discharge their respective obligations merely from a cold sense of duty, that the inferiority of their actuating principle would not be confined to its *nature,* but would be discoverable also in its *effects*? Who is there that does not feel that these domestic services, thus robbed of their vital spirit, would be so debased and degraded in our estimation, as to become not barely lifeless and uninteresting, but even distasteful and loathsome? Who will deny that these would be performed in fuller measure, with more wakeful and unwearied attention, as well as with more *heart;* where, with the same sense of duty, the enlivening principle of affection should be also associated?

The enemies of Religion are sometimes apt to compare the irreligious man of a temper naturally sweet and amiable, with the religious man of natural roughness and severity; the irreligious man of natural activity, with the religious man who is naturally indolent; and thence to draw their inferences. But this mode of reasoning is surely unjust. If they would argue the question fairly, they should make their comparisons between persons of similar natural qualities, not in one or two examples, but in a mass of instances. They would then be compelled to confess the efficacy of Religion, in heightening the benevolence and increasing the usefulness of men; and to admit that, granting the occasional but rare existence of genuine and persevering benevolence of disposition and usefulness of life, where the religious principle is wanting; yet that experience gives us reason to believe, that true Religion, while it would have implanted these qualities in persons in whom before they had no place, would in general have given to these very characters in whom they do exist, additional force in the same direction. It would have rendered the amiable more amiable, the useful more useful, with fewer inconsistencies, with less abatement.

Let *true Christians* meanwhile be ever mindful that *they* are loudly called upon to make this argument still more clear, these positions still less questionable. You are every where commanded to be tender and sympathetic, diligent and useful; and it is the character of that "wisdom from above" [James 3:17], in which you are to be proficients, that it "is gentle and easy to be intreated, full of mercy and good fruits" [James 3:17]. Could the efficacy of Christianity in softening the heart be denied by those, who saw in the instance of the great Apostle of the Gentiles [Paul], that it was able to transform a bigoted, furious, and cruel persecutor, into an almost unequalled example of candour, and gentleness, and universal tenderness and love? Could its spirit of active beneficence be denied by those who saw its Divine Author so diligent and unwearied in his benevolent labours, as to justify the compendious description which was given of him by a personal witness of his exertions, that he "went about doing good?" [Acts 10:38]. Imitate these blessed examples: so shall you vindicate the honour of your profession, and "put to silence the ignorance of foolish men" [Matthew 5:16]: so shall you obey those Divine injunctions of adorning the doctrine of Christ, and of "letting your light shine before men, that they may see your good works, and glorify your Father which is in heaven" [Matthew 5:16]. Beat the world at its own best weapons. Let your love be more affectionate, your mildness less open to irritation, your diligence more laborious, your activity more wakeful and persevering. Consider sweetness of temper and activity of mind, if they naturally belong to you, as talents of special worth and utility, for which you will have to give account. Carefully watch against whatever might impair them, cherish them with constant assiduity, keep them in continual exercise, and direct them to their noblest ends. The latter of these qualities renders it less difficult, and therefore more incumbent on you to be ever abounding in the work of the Lord; and to be copious in the production of that species of good fruit of which mankind in general will the most ready to allow the excellence, because they best understand its nature. In *your* instance, the solid substance of Christian practice is easily susceptible of that high and beautiful polish, which may attract the attention, and extort the admiration of a careless and undiscerning world, so slow to notice, and so backward to acknowledge intrinsic worth, when concealed under a less sightly exterior. Know then, and value as ye ought, the honourable office which is especially devolved on you. Let it be your acceptable service to recommend the discredited cause, and sustain the fainting interests of Religion, to furnish to her friends matters of sound and obvious argument, and of honest triumph; and if your best endeavours cannot conciliate, to refute at least, and confound her enemies.

If on the other hand, you are conscious that you are naturally rough and austere, that disappointments have soured, or prosperity has elated you, or that habits of command have rendered you quick in expression, and impatient of contradiction; or if, from whatever other cause, you have contracted an unhappy peevishness of temper, or asperity of manners, or harshness and severity of language, (remember that these defects are by no means incompatible with an aptness to perform services of substantial kindness); if nature has been confirmed by habit till at length your soul seems thoroughly tinctured with these evil dispositions, yet do not despair. Remember that the Divine Agency is promised "to take away the heart of stone, and give a heart of flesh" [Ezekiel 11:19], of which it is the natural property to be tender and susceptible. Pray then earnestly and perseveringly that the blessed aid of Divine Grace may operate effectually on your behalf. Beware of acquiescing in the evil tempers in question, under the idea that they are the ordinary imperfections of the best of men; that they shew themselves only in little instances; that they are only occasional, hasty, and transient effusions [unrestrained outpourings of thought or feeling], when you are taken off your guard; the passing shade of your mind, and not the settled colour. Beware of excusing or allowing them in yourself under the notion of warm zeal for the cause of Religion and virtue, which you perhaps own is now and then apt to carry you into somewhat over-great severity of judgment or sharpness of reproof. Listen not to these, or any other such flattering excuses, which your own heart will be but too ready to suggest to you. Scrutinize yourself rather with rigorous strictness; and where there is so much room for self-deceit, call in the aid of some faithful friend, and unbosoming [revealing of thoughts or feelings] yourself to him without concealment, ask his impartial and unreserved opinion of your behaviour and condition. Our unwillingness to do this, often betrays to others (not seldom it first discovers to ourselves) that we entertain a secret distrust of our own character and conduct. Instead also of extenuating to yourself the criminality of the vicious tempers under consideration, strive to impress your mind deeply with a sense of it. For this end, often consider seriously that these rough and churlish [rude] tempers are a direct contrast to the "meekness and gentleness of Christ" [2 Corinthians 10:1]; and that Christians are strongly and repeatedly enjoined to copy after their great Model in these particulars, and to be themselves patterns of "mercy and kindness, and humbleness of mind, and meekness, and long-suffering" [Colossians 3:12]. They are to "put away all bitterness, and wrath, and anger, and clamour, and evil-speaking" [Ephesians 4:31]; not only "being ready to every good work, but being *gentle* unto *all* men" [Titus 3:1–2]; "showing, *all* meekness unto *all* men" [Titus 3:2]; "forbearing, forgiving" [Colossians 3:13], tender hearted. Remember the Apostle's [James's] declaration, that "if any man bridleth not his tongue, he only seemeth to be religious, and deceiveth his own heart" [James 1:26]; and that it is one of the characters of that love, without which all pretensions to the name of Christian are but vain, that "it doth not behave itself unseemly" [1 Corinthians 13:5].

Consider how much these acrimonious [bitter] tempers must break in upon the peace, and destroy the comfort, of those around you. Remember also that the honour or your Christian profession is at stake, and be solicitous not to discredit it; justly dreading lest you should disgust those whom you ought to conciliate, and by conveying an unfavourable impression of your principles and character, should incur the guilt of putting an "offence in your brother's way" [Romans 14:13]; thereby "hindering the Gospel of Christ" [1 Corinthians 9:12], the advancement of which should be your daily and assiduous care.

Thus having come to the full knowledge of your disease, and to a just impression of its malignity, strive against it with incessant watchfulness. Guard with the most jealous circumspection against its breaking forth into act. Force yourself to abound in little offices of courtesy and kindness; and you shall gradually experience in the performance of these a pleasure hitherto unknown, and awaken in yourself the dormant principles of sensibility. But take not up with external amendment; guard against a false show of sweetness of disposition;

and remember that the Christian is not to be satisfied with the
world's superficial courtliness [dignified politeness] of demeanor,
but that his "Love is to be without dissimulation [qualification]"
[Romans 12:9]. Examine carefully, whether the unchristian
tempers which you would eradicate, are not maintained in
vigour by selfishness and pride; and strive to subdue them
effectually, by extirpating [destroying] the roots from which
they derive their nutriment. Accustom yourself to endeavour to
look attentively upon a careless and inconsiderate world, which
while it is in such eminent peril, is so ignorant of its danger.
Dwell upon this affecting scene, till it has excited your pity; and
this pity, while it melts the mind to Christian love, shall insensibly produce a temper of habitual sympathy and softness.
By means like these, perseveringly used in constant dependence on Divine aid, you may confidentally hope to make continual progress. Among men of the world, a youth of softness and
sweetness will often, as we formerly remarked, harden into
insensibility, and sharpen into moroseness [sullenness, gloomi-
ness]. But it is the office of Christianity to reverse this order. It
is pleasing to witness this blessed renovation: to see, as life
advances, asperities [rough or harsh aspects of the personality]
gradually smoothing down, and roughnesses mellowing away:
while the subject of this happy change experiences within,
increasing measures of the comfort which he diffuses around
him; and feeling the genial influences of that heavenly flame
which can thus give life, and warmth, and action, to what had
been hitherto rigid and insensible, looks up with gratitude to
Him who has shed abroad this principle of love in his heart;

> Miraturque novas frondes et non sua poma.

> [And marvels at strange leaves and fruits not its own.

> —Virgil][17]

Let it not be thought that in the foregoing discussion,
the amiable and useful qualities where they are not prompted
and governed by a principle of religion, have been spoken of in
too disparaging terms. Nor would I be understood as unwilling
to concede to those who are living in the exercise of them, their
proper tribute of commendation: Inest sua gratia ["Its favor is
present"]. Of such persons it must be said, in the language of
Scripture, "they have their reward" [Matthew 6:2]. They have it
in the inward complacency, which a sweet temper seldom fails

to inspire; in the comforts of the domestic or social circle; in the pleasure which from the constitution of our nature accompanies pursuit and action. They are always beloved in private, and generally respected in public life. But when devoid of Religion, if the word of God be not a fable, "they cannot enter into the kingdom of Heaven" [cf. Matthew 19:21]. True practical Christianity (never let it be forgotten) consists in devoting the heart and life to God; in being supremely and habitually governed by a desire to know, and a disposition to fulfill his will, and in endeavouring under the influence of *these motives* to "live to his glory." Where these essential requisites are wanting, however amiable the character may be, however creditable and respectable among men; yet, as it possesses not the grand distinguishing essence, it must not be complimented with the name of Christianity. This however, when the external decorums of Religion are not violated, must commonly be a matter between God and a man's own conscience; and we ought never to forget how strongly we are enjoined to be candid and liberal in judging the motives of others, while we are strict in scrutinizing and severe in questioning our own. And this strict scrutiny is no where more necessary, because there is no where more room for the operation of self-deceit. We are all extremely prone to lend ourselves to the good opinion which, however falsely, is entertained of us by others: and though we at first confusedly suspect, or even indubitably [beyond doubt] know, that their esteem is unfounded, and their praises undeserved, and that they would have thought and spoken of us very differently if they had discerned our secret motives, or had been accurately acquainted with all the circumstances of our conduct; we gradually suffer ourselves to adopt their judgment of us, and at length feel that we are in some sort injured or denied our due, when these false commendations are contradicted or with-held. Without the most constant watchfulness, and the most close and impartial self-examination, irreligious people of amiable tempers, and still more those of useful lives, from the general popularity of their character, will be particularly liable to become the dupes [those who have been deceived or tricked] of this propensity. Nor is it they only who have here need to be on their guard: men of real religion will also do well to watch against this delusion. There is however another danger to which these are still more exposed, and against which it is the rather necessary to warn them, because of our having insisted so strongly on their being bound to be diligent in the discharge of the active duties of life. In their endeavours to fulfill this obligation, let them specially beware, lest setting out on right principles, they insensibly lose them in the course of their progress; lest, engaging originally in the business and bustle of the world, from a sincere and earnest desire to promote the glory of God, their minds should become so heated and absorbed in the pursuit of their object, as that the true motive of action should either altogether cease to be an habitual principle, or should at least lose much of its life and vigour; lest their thoughts and affections being engrossed by temporal concerns, their sense of the reality of "unseen things" [2 Corinthians 4:18] should fade away, and they should lose their relish for the employments and offices of Religion.

The Christian's path is beset with dangers—On the one hand, he justly dreads an inactive and unprofitable life; on the other, he no less justly trembles for the loss of spiritual-mindedness, which is the very essence and power of his profession. This is not quite the place for the full discussion of the difficult topic here in question: and if it were, the writer of these sheets is too conscious of his own incompetencies, not to be desirous of asking rather than of giving advice respecting it. Yet, as it is a matter which has often engaged his most serious consideration, and has been the frequent subject of his anxious inquiry into the writings and opinions of far better instructors, he will venture to deliver a few words on it, offering them with unaffected diffidence [hesitation to put oneself or one's ideas forward].

Does then the Christian discover in himself, judging not from accidental or occasional feelings, on which little stress is either way to be laid, but from the permanent and habitual temper of his mind, a settled, and still more, a growing coldness and indisposition towards the considerations and offices of Religion? And has he reason to apprehend, that this coldness and indisposition are owing to his being engaged too much or too earnestly in worldly business, or to his being too keen in the pursuit of worldly objects? Let him carefully examine the state of his own heart, and seriously and impartially survey the circumstances of his situation in life; humbly praying to the Father of light and mercy, that he may be enabled to see his way clearly in this difficult emergency. If he finds himself pursuing wealth, or dignity, or reputation, with earnestness and solicitude; if these things engage many of his thoughts; if his mind naturally and inadvertently runs out into contemplations of them; if success in these respects greatly gladdens, and disappointments dispirit and distress his mind; he has but too plain grounds for self-condemnation. "No man can serve two masters" [Luke 16:13]. The world is evidently in possession of his heart, and it is no wonder that he finds himself dull, or rather dead, to the impression and enjoyment of spiritual things.

But though the marks of predominant estimation and regard for earthly things are much less clear and determinate, yet if the object he is pursuing be one which, by its attainment, would bring him a considerable accession of riches, station and honour, let him soberly and fairly question and examine whether the pursuit be warrantable? Here also, asking the advice of some judicious friend; his backwardness to do which, in instances like these, should justly lead him, as was before remarked, to distrust the reasonableness of the schemes which he is prosecuting. In such a case as this, we have good cause to distrust ourselves. Though the inward hope that we are chiefly promoted by a desire to promote the glory of our Maker, and the happiness of our fellow-creatures, by increasing our means of usefulness, may suggest itself to allay, yet let it not altogether remove, our suspicions. It is not improbable, that beneath this plausible mask we conceal, more successfully perhaps from ourselves than from others, an inordinate attachment to the pomps [stately and splendid ceremonies] and transitory distinctions of this life; and as this attachment gains the ascendancy, it will ever be found, that our perception and feeling of the supreme excellence of heavenly things will proportionably subside.

But when the consequences which would follow from the success of our worldly pursuits do not render them so questionable, as in the case we have been just considering; yet, having such good reason to believe that there is somewhere a flaw, let us carefully scrutinize the whole of our conduct, taking that word in its largest sense; in order to discover whether we may not be living either in the breach or in the omission of some known duty, and whether it may not therefore have pleased God to withdraw from us the influence of his Holy Spirit; particularly inquiring, whether the duties of self-examination, of secret and public prayer, the reading of the Holy Scriptures, and the other prescribed means of Grace, have not been either wholly intermitted at their proper seasons, or performed with precipitation [hastiness or rashness] or distraction? And if we find reason to believe, that the allotment of time, which it would be most for our spiritual improvement to assign to our religious offices, is often broken in upon and curtailed, let us be extremely backward to admit excuses for such interruptions and abridgments. It is more than probable, for many obvious reasons, that even our worldly affairs themselves will not, on the long run, go on the better for encroaching upon those hours which ought to be dedicated to the more immediate service of God, and to the cultivation of the inward principles of Religion. Our hearts at least and our conduct will soon exhibit proofs of the sad effects of this fatal negligence. They who in a crazy vessel navigate a sea wherein are shoals and currents innumerable, if they would keep their course or reach their port of safety, must carefully repair the smallest injuries, and often throw out their line and take their observations.[18] In the voyage of life also the Christian who would not make shipwreck of his faith, while he is habitually watchful and provident, must often make it his express business to look into his state, and ascertain his progress.

But to resume to my subject, let us when engaged in this important scrutiny, impartially examine ourselves whether the worldly objects which engross us, are all of them such as properly belong to our profession, or station, or circumstances in life; which therefore we could not neglect with a good conscience. If they be, let us consider whether they do not consume a larger share of our time than they really require; and whether, by not trifling over our work, by deducting somewhat which might be spared from our hours of relaxation, or by some other little management, we might not fully satisfy their just claims, and yet have an increased overplus of leisure, to be devoted to the offices of Religion.

But if we deliberately and honestly conclude that we ought not to give these worldly objects less of our *time,* let us endeavour at least to give them less of our *hearts;* striving that the settled frame of our desires and affections may be more spiritual, and that in the motley intercourses of life, we may constantly retain a more lively sense of the Divine presence, and a stronger impression of the reality of unseen things; thus corresponding with the Scripture description of true Christians, "walking by faith and not by sight" [2 Corinthians 5:7], and "having our conversation in Heaven" [Philippians 3:20].

Above all, let us guard against the temptation to which we shall certainly be exposed, of lowering down our views to our state, instead of endeavouring to rise to the level of our views. Let us rather determine to know the worst of our case, and strive to be suitably affected with it; not forward to speak peace to ourselves, but patiently carrying about with us a deep conviction of our backwardness and inaptitude to Religious duties, and a just sense of our great weakness and numerous infirmities. This cannot be an unbecoming temper in those who are commanded to "work out their salvation with fear and trembling" [Philippians 2:12]. It prompts to constant and earnest prayer. It produces that sobriety, and lowliness and tenderness of mind, that meekness of demeanor and circumspection in conduct, which are such eminent characteristics of the true Christian.

Nor is it a state devoid of consolation—"O tarry thou the Lord's leisure, be strong and he shall comfort thy heart" [Isaiah 35:4]. "They that wait on the Lord shall renew their strength" [Isaiah 40:31]. "Blessed are they that mourn, for they shall be comforted" [Matthew 5:4]. These Divine assurances soothe and encourage the Christian's disturbed and dejected mind, and insensibly diffuse a holy composure. The tint may be solemn, nay even melancholy, but it is mild and grateful. The tumult of his soul has subsided, and he is possessed by complacency, and hope, and love. If a sense of undeserved kindness fill his eyes with tears, they are tears of reconciliation and joy: while a generous ardour springing up within him, sends him forth to his worldly labours "fervent in spirit" [Romans 12:11], resolving through the Divine aid, to be henceforth more diligent and exemplary in living to the Glory of God, and longing meanwhile for that blessed time, when, "being freed from the bondage of corruption" [Romans 8:21], he shall be enabled to render to his Heavenly Benefactor more pure and acceptable service [cf. Romans 12:1].

After having discussed so much the whole question concerning amiable tempers in general, it may be scarcely necessary to dwell upon that particular class of them which belongs to the head of generous emotions, or of exquisite sensibility. To these almost all which has been said above, is strictly applicable; to which it may be added, that the persons in whom the latter qualities most abound, are often far from conducing [contributing] to the peace and comfort of their nearest connections. These qualities indeed may be rendered highly useful instruments, when enlisted into the service of Religion. But we ought to except [exclude] against them the more strongly when not under her controul, because there is still greater danger than in the former case, that persons in whom they abound, may be flattered into a false opinion of themselves by the excessive commendations often paid to them by others, and by the beguiling complacencies of their own minds, which are apt to be puffed up with a proud though secret consciousness of their own superior acuteness and sensibility. But it is the less requisite to enlarge on this topic, because it has been well discussed by many, who have unfolded the real nature of those fascinating qualities; who have well remarked, that though shewy and apt to catch the eye, they are of a flimsy and perishable fabric, not of that less gaudy, but more substantial and durable texture, which, imparting permanent warmth and comfort, will long preserve its more sober honours, and stand the wear and tear of life, and the vicissitudes [changes] of seasons. It has been shewn, that these qualities often fail us when most we want their aid; that their possessors can solace themselves with their imaginary exertions in behalf of ideal misery, and yet shrink from the labours of active benevolence, or retire with disgust from the homely forms of real poverty and wretchedness. In fine [in summary], the superiority of Christian charity and of plain practical beneficence has been ably vindicated, and the school of Rousseau[19] has been forced to yield to the school of Christ, when the question has been concerning the best means of promoting the comfort of family life or the temporal well-being of society.[20]

SECTION FIVE ↶

Some Other Grand Defects in the Practical System of the Bulk of Nominal Christians

In the imperfect sketch which has been drawn of the Religion of the bulk of nominal Christians, their fundamental error respecting the nature of Christianity has been discussed, and traced into some of its many mischievous consequences. Several of their particular misconceptions and allowed defects have also been pointed out and illustrated. It may not be improper to close the survey by noticing some others, for the existence of which we may now appeal to almost every part of the preceding delineation.

In the first place, then, there appears throughout, both in the principles and allowed conduct of the bulk of nominal Christians, a most inadequate idea of the *guilt and evil of sin*. We every where find reason to remark, that, as was formerly observed, Religion is suffered to dwindle away into a mere matter of *police*. Hence the guilt of actions is estimated, not by the proportion in which, according to Scripture, they are offensive to God, but by that in which they are injurious to society. Murder, theft, fraud in all its shapes, and some species of lying, are manifestly and in an eminent degree, injurious to social happiness. How different accordingly, in the moral scale, is the place they hold, from that which is assigned to idolatry, to general irreligion, to swearing, drinking, fornication, lasciviousness [lustfulness], sensuality, excessive dissipation, and, in particular circumstances, to pride, wrath, malice, and revenge!

Indeed, several of the above-mentioned vices are held to be grossly criminal in the lower ranks, because manifestly ruinous to their temporal interests; but in the higher, they are represented as "losing half their evil by losing all their grossness," as flowing naturally from great prosperity, from the excess of gaiety and good humour; and they are accordingly "regarded with but a small degree of disapprobation, and censured very slightly or not at all."[21] "Non meus hic sermo est" ["This is not my speech"]. These are the remarks of authors who have surveyed the stage of human life with more than ordinary observation; one of whom in particular, cannot be suspected of having been misled by religious prejudices, to form a judgment of the superior orders too unfavourable and severe.

Will these positions however be denied? Will it be maintained that there is not the difference already stated, in the moral estimation of these different classes of vices? Will it be said that the one class is indeed more generally restrained, and more severely punished by human laws, because more properly cognizable by human judicatures, and more directly at war with the well being of society; but that when brought before the tribunal of internal opinion they are condemned with equal rigour?

Facts may be denied, and charges laughed out of countenance: but where the general sentiment and feeling of mankind are in question, our common language is often the clearest and most impartial witness; and the conclusions thus furnished, are not to be parried by wit, or eluded by sophistry. In the present case, our ordinary modes of speech furnish sufficient matter for the determination of the argument; and abundantly prove our disposition to consider as matters of small account, such sins as are not held to be injurious to the community. We invent for them diminutive and qualifying terms, which, if not, as in the common uses of language,[22] to be admitted as signs of approbation and good will, must at least be confessed to be proofs of our tendency to regard them with palliation [as if less serious] and indulgence. Free-thinking, gallantry, jollity,[23] and a thousand similar phrases, might be adduced as instances. But it is worthy of remark, that no such soft and qualifying terms are in use for expressing the smaller degrees of theft or fraud, or forgery, or any other of those offences, which are committed by men against their fellow-creatures, and in the suppression of which we are interested by our regard to our temporal concerns.

The charge which we are urging is indeed undeniable. In the case of any question of honour, or of moral honesty, we are sagacious in discerning and inexorable in judging the offence. No allowance is made for the suddenness of surprize, or the strength of temptations. One single failure is presumed to imply the absence of the moral or honourable principle. The memory is retentive on these occasions, and the man's character is blasted for life. Here, even mere suspicion of having once offended can scarcely be got over: "There is an awkward story about that man, which must be explained before he and I can become acquainted." But in the case of sins against God, there is no such watchful jealousy, none of this rigorous logic. A man may go on in the frequent commission of known sins, yet no such inference is drawn respecting the absence of the religious principle. On the contrary, we say of him, that "though his *conduct* be a little incorrect, his *principles* are untouched;" "that he has a good heart:" and such a man may go quietly through life, with the titles of a *mighty worthy creature,* and a *very good Christian.*

But in the Word of God, actions are estimated by a far less accommodating standard. There we read of no little sins. Much of our Saviour's sermon on the mount [Matthew 5:1–7:29], which many of the class we are condemning affect highly to admire, is expressly pointed against so dangerous a misconception. *There,* no such distinction is made between the rich and the poor. No notices are to be traced of one scale of morals for the higher, and of another for the lower classes of society. Nay, the former are expressly guarded against any such vain imagination, and are distinctly warned, that their condition in life is the more dangerous because of the more abundant temptations to which it exposes them. Idolatry, fornication, lasciviousness, drunkenness, revellings, inordinate affection, are classed with theft and murder, and with what we hold in even still greater abomination; and concerning them all it is pronounced alike, that "they which do such things shall not inherit the kingdom of God" [Galatians 5:19–21; Colossians 3:5–9].

In truth, the instance which we have lately specified of the loose system of these nominal Christians, betrays a fatal absence of the principle which is the very foundation of all Religion. Their slight notions of the guilt and evil of sin discover an utter want of all suitable reverence for the Divine Majesty. This principle is justly termed in Scripture, "the beginning of wisdom" [Psalm 111:10], and there is perhaps no one quality which it is so much the studious endeavour of the sacred writers to impress upon the human heart [Job 28:28; Psalm 110:10; Proverbs 1:7–9:10].

Sin is considered in Scripture as rebellion against the sovereignty of God, and every different act of it equally violates his law, and, if persevered in, disclaims his supremacy. To the inconsiderate and the gay this doctrine may seem harsh, while, vainly fluttering in the sunshine of worldly prosperity, they lull themselves into a fond security. "But the day of the Lord will come as a thief in the night; in which the Heavens shall pass away with a great noise, and the elements shall melt with fervent heat; the earth also and the works that are therein shall be burned up. Seeing, then, that all these things shall be dissolved, what manner of persons ought we to be in all holy conversation and Godliness?" [2 Peter 3:10–11]. We are but an atom in the universe.—Worlds upon worlds surround us, all probably full of intelligent creatures, to whom, now or hereafter, we may be a spectacle, and afford an example of the Divine procedure. Who then shall take upon him to pronounce what might be the issue, if sin were suffered to pass unpunished in one corner of this universal empire? Who shall say what confusion might be the consequence, what disorder it might spread through the creation of God? Be this however as it may, the language of Scripture is clear and decisive; —"The wicked shall be turned into hell, and all the nations that forget God" [Psalm 9:17].

It should be carefully observed too, that these awful denunciations of the future punishment of sin derive additional weight from this consideration, that they are represented, not merely as a judicial sentence, which, without violence to the settled order of things, might be remitted through the mere mercy of our Almighty Governor, but as arising out of the established course of nature; as happening in the way of natural consequence, just as a cause is necessarily connected with its effect; as resulting from certain connections and relations which rendered them suitable and becoming. It is stated, that the kingdom of God and the kingdom of Satan are both set up in the world, and that to the one or the other of these we must belong. "The righteous have *passed* from death unto life" [cf. John 5:24 and 1 John 3:14] —"they are delivered from the power of darkness, and are translated into the kingdom of God's dear Son" [Colossians 1:13]. They are become "the children" and "the subjects of God." While on earth, they love his day, his service, his people; they "speak good of his name" [Psalm 66:2]; they abound in his works. Even here they are in some decree possessed of his image: by and by it shall be perfected; "they shall awake up after his likeness" [Psalm 17:15], and being "heirs of eternal life" [Titus 3:7], they shall receive "an inheritance incorruptible and undefiled, and that fadeth not away" [1 Peter 1:4].

Of sinners, on the other hand, it is declared, that "they are of their father the devil" [John 8:44]; while on earth, they are styled "his children" [1 John 3:10], "his servants;" they are said "to do his works" [1 John 3:8], "to hold to his side" [cf. John 20:24–28], to be "subjects of his kingdom" [cf. John 12:31]: at length "they shall partake his portion" [cf. Matthew 25:41], when the merciful Saviour shall be changed into an avenging judge, and shall pronounce that dreadful sentence, "depart from me, ye cursed, into everlasting fire, prepared for the devil and his angels" [see Matthew 25:41].

Is it possible that these declarations should not strike terror, or at least excite serious and fearful apprehension in the lightest and most inconsiderate mind? But the imaginations of men are fatally prone to suggest to them fallacious hopes in the very face of these positive declarations. We cannot persuade ourselves that God will in fact, prove so severe. It was the very delusion to which our first parents listened: "Ye shall not surely die" [Genesis 3:4].

Let me ask these rash men, who are thus disposed to trifle with their immortal interests, had they lived in the antideluvian [the time before the flood of Noah] world, would they have conceived it possible that God would then execute his predicted threatening? Yet the event took place at the appointed time; the flood came and swept them all away: and this aweful instance of the anger of God against sin is related in the inspired writings for our instruction. Still more to rouse us to attention, the record is impressed in indelible characters on the solid substance of the very globe we inhabit; which thus, in every country upon earth, furnishes practical attestations to the truth of the sacred writings, and to the actual accomplishment of their aweful predictions. For myself I must declare, that I never can read without awe the passage in which our Saviour is speaking of the state of the world at the time of this memorable event. The wickedness of men is represented to have been great and prevalent; yet not as we are ready to conceive, such as to interrupt the course, and shake the very frame of society. The general face of things was, perhaps, not very different from that which is exhibited in many of the European nations. It was a selfish, a luxurious, an irreligious, and an inconsiderate world. They were called, but they would not hearken; they were warned, but they would not believe—"They did eat, they drank, they married wives, they were given in marriage" [Luke 17:27]: such is the account of one of the Evangelists [Luke]; in that of another [Matthew] it is stated nearly in the same words; "They were eating and drinking, marrying and giving in marriage, and knew not until the flood came and swept them all away" [Matthew 24:38–39].

Again, we see throughout, in the system which we have been describing, a most inadequate conception of the difficulty of becoming true Christians; and an utter forgetfulness, of its being the great business of life to secure our admission into Heaven, and to prepare our hearts for its service and enjoyments. The general notion appears to be, that, if born in a country of which Christianity is the established religion, we are born Christians. We do not therefore look out for positive evidence of our really being of that number; but putting the *onus probandi* ["the burden of proving"], (if it may be so expressed) on the wrong side, we conceive ourselves such *of course*, except our title be disproved by positive evidence to the contrary. And we are so slow in giving ear to what conscience urges to us on this side; so dexterous in justifying what is clearly wrong, in palliating [means making less intense or severe] what we cannot justify, in magnifying the merit of what is fairly commendable, in flattering ourselves that our habits of vice are only occasional acts, and in multiplying our single acts into habits of virtue, that we must be bad indeed, to be compelled to give a verdict against ourselves. Besides, having no suspicion of our state, we do not set ourselves in earnest to the work of self-examination; but only receive in a confused and hasty way some occasional notices of our danger, when sickness, or the loss of a friend, or the recent commission of some act of vice of greater size than ordinary, has awakened in our consciences a more than usual degree of sensibility.

Thus, by the generality, it is altogether forgotten, that the Christian has a great work to execute; that of forming himself after the pattern of his Lord and Master, through the operation of the Holy Spirit of God, which is promised to our fervent prayers and diligent endeavours. Unconscious of the obstacles which impede, and of the enemies which resist their advancement; they are naturally forgetful also of the ample provision which is in store, for enabling them to surmount the one, and to conquer the other. The scriptural representations of the state of the Christian on earth, by the images of "a race" [cf. Hebrews 12:1], and "a warfare" [cf. Ephesians 6:12]; of its being necessary to rid himself of every encumbrance which might retard him in the one [cf. Hebrews 12:1], and to furnish himself with the whole armor of God for being victorious in the other [cf. Ephesians 6:13], are, so far as these nominal Christians are concerned, figures of no propriety or meaning. As little (as was formerly shewn) have they, in correspondence with the Scripture descriptions of the feelings and language of real Christians, any idea of acquiring a relish, while on earth, for the worship and service of Heaven. If the truth must be told, their notion is rather a confused idea of future gratification in Heaven, in return for having put a force upon their inclinations, and endured so much religion while on earth.

But all this is only *nominal* Christianity, which exhibits a more inadequate image of her real excellences, than the cold copyings, by some insipid pencil, convey of the force and grace of Nature, or of Raphael [a renaissance artist whose work was distinguished by its harmony and balance]. In the language of Scripture, Christianity is not a geographical, but a moral term. It is not the being a native of a Christian country: it is *a condition, a state;* the possession of a *peculiar nature* [1 Peter 2:9], with the *qualities* and *properties* which belong to it.

Farther than this; it is a state into which we are not *born*, but into which we must be *translated;* a nature which we do not *inherit*, but into which we are to be *created anew*. To the undeserved grace of God, which is promised on our use of the appointed means, we must be indebted for the attainment of this nature; and, to acquire and make sure of it, is that great "work of our salvation" [cf. Hebrews 2:3] which we are commanded to "work out with fear and trembling" [Philippians 2:12]. We are every where reminded, that this is a matter of labour and difficulty, requiring continual watchfulness, and unceasing effort, and unwearied patience. Even to the very last, towards the close of a long life consumed in active service, or in cheerful suffering, we find St. Paul himself declaring, that he conceived bodily self-denial and mental discipline to be indispensably necessary to his very safety. Christians, who are really worthy of the name, are represented as being "made meet for the inheritance of the Saints in light" [Colossians 1:12]; as "waiting for the coming of our Lord Jesus Christ" [1 Corinthians 1:7]; as "looking for and hasting unto the coming of the day of God" [2 Peter 3:12]. It is stated as being enough to make them happy, that "Christ should receive them to himself" [cf. Colossians 1:20]; and the songs of the blessed Spirits in Heaven are described to be the same as those in which the servants of God on earth pour forth their gratitude and adoration.

Conscious therefore of the indispensable necessity, and of the arduous nature of the service in which he is engaged, the true Christian sets himself to the work with vigour, and prosecutes it with diligence. His motto is that of the painter: "Nullus dies sine linea" ["Never a day without a sketch"]. Fled as it were from a country in which the plague is raging, he thinks it not enough just to pass the boundary line, but would put out of doubt his escape beyond the limits of infection. Prepared to meet with difficulties, he is not discouraged when they occur; warned of his numerous adversaries, he is not alarmed on their approach, or unprovided for encountering them. He knows that the beginning of every new course may be expected to be rough and painful; but he is assured that the paths on which he is entering will ere long seem smoother, and become indeed "paths of pleasantness and peace" [Proverbs 3:17].

Now of the state of such an one the expressions of Pilgrim and Stranger are a lively description; and all the other figures and images, by which Christians are represented in Scripture, have in his case a determinate meaning and a just application. There is indeed none by which the Christian's state on earth is in the word of God more frequently imaged, or more happily illustrated, than by that of a journey; and it may not be amiss to pause for a while in order to survey it under that resemblance.[24] The Christian is travelling on business through a strange country, in which he is commanded to execute his work with diligence, and pursue his course homeward with alacrity. The fruits which he sees by the way side he gathers with caution; he drinks of the streams with moderation; he is thankful when the sun shines, and his way is pleasant; but if it be rough and rainy, he cares not much, he is but a traveller. He is prepared for vicissitudes; he knows that he must expect to meet with them in the stormy and uncertain climate of this world. But he is traveling to a "better country" [Hebrews 11:16], a country of unclouded light and undisturbed serenity. He finds also by experience, that when he has had the least of external comforts, he has always been least disposed to loiter; and if for the time it be a little disagreeable, he can solace himself with the idea of his being thereby forwarded in his course. In a less unfavourable season, he looks round with an eye of observation: he admires what is beautiful; he examines what is curious; he receives with complacency the refreshments which are set before him, and enjoys them with thankfulness. Nor does he churlishly refuse to associate with the inhabitants of the country through which he is passing; nor, so far as he may, to speak their language, and adopt their fashions. But he neither suffers pleasure, nor curiosity, nor society, to take up too much of his time; and is still intent on transacting the business he has to execute, and on prosecuting the journey which he is ordered to pursue. He knows also that, to the very end of life, his journey will be through a country in which he has many enemies; that his way is beset with snares; that temptations throng around him, to seduce him from his course, or check his advancement in it; that the very air disposes to drowsiness, and that therefore to the very last it will be requisite for him to be circumspect and collected. Often therefore he examines whereabouts he is, how he has got forward, and whether or not he is travelling in the right direction. Sometimes he seems to himself to make considerable progress; sometimes he advances but slowly; too often he finds reason to fear that he has fallen backward in his course. Now he is cheered with hope, and gladdened by success; now he is disquieted by doubts, and damped by disappointments. Thus while to nominal Christians, Religion is a dull uniform thing, and they have no conception of the desires and disappointments, the hopes and fears, the joys and sorrows, which it is calculated to bring into exercise; in the true Christian all is life and motion, and his great work calls forth alternately the various passions of the soul. Let it not therefore be imagined that his is a state of unenlivened toil and hardship. His very labours are "the labours of love" [1 Thessalonians 1:3]; if "he has need of patience" [cf. Hebrews 10:36], it is "the patience of hope" [1 Thessalonians 1:3], and he is cheered in his work by the constant assurance of present support, and of final victory. Let it not be forgotten that this is the very idea given us of happiness by one of the ablest examiners of the human mind; "a constant employment for a desired end, with the consciousness of continual progress." So true is the Scripture declaration, that "Godliness has the promise of the life that now is, as well as of that which is to come" [1 Timothy 4:8].

Our review of the character of the bulk of nominal Christians has exhibited abundant proofs of their defectiveness in that great constituent of the true Christian character, *the love of God.* Many instances, in proof of this assertion, have been incidentally pointed out, and the charge is in itself so obvious, that it were superfluous to spend much time in endeavouring to establish it. Put the question fairly to the test. Concerning the proper marks and evidences of affection, there can be little dispute. Let the most candid investigator examine the character, and conduct, and language of the persons of whom we have been speaking, and he will be compelled to acknowledge, that so far as love towards the Supreme Being is in question, these marks and evidences are no where to be met with. It is in itself a decisive evidence of a contrary feeling in these nominal Christians, that they find no pleasure in the service and worship of God. Their devotional acts resemble less the free will offerings of a grateful heart, than that constrained and reluctant homage which is exacted by some hard master from his oppressed dependents, and paid with cold sullenness, and slavish apprehension. It was the very charge brought by God against his ungrateful people of old, that while they called him Sovereign and Father, they withheld from him the regards which severally belong to those respected and endearing appellations. Thus we likewise think it enough to offer to the most excellent and amiable of Beings, to our supreme and unwearied Benefactor, a dull, artificial, heartless gratitude, of which we should be ashamed in the case of a fellow-creature who had ever so small a claim on our regard and thankfulness.

It may be of infinite use to establish in our minds a strong and habitual sense of that first and great commandment—"Thou shalt love the Lord thy God with all thy heart, and with all thy mind, and with all thy soul, and with all thy strength" [Mark 12:30, 33]. This passion, operative and vigorous in its very nature, like a master spring, would put and maintain in action all the complicated movements of the human soul. Soon also would it terminate many practical questions concerning the allowableness of certain compliances; questions which, with other similar difficulties, are often only the cold offspring of a spirit of reluctant submission, and cannot stand the encounter of this trying principle. If, for example, it were disputed whether or not the law of God were *so* strict, as had been stated in condemning the slightest infraction of its precepts, yet when, from the precise demands of justice, the appeal should be made to the more generous principle of love, there would be at once an end of the discussion. Fear will deter from acknowledged crimes, and self-interest will bribe to laborious services. But it is the peculiar glory, and the very characteristic of this more generous passion, to shew itself in ten thousand little and undefinable acts of sedulous attention, which love alone can pay, and of which, when paid, love alone can estimate the value. Love outruns the deductions of reasoning; it scorns the refuge of casuistry; it requires not the slow process of laborious and undeniable proof that an action would be injurious and offensive, or another beneficial or gratifying to the object of affection. The least hint, the slightest surmise, is sufficient to make it start from the one, and fly with eagerness to the other.

I am well aware that I am now about to tread on very tender ground; but it would be an improper deference to the opinions and manners of the age to altogether avoid it. There has been much argument concerning the lawfulness of theatrical amusements.[25] Let it be sufficient to remark, that the controversy would be short indeed, if the question were to be tried by this criterion of love to the Supreme Being. If there were any thing of that sensibility for the honour of God, and of that zeal in his service, which we show in behalf of our earthly friends, or of our political connections, should we seek our pleasure in that place which the debauchee, inflamed with wine, or bent on the gratification of other licentious appetites, finds most congenial to his state and temper of mind? In that place, from the neighbourhood of which (how justly termed a school of morals might hence alone be inferred) decorum, and modesty, and regularity retire, while riot and lewdness are invited to the spot, and invariably select it for their chosen residence; where the sacred name of God is often profaned; where sentiments are often heard with delight, and motions and gestures often applauded, which would not be tolerated in private company, but which may far exceed the utmost license allowed in the social circle, without at all transgressing the large bounds theatrical decorum; where, when moral principles are inculcated, they are not such as a Christian ought to cherish in his bosom, but such as it must be his daily endeavour to extirpate; not those which Scripture warrants, but those which it condemns as false and spurious, being founded in pride and ambition, and the overvaluation of human favour; where surely, if a Christian should trust himself at all, it would be requisite for him to prepare himself with a double portion of watchfulness and seriousness of mind, instead of selecting it as the place in which he may throw off his guard, and unbend without danger. The justness of this last remark, and the general tendency of theatrical amusements, is attested by the same well-instructed master in the science of human life, to whom we had before occasion to refer [Adam Smith]. By him they are recommended as the most efficacious expedient for relaxing, among any people, that *"preciseness and austerity* of morals," to use his own phrase, which, under the name of holiness, it is the business of Scripture to inculcate and enforce. Nor is this position merely theoretical. The experiment was tried, and tried successfully, in a city upon the continent,[26] in which it was wished to corrupt the simple morality of purer times.

Let us try the question by a parallel instance.

What judgment should we form of the warmth of that man's attachment to his Sovereign, who, at seasons of recreation, should seek his pleasures in scenes as ill accordant with the principle of loyalty, as those of which we have been speaking with the genius of religion? If for this purpose he were to select the place, and frequent the amusements to which Democrats and Jacobins[27] should love to resort for entertainment, and in which they should find themselves so much at home, as invariably to select the spot for their abiding habitation; where dialogue and song, and the intelligible language of gesticulation [expressive movement of the hands and arms], should be used to convey ideas and sentiments, not perhaps palpably treasonable, or directly falling within the strict precision of any legal limits, but yet palpably contrary to the spirit of the monarchical government; which, further, the highest authorities had recommended as sovereign specifics for cooling the warmth, and enlarging the narrowness of an excessive loyalty. What opinion should we form of the delicacy of that friendship, or of the fidelity of that love, which, in relation to their respective objects, should exhibit the same contradictions?

In truth, the *hard measure*, if the phrase may be pardoned, which, as has been before remarked, we give to God; and the very different way in which we allow ourselves to act, and speak, and feel, where he is concerned from that which we require, or even practice in the case of our fellow-creatures, is in itself the most decisive proof that the principle of the love of God, if not altogether extinct in us, is at least in the lowest possible degree of languor.

From examining the degree in which the bulk of nominal Christians are defective in the love of God, if we proceed to inquire concerning the strength of their love towards their fellow-creatures, the writer is well aware of its being generally held, that here at least they may rather challenge praise than submit to censure. And the many beneficent institutions in which this country abounds, probably above every other, whether in ancient or modern times, may be perhaps appealed to in proof of the opinion. Much of what might have been otherwise urged in the discussion of this topic has been anticipated in the inquiry into the grounds of the extravagant estimation assigned to amiable tempers and useful lives, when unconnected with religious principle. What was then stated may serve in many cases to lower, in the present instance, the loftiness of the pretensions of these nominal Christians; and we shall hereafter have occasion to mention another consideration, of which the effect must be, still further to reduce their claims. Meanwhile, let it suffice to remark, that we must not rest satisfied with merely superficial appearances, if we would form a fair estimate of the degree of purity and vigour, in which the principle of good will towards men warms the bosoms of the bulk of nominal Christians in the higher and more opulent classes in this country. In a highly polished state of society, for instance, we do not expect to find moroseness. But in an age of great profusion, though we may reflect with pleasure on those numerous charitable institutions, which are justly the honour of Great Britain, we are not too hastily to infer a strong principle of internal benevolence, from liberal contributions to the relief of indigence [poverty] and misery. When these contributions are indeed equally abundant in times or in individuals personally oeconomical, the source from which they originate becomes less questionable. But a vigorous principle of philanthropy must not be at once conceded on the ground of liberal benefactions to the poor, in the case of one who, by his liberality in this respect, is curtailed in no necessary, is abridged of no luxury, is put to no trouble either of thought or of action; who, not to impute a desire of being praised for his benevolence, is injured in no man's estimation; in whom also familiarity with large sums has produced that freedom in the expenditure of money, which, thereby affording a fresh illustration of the justice of the old proverb, "Familiarity breeds contempt,"[28] it never fails to operate, except in minds under the influence of a strong principle of avarice.

Our conclusion, perhaps, would be less favourable, but not less fair, if we were to try the characters in question by those surer tests which are stated by the Apostle [most likely Paul, cf. 1 Corinthians 13] to be less ambiguous marks of a real spirit of philanthropy. The strength of every passion is to be estimated by its victory over passions of an opposite nature. What judgment then shall we form of the force of the benevolence of the age, when measured by this standard? How does it stand the shock when it comes into encounter with our pride, our vanity, our self-love, our self-interest, our love of ease or of pleasure, with our ambition, with our desire of worldly estimation? Does it make us self-denying, that we may be liberal in relieving others? Does it make us persevere in doing good in spite of ingratitude; and only pity the ignorance, or prejudice, or malice which misrepresents our conduct, or misconstrues our motives? Does it make us forbear from what we conceive may probably prove the occasion of harm to a fellow-creature; though the harm should not seem naturally or even fairly to flow from our conduct, but to be the result only of his own obstinacy or weakness? Are we slow to believe any thing to our neighbour's disadvantage; and when we cannot but credit it, are we disposed to cover, and as far as we justly can, rather to palliate [to make less intense or severe], than to divulge or aggravate it? Suppose an opportunity to occur of performing a kindness to one who from pride or vanity, should be loth to receive, or to be known to receive, a favour from us; should we honestly endeavour, so far as we could with truth, to lessen in his own mind and in that of others the merit of our good offices, and by so doing dispose him to receive them with diminished reluctance, and a less painful weight of obligation? This end, however, must be accomplished, if to be accomplished at all, by a simple and fair explanation of the circumstances, which may render the action in no wise inconvenient to ourselves, though highly beneficial to another; not by speeches of affected disparagement, which we might easily foresee, and in fact do foresee, must produce the contrary effect. Can we, from motives of kindness, incur or risk the charge of being deficient in spirit, in penetration, or in foresight? Do we tell another of his faults, when the communication, though probably beneficial to *him*, cannot be made without embarrassment or pain to ourselves, and may probably lessen his regard for our person, or his opinion of our judgment? Can we stifle a repartee which would wound another, though the utterance of it would gratify our vanity, and the suppression of it may disparage our character for wit? If any one advance a mistaken proposition in an instance wherein the error may be mischievous to him, can we, to the prejudice perhaps of our credit for discernment, forbear to contradict him in public, if it be probable that in so doing, by piquing [injuring] his pride we might only harden him in his error? and can we reserve our counsel for some more favourable season, the "mollia tempora fandi" ["the favourable occasions for speaking"], when it may be communicated without offence? If we have recommended to any one a particular line of conduct, or have pointed out the probable mischiefs of the opposite course, and if our admonitions have been neglected, are we *really hurt* when our predictions of evil are accomplished? Is our love superior to envy, and jealousy, and emulation? Are we acute to discern and forward to embrace any fair opportunity of promoting the interest of another; if it be in a line wherein we ourselves also are moving, and in which we think our progress has not been proportioned to our desert [what one deserves]? Can we take pleasure in bringing his merits into notice, and in obviating the prejudices which may have damped his efforts, or in removing the obstacles which may have retarded his advancement? If even to this extent we should be able to stand the scrutiny, let it be farther asked how, in the case of our enemies, do we correspond with the Scripture representations of love? Are we meek under provocations, ready to forgive, and apt to forget injuries? Can we, with sincerity, "bless them that curse us, do good to them that hate us, and pray for them which despitefully use us, and persecute us?" [Matthew 5:44; cf. Luke 6:28]. Do we prove to the Searcher of hearts a real spirit of forgiveness, by our forbearing not only from avenging an injury when it is in our power, but even from telling to any one how ill we have been used; and that too when we are not kept silent by a consciousness that we should lose credit by divulging the circumstance? And lastly, Can we not only be content to return our enemies good for evil (for this return. as has been remarked by one of the greatest of uninspired authorities,[29] may be prompted by pride and repaid by self-complacency) but, when they are successful or unsuccessful without our having contributed to their good or ill fortune, can we not only be content, but cordially rejoice in their prosperity, or sympathize with their distresses?

These are but a few specimens of the characteristic marks which might be stated, of a true predominant benevolence: yet even these may serve to convince us how far the bulk of nominal Christians fall short of the requisitions of Scripture, even in that particular, which exhibits their character in the most favourable point of view. The truth is, we do not enough call to mind the exalted tone of Scripture morality; and are therefore apt to value ourselves on the heights to which we attain, when a better acquaintance with our standard would have convinced us of our falling far short of the elevation prescribed to us. It is in the very instance of the most difficult of the duties lately specified, the forgiveness and love of enemies, that our Saviour points out to our imitation the example of our Supreme Benefactor. After stating that, by being kind and courteous to those who, even in the world's opinion, had a title to our good offices and good will, we should in vain set up a claim to *Christian* benevolence, he emphatically adds, "Be ye therefore perfect, even as your Father which is in heaven is perfect" [Matthew 5:48].

We must here again resort to the topic which was lately touched on, that of theatrical amusements; and recommend it to their advocates to consider them in connection with the duty, of which we have now been exhibiting some of the leading characters.

It is an undeniable fact, for the truth of which we may safely appeal to every age and nation, that the situation of the performers, particularly those of the female sex, is remarkably unfavourable to the maintenance and growth of religious and moral principle, and of course highly dangerous to their eternal interests. Might it not then be fairly asked, how far, in all who confess the truth of this position, it is consistent with the sensibility of Christian benevolence, merely for the entertainment of an idle hour, to encourage the continuance of any of their fellow-creatures in such a way of life, and to take a part in tempting any others to enter into it? how far, considering that, by their own concession, they are employing whatever they spend in this way in sustaining and advancing the cause of vice, and consequently in promoting misery; they are herein bestowing this share of their wealth in a manner agreeable to the intentions of their holy and benevolent benefactor? how far also they are not in this instance the rather criminal, from there being so many sources of innocent pleasure open to their enjoyment? how far they are acting conformably to that golden principle of doing to others as we would they should do to us? [cf. Luke 6:31] how far they harmonize with the spirit of the Apostle's [Paul's] affectionate declaration, that he would deny himself for his whole life the most innocent indulgence, nay, what might seem almost an absolute necessary, rather than cause his weak fellow Christian to offend! [cf. Romans 14:13] or lastly, how far they are influenced by the solemn language of our Saviour himself? "It needs must be that offences come, but woe to that man by whom the offence cometh; it were better for him that a millstone were hanged about his neck, and that he were cast into the depths of the sea?" [cf. Matthew 18:6; see also Mark 9:42 and Luke 17:2]. The present instance is perhaps another example of our taking greater concern in the temporal than in the spiritual interests of our fellow creatures. That man would be deemed, and justly deemed, of an inhuman temper, who in these days were to seek his amusement in the combat of gladiators and prize-fighters: yet *Christians* appear conscious of no inconsistency in finding their pleasure in spectacles maintained at the risk at least, if not the ruin, of the eternal happiness of those who perform in them.

SECTION SIX ↵

Grand Defect—Neglect of the Peculiar Doctrines of Christianity

But the grand radical defect in the practical system of these nominal Christians, is their forgetfulness of all the peculiar doctrines of the Religion which they profess—the corruption of

human nature—the atonement of the Saviour—and the sanctifying influence of the Holy Spirit.

Here then we come again to the grand distinction
between the Religion of Christ and that of the bulk of nominal
Christians in the present day. The point is of the utmost
practical importance, and we would therefore trace it into its
actual effects.

There are, it is to be apprehended, not a few, who
having been for some time hurried down the stream of dissipation in the indulgence of all their natural appetites, (except,
perhaps, that they were restrained from very gross vice by a
regard to character, or by the yet unsubdued voice of conscience) and who, having all the while thought little, or scarce at
all, about Religion, "living," to use the emphatical language of
Scripture, "without God in the world" [Ephesians 2:12], become
in some degree impressed with a sense of the infinite importance of Religion. A fit of sickness, perhaps, or the loss of some
friend or much loved relative, or some other stroke of adverse
fortune, damps their spirits, awakens them to a practical conviction of the precariousness of all human things, and turns them
to seek for some more stable foundation of happiness than this
world can afford. Looking into themselves ever so little, they
become sensible that they must have offended God. They resolve accordingly to set about the work of reformation.—Here it
is that we shall recognize the fatal effects of the prevailing
ignorance of the real nature of Christianity, and the general
forgetfulness of its grand peculiarities. These men *wish* to reform, but they know neither the real *nature* of their distemper
nor its true remedy. They are aware, indeed, that they must
"cease to do evil, and learn to do well" [Isaiah 1:16–17]; that
they must relinquish their habits of vice, and attend more or less
to the duties of Religion; but having no conception of the actual
malignity [harm] of the disease under which they labour, or of
the perfect cure which the Gospel has provided for it, or of the
manner in which that cure is to be effected,

> They do but skim and film the ulcerous place,
> While rank corruption, mining all within,
> Infects unseen.
>
> [—William Shakespeare][30]

It often happens therefore but too naturally in this
case, that where they do not soon desist from their attempt at

reformation, and relapse into their old habits of sin; they take up with a partial and scanty amendment, and fondly flatter themselves that it is a thorough change. They now conceive that they have a right to take to themselves the comforts of Christianity. Not being able to raise their practice up to their standard of right, they lower their standard to their practice: they sit down for life contented with their present attainments, beguiled by the complacencies of their own minds, and by the favourable testimony of surrounding friends; and it often happens, particularly where there is any degree of strictness in formal and ceremonial observances, that there are no people more jealous of their character for Religion.

Others perhaps go farther than this. The dread of the wrath to come has sunk deeper into their hearts; and for a while they strive with all their might to resist their evil propensities, and to walk without stumbling in the path of duty. Again and again they resolve: again and again they break their resolutions.[31] All their endeavours are foiled, and they have become more and more convinced of their own moral weakness, and of the strength of their indwelling corruption. Thus groaning under the enslaving power of sin, and experiencing the futility of the utmost efforts which they can use for effecting their deliverance, they are tempted (sometimes it is to be feared they yield to the temptation) to give up all in despair, and to aquiesce under their wretched captivity, conceiving it impossible to break their chains. Sometimes, probably, it even happens that they are driven to seek for refuge from their disquietude in the suggestions of infidelity; and to quiet their troublesome consciences by arguments which they themselves scarcely believe, at the very moment in which they suffer themselves to be lulled asleep by them. In the mean time, while this conflict has been going on, their walk is sad and comfortless, and their couch is nightly watered with tears. These men are pursuing the right object, but they mistake the way in which it is to be obtained. *The path in which they are now treading is not that which the Gospel has provided for conducting them to true holiness, nor will they find in it any solid peace.*

Persons under these circumstances naturally seek for religious instruction. They turn over the works of our modern Religionists, and as well as they can collect the advice addressed to men in their situation, the substance of it is, at the best, of this sort; "Be sorry indeed for your sins, and discontinue the practice of them, but do not make yourselves so uneasy. Christ died for the sins of the whole world. Do your utmost; discharge with fidelity the duties of your stations, not neglecting your religious offices; and fear not but that in the end all will go well; and that having thus performed the conditions required on your part, you will at last obtain forgiveness of our merciful Creator through the merits of Jesus Christ, and be aided, where your own strength shall be insufficient, by the assistance of his Holy Spirit. Meanwhile you cannot do better than read carefully such books of practical divinity as will instruct you in the principles of a Christian life. We are excellently furnished with works of this nature; and it is by the diligent study of them that you will gradually become a proficient in the lessons of the Gospel."

But the holy Scriptures, and with them the Church of England, call upon those who are in the circumstances above stated, to *lay afresh the whole foundation of their Religion.* In concurrence with the Scripture, that the Church calls upon them, in the first place, gratefully to adore that undeserved goodness which has awakened them from the sleep of death; to prostrate themselves before the Cross of Christ with humble penitence and deep self-abhorrence; solemnly resolving to forsake all their sins, but relying on the Grace of God alone for power to keep their resolution. Thus, and thus only, she assures them that all their crimes will be blotted out, and that they will receive from above a new living principle of holiness. She produces from the Word of God the ground and warrant of her counsel; "Believe in the Lord Jesus Christ, and thou shalt be saved" [Acts 16:31]. —"No man," says our blessed Saviour, "cometh unto the Father but by me" [John 14:6]. —"I am the true Vine. As the branch cannot bear fruit of itself except it abide in the vine, no more can ye except ye abide in me" [John 15:4]. —"He that abideth in me and I in him the same bringeth forth much fruit; for without (or severed from) me, ye can do nothing" [John 15:5]. —"By grace are ye saved through faith, and that not of yourselves, it is the gift of God; not of works, lest any man should boast: for we are his workmanship, created in Christ Jesus unto good works" [Ephesians 2:9–10].

Let us not be thought tedious, or be accused of running into needless repetitions, in pressing this point with so much earnestness. It is in fact a point which can never be too much insisted on. It is the cardinal point on which the whole of Christianity turns; on which it is peculiarly proper is this place to be perfectly distinct. There have been some who have imagined that the wrath of God was to be deprecated, or his favour conciliated by austerities and penances, or even by forms and ceremonies, and external observances. But all men of enlightened understandings who acknowledge the moral government of God, must also acknowledge, that vice must offend and virtue delight him. In short they must, more or less, assent to the Scripture declaration, "without holiness no man shall see the Lord" [Hebrews 12:14]. But the grand distinction which subsists between the true Christian and all other Religionists, (the class of persons in particular whom it is our object to address) is concerning the *nature* of this holiness, and the *way in which it is to be obtained*. The views entertained by the latter, of the *nature* of holiness, are of all degrees of inadequateness; and they conceive it is to be *obtained* by their own natural unassisted efforts: or if they admit some vague indistinct notion of the assistance of the Holy Spirit, it is unquestionably obvious, on conversing with them, that this does not constitute the *main practical* ground of their dependence. *But the nature of the holiness to which the desires of the true Christian are directed, is no other than the restoration of the image of God: and as to the manner of acquiring it, disclaiming with indignation every idea of attaining it by his own strength, all his hopes of possessing it rest altogether on the divine assurances of the operation of the Holy Spirit, in those who cordially embrace the Gospel of Christ. He knows therefore that this holiness is not to* PRECEDE *his reconciliation to God, and be its* CAUSE; *but to* FOLLOW *it, and be its* EFFECT. *That, in short, it is by* FAITH IN CHRIST *only*[32] *that he is to be justified in the sight of God; to be delivered from the condition of a child of wrath, and a slave of Satan; to be adopted into the family of God; to become an heir of God and a joint heir with Christ, entitled to all the privileges which belong to this high relation; here, to the Spirit of Grace, and a partial renewal after the image of his Creator; hereafter, to the more perfect possession of the Divine likeness, and an inheritance of eternal glory.*

And as it is in this way, that, in obedience to the dictates of the Gospel, the true Christian must originally become possessed of the vital spirit and living principle of universal holiness; so, in order to grow in grace, he must also study in the same school; finding in the consideration of the peculiar doctrines of the Gospel, and in the contemplation of the life, and character, and sufferings of our blessed Saviour, the elements of all practical wisdom, and an inexhaustible storehouse of instructions and motives, no otherwise to be so well supplied. From the neglect of these peculiar doctrines arise the main practical errors of the bulk of professed Christians. These gigantic truths retained in view, would put to shame the littleness of their dwarfish morality. It would be impossible for them to make these harmonize with their low conceptions of the wretchedness and danger of their natural state, which is represented in Scripture as having so powerfully called forth the compassion of God, that he sent his only begotten Son to rescue us. Where *now* are their low conceptions of the worth of the soul, when means like these were taken to redeem it? Where *now* their inadequate conceptions of the guilt of sin, for which in the divine counsels it seemed requisite that an atonement no less costly should be made than that of the blood of the only begotten Son of God? How can they reconcile their low standard of Christian practice with the representation of our being "temples of the Holy Ghost?" [1 Corinthians 6:19]. Their cold sense of obligation, and scanty grudged returns of service, with the glowing gratitude of those who, having been "delivered from the power of darkness, and translated into the kingdom of God's dear Son" [Colossians 1:13], may well conceive that the labours of a whole life will be but an imperfect expression of their thankfulness.

The peculiar doctrines of the Gospel being once admitted, the conclusions which have been now suggested are clear and obvious deductions of reason. But our neglect of these important truths is still less pardonable, because they are distinctly and repeatedly applied in Scripture to the very purposes in question, and the whole superstructure of Christian morals is grounded on their deep and ample basis. Sometimes these truths are represented in Scripture, *generally,* as furnishing Christians with a vigorous and ever present principle of universal obedience. And our slowness in learning the lessons of heavenly wisdom is still further stimulated by almost every particular Christian duty being occasionally traced to them as to its proper source. They are every where represented as warming the hearts of the people of God on earth with continual admiration, and thankfulness, and love, and joy; as triumphing over the attack of the last great enemy, and as calling forth afresh in Heaven the ardent effusions of their unexhausted gratitude.

If then we would indeed be "filled with wisdom and spiritual understanding" [Colossians 1:9]; if we would "walk worthy of the Lord unto all well pleasing, being fruitful in every good work, and increasing in the knowledge of God"

[Colossians 1:10]; here let us fix our eyes! "laying aside every weight, and the sin which doth so easily beset us, and let us run with patience the race that is set before us, LOOKING UNTO JESUS, the author and finisher of our faith; who, for the joy that was set before him, endured the cross, despising the shame, and is set down at the right hand of the throne of God" [Hebrew 12:1–2].

Here best we may learn the infinite *importance* of Christianity. How little it can deserve to be treated in that slight and superficial way in which it is in these days regarded by the bulk of nominal Christians, who are apt to think it may be enough, and almost equally pleasing to God, to be religious *in any way,* and upon *any* system. What exquisite folly it must be to risk the soul on such a venture, in direct contradiction to the dictates of reason, and the express declaration of the word of God! "How shall we escape, if we neglect so great salvation?" [Hebrews 2:3].

LOOKING UNTO JESUS!

Here we shall best learn the duty and reasonableness of an absolute and unconditional surrender of soul and body to the will and service of God—"We are not our own, for we are bought with a price," and must therefore make it our grand concern to "glorify God with our bodies and our spirits, which are God's" [1 Corinthians 6:20]. Should we be base enough, even if we could do it with safety, to make any reserves in our returns of service to that gracious Saviour who "gave up *himself* for us?" [cf. Hebrews 7:27]. If we have formerly talked of compounding by the performance of some commands for the breach of others, can we now bear the mention of a *composition* of duties, or of retaining to ourselves the right of practicing *little* sins? The very suggestion of such an idea fills us with indignation and shame, if our hearts be not dead to every sense of gratitude.

LOOKING UNTO JESUS!

Here we find displayed, in the most lively colours, the guilt of sin, and how hateful it must be to the perfect holiness of that Being who is of purer eyes than to behold iniquity [cf. Habakkuk 1:13]. When we see that, rather than sin should go unpunished, "God spared not his own Son" [Romans 8:32], but "was *pleased* to bruise and put him to grief" [Isaiah 53:10][33] for our sake, how vainly must impenitent sinners flatter themselves with the hope of escaping the vengeance of Heaven, and buoy themselves up with I know not what desperate dreams of the Divine benignity.

Here too we may anticipate the dreadful sufferings of that state "where shall be weeping and gnashing of teeth" [Matthew 8:12]; when rather than that we should undergo them, "the Son of God" himself, who "thought it no robbery to be equal with God" [Philippians 2:6], consented to take upon him our degraded nature with all its weaknesses and infirmities; to be "a man of sorrows" [Isaiah 53:3]; "to hide not his face from shame and spitting" [Isaiah 50:6]; "to be wounded for our transgressions, and bruised for our iniquities" [Isaiah 53:5]; and at length to endure the sharpness of death, "even the death of the Cross" [Philippians 2:8], that he might "deliver us from the wrath to come" [1 Thessalonians 1:10], and open the kingdom of Heaven to all believers.

LOOKING UNTO JESUS!

Here best we may learn to grow in the love of God! The certainty of his pity and love towards repenting sinners, thus irrefragably demonstrated, chases away the sense of tormenting fear, and best lays the ground in us of a reciprocal affection. And while we steadily contemplate this wonderful transaction, and consider in its several relations the amazing truth, that "God spared not his own Son, but delivered him up for us all" [Romans 8:32]; if our minds be not utterly dead to every impulse of sensibility, the emotions of admiration, of preference, of hope, and trust, and joy cannot but spring up within us, chastened with reverential fear, and softened and quickened by overflowing gratitude.[34] *Here* we shall become animated by an abiding disposition to endeavour to please our great Benefactor, and by a humble persuasion, that the weakest endeavours of this nature will not be despised by a Being who has already proved himself so kindly affected towards us [cf. Romans 5:9–10]. *Here* we cannot fail to imbibe an earnest desire of possessing his favour, and a conviction, founded on his own declarations, thus unquestionably confirmed, that the desire shall not be disappointed. Whenever we are conscious that we have offended this gracious Being, a single thought of the great work of Redemption will be enough to fill us with compunction [uneasiness due to guilt]. We shall feel a deep concern, grief mingled with indignant shame, for having conducted ourselves so unworthily towards one who to us has been infinite in kindness: we shall not rest till we have reason to hope that he is reconciled to us; and we shall watch over our hearts and conduct in future with a renewed jealousy, lest we should again offend him. To those who are ever so little acquainted with the nature of the human mind, it were superfluous to remark that the affections and tempers which have been enumerated are the infallib[l]e marks and the constituent properties of love. Let *him* then who would abound and grow in this Christian principle, be much conversant with the great doctrines of the Gospel.

It is obvious, that the attentive and frequent consideration of these great doctrines must have a still more direct tendency to produce and cherish in our minds the principle of the love of Christ. But on this head, so much was said in a former chapter, as to render any further observations unnecessary.

Much also has been already observed concerning the love of our fellow-creatures, and it has been distinctly stated to be the indispensable, and indeed the characteristic duty of Christians. It remains, however, to be here farther remarked, that this grace can no where be cultivated with more advantage than at the foot of the Cross. No where can our Saviour's dying injunction to the exercise of this virtue be recollected with more effect; "This is my commandment, that ye love one another as I have loved you" [John 13:34]. No where can the admonition of the Apostle more powerfully affect us; "Be ye kind one to another, tender-hearted, forgiving one another, even as God, for Christ's sake, hath forgiven you" [Ephesians 4:32]. The view of mankind which is here presented to us, as having been all involved in one common ruin, and the offer of deliverance held out to all, by the Son of God's giving of himself up to pay the price of our reconciliation, produce that sympathy towards our fellow-creatures, which, by the constitution of our nature, seldom fails to result from the consciousness of an identity of interests and a similarity of fortunes. Pity for an unthinking world assists this impression. Our enmities soften and melt away: we are ashamed of thinking much of the *petty injuries* which we may have suffered, when we consider what the Son of God, "who did no wrong, neither was guile found in his mouth" [1 Peter 2:22], patiently underwent. Our hearts become tender while we contemplate this signal act of loving-kindness. We grow desirous of imitating what we cannot but admire. A vigorous principle of enlarged and active charity springs up within us; and we go forth with alacrity, desirous of treading in the steps of our blessed Master, and of manifesting our gratitude for his unmerited goodness, by bearing each other's burthens, and abounding in the disinterested labours of benevolence.

LOOKING UNTO JESUS!

He was meek and lowly of heart, and from the study of *his* character we shall best learn the lessons of humility. Contemplating the work of Redemption, we become more and more impressed with the sense of our natural darkness, and helplessness, and misery, from which it was requisite to ransom us at such a price; more and more conscious that we are utterly unworthy of all the amazing condescension and love which have been manifested towards us; ashamed of the callousness of our tenderest sensibility, and of the poor returns of our most active services. Considerations like these, abating our pride and reducing our opinion of *ourselves,* naturally moderate our pretensions towards *others.* We become less disposed to exact that respect for our persons, and that deference for our authority, which we naturally covet; we less sensibly feel a slight, and less hotly resent it; we grow less irritable, less prone to be dissatisfied, more soft, and meek, and courteous, and placable, and condescending.[35] We are not literally required to practice the same humiliating submissions to which our blessed Saviour himself was not ashamed to stoop;[36] but the *spirit* of the remark applies to us, "the servant is not greater than his lord" [John 13:16]: and we should especially bear this truth in mind, when the occasion calls upon us to discharge some duty, or patiently to suffer some ill treatment, whereby our pride will be wounded, and we are likely to be in some degree degraded from the rank we had possessed in the world's estimation. At the same time the Holy Scriptures assuring us, that to the powerful operations of the Holy Spirit, purchased for us by the death of Christ, we must be indebted for the success of all our endeavours after improvement in virtue; the conviction of this truth tends to render us diffident of our own powers, and to suppress the first risings of vanity. Thus, while we are conducted to heights of virtue no otherwise attainable, due care is taken to prevent our becoming giddy from our elevation.[37] It is the Scripture characteristic of the Gospel system, that by it all disposition to exhalt ourselves is excluded; and if we really grow in grace, we shall grow also in humility.

Looking unto Jesus!

"He endured the cross, despising the shame" [Hebrews 12:2]. —While we steadily contemplate this solemn scene, that sober frame of spirit is produced within us which best befits the Christian, militant here on earth. We become impressed with a sense of the shortness and uncertainty of time, and that it behoves us to be diligent in making provision for eternity. In such a temper of mind, the pomps and vanities of life are cast behind us as the baubles of children.—We lose our relish for the frolics of gaiety, the race of ambition, or the grosser gratifications of voluptuousness [luxurious living]. In the case even of those objects, which may more justly claim the attention of reasonable and immortal beings, in our family arrangements, in our plans of life, in our schemes of business, we become, without relinquishing the path of duty, more moderate in pursuit, and more indifferent about the issue. Here also we learn to correct the world's false estimate of things, and to "look through the shallowness of earthly grandeur;"[38] to venerate what is truly excellent and noble, though under a despised and degraded form; and to cultivate within ourselves that true magnanimity which can make us rise superior to the smiles or frowns of this world; that dignified composure of soul which no earthly incidents can destroy or ruffle. Instead of repining at any of the little occasional inconveniences we may meet with in our passage through life; we are almost ashamed of the multiplied comforts and enjoyments of our condition, when we think of him, who, though "the Lord of glory" [cf. 1 Corinthians 2:8], "had not where to lay his head" [Matthew 8:20]. And if it be our lot to undergo evils of more than ordinary magnitude, we are animated under them by reflecting that we are hereby more conformed to the example of our blessed Master: though we must ever recollect one important difference, that the sufferings of Christ were voluntarily borne for *our* benefit, and were probably far more exquisitely agonizing than any which we are called upon to undergo. Besides, it must be a solid support to us amidst all our troubles to know that they do not happen to us by chance; that they are not even merely the punishment of sin; but that they are the dispensations of a kind Providence, and sent on messages of mercy.—"The cup that our Father hath given us, shall we not drink it?" [cf. John 18:11]. —"Blessed Saviour! by the bitterness of thy pains we may estimate the force of thy love; we are *sure* of thy kindness and compassion; *thou* wouldst not willingly call on us to suffer; thou hast declared unto us, that all things shall finally work together for good to them that love thee [Romans 8:28]; and therefore, if thou so ordainest it, welcome disappointment and poverty, welcome sickness and pain, welcome even shame, and contempt, and calumny. If this be a rough and thorny path, it is one in which thou hast gone before us. Where we see thy footsteps we cannot repine. Meanwhile, thou wilt support us with the consolations of thy grace; and even here thou canst more than compensate to us for any temporal sufferings, by the possession of that peace which the world can neither give nor take away" [cf. John 14:27].

Looking unto Jesus!

"The Author and Finisher of our faith, who for the joy that was set before him endured the cross, despising the shame, and is set down at the right hand of God" [Hebrews 12:2]. From the scene of our Saviour's weakness and degradation we follow him, in idea, into the realms of glory, where "he is on the right hand of God; angels, and principalities, and powers being made subject unto him" [1 Peter 3:22]. —But though changed in place, yet not in nature, he is still full of sympathy and love; and having died "to save his people from their sins" [Matthew 1:21], "he ever *liveth* to make intercession for them" [Hebrews 7:25]. Cheered by this animating view, the Christian's fainting spirits revive. Under the heaviest burthens he feels his strength recruited: and when all around him is dark and stormy, he can lift up an eye to Heaven, radiant with hope, and glistening with gratitude. At such a season no dangers can alarm, no opposition can move, no provocations can irritate. He may almost adopt, as the language of his sober exultation, what in the philosopher was but idle rant: and, considering that it is only the garment of mortality which is subject to the rents of fortune, while his spirit, cheered with the divine support, keeps its place within, secure and unassailable, he can sometimes almost triumph at the stake, or on the scaffold, and cry out amidst the severest buffets of adversity, "Thou beatest but the case of Anaxarchus."[39] But it is rarely that the Christian is elevated with this "joy unspeakable and full of glory" [1 Peter 1:8]: he even lends himself to these views with moderation and reserve. Often alas! emotions of another kind fill him with grief and confusion; and conscious of having acted unworthy of his high calling, perhaps of having exposed himself to the just censure of a world ready enough to spy out his infirmities, he seems to himself almost "to have crucified the Son of God afresh, and put him to an open shame" [Hebrews 6:6]. But let neither his joys intoxicate, nor his sorrows too much depress him. Let him still remember that his *chief* business while on earth is not to meditate, but to act; that the seeds of moral corruption are apt to spring up within him, and that it is requisite for him to watch over his own heart with incessant care; that he is to discharge with fidelity the duties of his particular station, and to conduct himself according to his measure, after the example of his blessed Master, whose meat and drink it was to do the work of his heavenly Father [cf. John 4:34]; that he is diligently to cultivate the talents with which God has entrusted him, and assiduously to employ them in doing justice and shewing mercy [cf. Micah 6:8], while he guards against the assaults of an internal enemy. In short, he is to demean himself, in all the common affairs of life, like an *accountable* creature, who, in correspondence with the Scripture character of Christians, is "waiting for the coming of the Lord Jesus Christ" [cf. Titus 2:13]. Often therefore he questions himself, "Am I employing my time, my fortune, my bodily and mental powers so as to be able to 'render up my account with joy, and not with grief?' [Hebrews 13:17]. Am I 'adorning the doctrine of God my Saviour in all things' [Titus 2:10]; and proving that the servants of Christ, animated by a principle of filial affection, which renders their work a service of perfect freedom, are capable of as active and as persevering exertions as the votaries of fame, or the slaves of ambition, or the drudges of avarice?"

Thus, without interruption to his labours, he may interpose occasional thoughts of things unseen; and amidst the many little intervals of business, may calmly look upwards to the heavenly Advocate, who is ever pleading the cause of his people, and obtaining for them needful supplies of grace and consolation. It is these realizing views which give the Christian a relish for the worship and service of the heavenly world. And if these blessed images, "seen but through a glass darkly" [1 Corinthians 13:12], can thus refresh the soul; what must be its state, when on the morning of the resurrection it shall awake to the unclouded vision of celestial glory, when "to them that look for him, the Son of God shall appear a second time without sin unto salvation!" [Hebrews 9:28] when "sighing and sorrow being fled away" [Isaiah 35:10], when doubts and fears no more disquieting, and the painful consciousness of remaining imperfections no longer weighing down the spirit, they shall enter upon the fruition of "those joys which eye hath not seen, nor ear heard, neither hath it entered into the heart of man to conceive" [1 Corinthians 2:9]; and shall bear their part in that blessed anthem—"Salvation to our God which sitteth upon the throne and unto the Lamb, for ever and ever!" [Revelation 7:10].

Thus (never let it be forgotten) the main distinction between real Christianity, and the system of the bulk of nominal Christians, chiefly consists in the different place which is assigned in the two schemes to the peculiar doctrines of the Gospel. These, in the scheme of nominal Christians, if admitted at all, appear but like the stars of the firmament to the ordinary eye. Those splendid luminaries draw forth perhaps occasionally a transient expression of admiration, when we behold their beauty, or hear their distances, magnitudes, or properties: now and then too we are led, perhaps, to muse upon their possible uses: but however curious as subjects of speculation, after all, it must be confessed, they twinkle to the common observer with a vain and "idle" lustre; and except in the dreams of the astrologer, have no influence on human happiness, or any concern with the course and order of the world. But to the *real* Christian, on the contrary, THESE *peculiar doctrines constitute the center to which he gravitates! the very sun of his system! the soul of the world! the origin of all that is excellent and lovely! the source of light, and life, and motion, and genial warmth, and plastic energy!* Dim is the light of reason, and cold and comfortless our state, while left to her unassisted guidance. Even the Old Testament itself, though a revelation from Heaven, shines but with feeble and scanty rays. But the blessed truths of the Gospel are now unveiled to *our* eyes, and *we* are called upon to behold, and to enjoy "the light of the knowledge of the glory of God, in the face of Jesus Christ" [2 Corinthians 4:6], in the full radiance of its meridian splendor. The words of inspiration best express our highly favoured state. "We all, with open face beholding as in a glass the glory of the Lord, are changed into the same image, from glory to glory, even as by the Spirit of the Lord" [2 Corinthians 3:18].

Thou art the source and center of all minds,
Their only point of rest, ETERNAL WORD;
From thee departing, they are lost, and rove
At random, without honour, hope, or peace:
From thee is all that soothes the life of man,
His high endeavour, and his glad success,
His strength to suffer, and his will to serve.
But O thou bounteous Giver of all good,
Thou art of all thy gifts, thyself the crown!
Give what thou canst, without thee we are poor;
And with thee rich, take what thou wilt away.

[—William Cowper][40]

Notes ↤

1. Deists think God's existence is proven in nature, but reject formal religion. Muslims have a holy book, the Koran, which builds on and surpasses the Bible. They also believe that Mohammed is the last and greatest of God's prophets, who include Adam, Noah, Abraham, Moses, and Jesus. Hindus accept the Veda as the most sacred scripture. Their goal is liberation from the cycle of rebirth and the suffering brought about by one's own actions.

2. Hamilcar Barca (d. c. 229 B.C.) was a general who led Carthage into the First Punic War against Rome. His son, Hannibal (247–c. 183 B.C.), one of the great miltary geniuses of all time, followed in his father's footsteps and fought the Second Punic War, during which he invaded Italy by crossing the Alps with elephants.

3. This Latin passage cited by Wilberforce is taken from Book VI, line 730–31 of *The Aeneid,* by the Roman poet Virgil (70–19 B.C.). I have inserted an English translation by H. Rushton Fairclough. Fairclough's translation appears in the Loeb Classical Library's edition of *The Aeneid* (Cambridge, Mass.: Harvard University Press, 1974), p. 557. I have corrected Wilberforce's slightly inaccurate citation of this Latin passage by inserting the word "seminibus."

4. Wilberforce writes,

> It will be remembered by the reader, that it is not the object of this work to animadvert on the vices, defects, and erroneous opinions of the times, except as they are received into the prevailing religious system, or are tolerated by it, and are not thought sufficient to prevent a man from being esteemed on the whole a very tolerable Christian.

5. This Latin passage cited by Wilberforce is taken from Book X, line 96 of *The Satires of Juvenal,* a work by the Roman writer Juvenal (A.D. 60–c. 130). I have inserted an English translation by G. G. Ram-

say. Ramsay's translation appears in the Loeb Classical Library's edition of *The Satires of Juvenal* (Cambridge, Mass.: Harvard University Press, 1940), p. 201. Again, Wilberforce appears to have quoted this passage somewhat inaccurately. I have corrected this citation using the Loeb Library edition as the authoritative text.

6. Wilberforce states, "Vide [See] *Tale of a Tub*." *A Tale of a Tub* was a work written by Jonathan Swift (1667–1745) in 1704. Swift was the Dean of St. Patrick's in Dublin, Ireland, and his most famous work was *Gulliver's Travels*. The story of the "unfortunate Brothers" to which Wilberforce refers occurs in section II of *A Tale of a Tub*. Here three brothers, named Martin, Jack, and Peter, are the main characters in an allegory about a Father, his will, and his three sons. This allegory traces the development of the Christian religion in Europe. Martin represents the Anglican tradition, Jack represents Protestant dissenters, and Peter represents Catholicism.

At one point in this allegory, Martin, Jack, and Peter find themselves in a town were everyone has shoulder-knots (an ornamental clothing accessory). Greatly desiring to acquire shoulder-knots, they consult their father's will to see if they are permitted to do so. Finding no mention of shoulder-knots in the will, one brother states he could find nothing in it about shoulder-knots, *totidem verbis* (in so many words), but that it might contain something about shoulder-knots *totidem syllabis* (in so many syllables). Failing to find the required syllables, this brother then proceeds to see if he can find mention of shoulder-knots in the will *totidem literis* (in so many letters). Having stretched the documentary interpretation of the will to this extreme, the brothers then proceed to acquire lavish shoulder-knots of their own. As the allegory goes on, the brothers resort to various other interpretive artifices to justify their acquisition of other items in addition to shoulder-knots—each successive interpretive device being more absurd than the one that preceeded it. In due course, mythical and allegorical means of interpretation are used. In the end, the brothers find that they can engage in almost any kind of behavior and assert that it is sanctioned in their father's will so long as it is understood *cum grano salis* (with a grain of salt). See Jonathan Swift, *Jonathan Swift: Selections* (Ed. Angus Ross and David Wooley; New York: Oxford University Press, 1990), pp. 38–42.

7. Wilberforce states, "Vide [See] Hey's *Tract,* Rousseau's *Eloisa,* and many periodical essays and sermons." English essayist and mathematician Richard Hey (1745–1835) was the author of *Disseration on Duelling,* published in 1784. French author Jean-Jacques Rousseau's (1712–78) *Julie: ou la nouvelle Heloise* (1761; *Julie: or, The New Eloise*) was a novel which was enormously popular in the second half of the eighteenth century.

8. Wilberforce states, "Vide [See] 'Whosoever looketh on a woman to lust after her, hath committed adultery with her,' &c."

9. Wilberforce states,

The writer cannot omit this opportunity of declaring that he should long ago have brought this subject before the notice of Parliament, but for a perfect conviction that he should probably thereby only give encouragement to a system he wishes to see at an end. The practice has been at different periods nearly stopped by positive laws, in various nations on the Continent; and there can be little doubt of the efficacy of what has been more than once suggested—a Court of Honour, to take cognizance of such offences as would naturally fall within its province. The effects of this establishment would doubtless require to be enforced by legislative provisions, directly punishing the practice; and by discouraging it at court, and in the military and naval institutions, all who should directly or indirectly be guilty of it.

10. Wilberforce states, "Vide [See], in a particular paper in *The Guardian,* by [Joseph] Addison [1672–1719], 'On Honour,' Vol. 2."

11. The words Epicurean, Stoic, and Cynic also refer to schools of philosophy which existed in ancient Greece.

12. According to a substantial tradition, the apostles Peter and Paul were martyred during Nero's reign.

13. Timon the Misanthrope became misanthropic as a result of disappointments and ingratitudes he suffered at the hands of early friends and companions. He resolved to cut himself off entirely from the world.

14. Wilberforce writes, "Vide [See] [Adam] Smith's *Theory of Moral Sentiments.*"

15. Wilberforce writes, "The writer hopes that the work to which he is referring is so well known, that he needs scarcely name Mrs. H. More." Wilberforce is here referring to one of the great friends of his life, the religious writer and philanthropist Hannah More (1745–1833).

16. Wilberforce writes, "See [Adam] Smith's *Theory of Moral Sentiments.*"

17. This Latin phrase is taken from Virgil's *Georgics,* II, 82. When selecting this phrase, Wilberforce may have been influenced by lines 427–29 of "The Garden," Book Three of William Cowper's epic poem "The Task." In a footnote accompanying these lines, Cowper cited Virgil's phrase. Moreover, the likelihood of Cowper's influence upon Wilberforce in this regard is buttressed by the fact that Cowper was Wilberforce's favorite poet, and that Wilberforce quoted from "The Task" several times throughout *A Practical View of Christianity* (p. 176, p. 180 n. 31, p. 256 n. 16). In "The Garden," Cowper wrote:

Hence summer has her riches, autumn hence,
And hence ev'n winter fills his wither'd hand
With blushing fruits, and plenty not his own.

18. It is tempting to speculate that Wilberforce's (lifelong) penchant for nautical allusions may have resulted from his close friendship with the ex-captain, slave trader, and parson John Newton. Newton was renowned for telling stories of his life at sea.

19. The philosopher Jean-Jacques Rousseau was a major figure of the eighteenth-century philosophical movement known as the Enlightenment.

20. Wilberforce writes:

> While all are worthy of blame who, to qualities like these, have assigned a more exalted place than to religious and moral principle; there is one writer who, eminently culpable in this respect, deserves, on another account, still severer reprehension. Really possessed of powers to explore and touch the finest strings of the human heart, and bound by his sacred profession to devote those powers to the service of religion and virtue, he every where discovers a studious solicitude to excite indecent ideas. We turn away our eyes with disgust from open immodesty: but even this is less mischievous than that more measured style, which excites impure images, without shocking us by the grossness of the language. Never was delicate sensibility proved to be more distinct from plain practical benevolence, than in the writings of the author to whom I allude. Instead of employing his talents for the benefit of his fellow-creatures, they were applied to the pernicious purposes of corrupting the national taste, and of lowering the standard of manners and morals. The tendency of his writings is to vitiate that purity of mind, intended by Providence as the companion and preservative of youthful virtue; and to produce, if the expression may be permitted, *a morbid sensibility in the perception of indecency*. An imagination exercised in this discipline is never *clean*, but seeks for and discovers something indelicate in the most common phrases and actions of ordinary life. If the general style of writing and conversation were to be formed on that model, to which Sterne used his utmost endeavours to conciliate the minds of men, there is no estimating the effects which should soon be produced on the manners and morals of the age.

21. Wilberforce writes, "Vide [See] Smith on the *Wealth of Nations,* Vol. III." Adam Smith's *The Wealth of Nations* is perhaps the best known text of economic science. It is universally regarded as a classic of Western Literature.

22. Wilberforce writes, "Vide [See] the Grammarians and Dialecticians on the Dimminutives of the Italian and other languages."

23. Wilberforce writes, "Many might be added, such as a good fellow, a good companion, a libertine, a little free, a little loose in talk, wild, gay, jovial, being no man's enemy but his own, &c. &c. &c. &c. (above all) *having a good heart.*"

24. Wilberforce profited greatly from reading John Bunyan's *Pilgrim's Progress.* It may be that perhaps his fondness for the metaphor

of a pilgrim (aside from the use of such in scripture) owes something to this fact.

25. Wilberforce writes, "It is almost unnecessary to remark, that the word is to be understood in the large sense, as including the opera, &c." In Wilberforce's time, vices such as prostitution were commonly part of the theater-going world.

26. Wilberforce writes,

> Geneva—It is worthy of remark, that the play-houses have multiplied extremely in Paris since the revolution [of 1789]; and that last winter there were twenty open every night, and all crowded. It should not be left unobserved, and it is seriously submitted to the consideration of those who regard the stage as a school of morals, that the pieces which were best composed, best acted, and most warmly and generally applauded, were such as abounded in touches of delicate sensibility. The people of Paris have never been imagined to be more susceptible, than the generality of mankind, of these emotions, and this is not the particular period when the Parisians have been commonly conceived most under their influence. Vide [See] Journal d'un Voyageur Neutre. The author of the work expresses himself as astonished by the phenomenon, and as unable to account for it.

27. Wilberforce writes, "The author is almost afraid of using the terms, lest they should convey an impression of party feelings, of which he wishes this book to exhibit no traces; but he here means by Democrats and Jacobins, not persons on whom party violence fastens the epithet, but persons who are really and avowedly such."

28. This proverb comes from the fable by Aesop (fifth century B.C.) entitled *The Fox and the Lion*.

29. Wilberforce cites Lord Francis Bacon [1561–1626], essayist, lawyer, orator, and philosopher.

30. William Shakespeare, *Hamlet*, act 3, scene 4, line 93.

31. Wilberforce writes,

> If any one would read a description of this process, enlivened and enforced by the powers of the most exquisite poetry, let him peruse the middle and latter part of the fifth book of [William] COWPER'S *Task*. My warm attachment to the exquisitely natural compositions of this truly Christian poet may perhaps bias my judgment; but the part of the work to which I refer appears to me to be scarcely surpassed by any thing in our language. The honorable epithet of *Christian* may be justly assigned to a poet, whose writings, while they fascinate the reader by their manifestly coming from the heart, breathe throughout the spirit of that character of Christianity, with which she was announced to the world, "Glory to God, peace on earth, good will towards men" (Luke 2:14).

The Book of "The Task" to which Wilberforce refers above is entitled "The Winter Morning Walk."

32. Wilberforce writes, "Here again let it be remarked, that faith, where genuine, always supposes repentance, abhorrence of sin, &c."

33. Wilberforce also writes, "It has been well remarked that the word used, where it is said that God 'was PLEASED to bruise,' and put to grief his only Son for us, is the same word as that wherein it was declared by a voice from Heaven, 'This is my beloved Son, in whom I am well pleased.' " See Matthew 17:5.

34. Wilberforce writes, "Vide [See] chapter 3 where these were shewn to be the elementary principles of the passion of love."

35. These amiable kinds of temperament represent a model of Christian behavior which Wilberforce himself constantly exhibited.

36. Wilberforce's footnote reads, "John 13:13–17. 'As I have washed your feet, so wash ye one another's feet,' &c."

37. Wilberforce writes, "Vide [See] Pascal's *Thoughts on Religion:* a book abounding in the deepest views of practical Christianity." Wilberforce is referring here to the French theologian, mathematician, and savant Blaise Pascal (1623–62).

38. Wilberforce refers the reader to the English writer Alexander Pope (1688–1744).

39. Anaxarchus (mid-fourth century B.C.) was a Greek philosopher from Abdera, of the school of Democritus. Following the death of Alexander the Great, Anaxarchus was thrown by shipwreck into the power of Nicocreon, king of Cyprus, to whom he had given mortal offence, and who had him pounded to death in a stone mortar. Reportedly, he endured this torturous death with great fortitude. At one point, the dying man said, "Thou beatest but the case of Anaxarchus."

40. Here Wilberforce has quoted lines 898–909 of "The Winter Morning Walk," Book Five of William Cowper's poem, "The Task."

$\curvearrowleft$Chapter Five

*On the Excellence of Christianity in Certain
Important Particulars—Argument Which
Results Thence in Proof of its Divine Origin*

THE WRITER OF THE PRESENT WORK, HAVING NOW
completed a faint delineation of the leading features of real
Christianity, may be permitted to suspend for a few moments
the farther execution of his plan, for the purpose of pointing
out some excellences which she really possesses; but which, as
they are not to be found in that superficial system which so
unworthily usurps her name, appear scarcely to have attracted
sufficient notice. If he should seem to be deviating from the
plan which he proposed to himself, he would suggest as his
excuse, that the observations which he is about to offer will
furnish a strong argument in favour of the correctness of his
preceding delineation of Christianity, since she will *now* appear
to exhibit more clearly, than as she is usually drawn, the characters of her Divine original.

It holds true, indeed, in the case of Christianity as in
that of all the works of God, that though a superficial and
cursory view cannot fail to discover to us somewhat of their
beauty; yet, when on a more careful and accurate scrutiny we
become better acquainted with their properties, we become
also more deeply impressed by a conviction of their excellence.
We may begin by referring to the last chapter for an instance of
the truth of this assertion. Therein was pointed out that intimate connection, that perfect harmony between the leading
doctrines and the practical precepts of Christianity, which is apt
to escape the attention of the ordinary eye.

It may not be improper also to remark, though the position be so obvious as almost to render the statement of it needless, that there is the same close connection and perfect harmony in the leading doctrines of Christianity among each other. It is self-evident, that the corruption of human nature, that our reconciliation to God by the atonement of Christ, and that the restoration of our primitive dignity by the sanctifying influence of the Holy Spirit, are all parts of one whole, united in close dependence and mutual congruity [agreement].

Perhaps, however, it has not been sufficiently noticed, that in the chief practical precepts of Christianity, there is the same essential agreement, the same mutual dependency of one upon another. Let us survey this fresh instance of the wisdom of that system, which is the only solid foundation of our present or future happiness.

The virtues most strongly and repeatedly enjoined in Scripture, and by our progress in which, we may best measure our advancement in holiness, are the fear and love of God and of Christ; love, kindness, and meekness towards our fellow-creatures; indifference to the possessions and events of this life, in comparison with our concern about eternal things; self-denial, and humility.

It has been already pointed out in many particulars, how essentially such of these Christian graces as respect the Divine Being are connected with those, which have more directly for their objects our fellow-creatures and ourselves. But in the case of these two last descriptions of Christian graces, the more attentively we consider them with reference to the acknowledged principles of human nature, and to indisputable facts, the more we shall be convinced that they afford mutual aid towards the acquisition of each other, and that when acquired, they all harmonize with each other in perfect and essential union. This truth may perhaps be sufficiently apparent from what has been already remarked; but it may not be useless to dwell on it a little more in detail. Take then the instances of loving-kindness and meekness towards others, and observe the solid foundation which is laid for them in self-denial, in moderation as to the good things of this life, and in humility. The chief causes of enmity among men are, pride and self-importance, the high opinion which men entertain of themselves, and the consequent deference which they exact from others, the over-valuation of worldly possessions and of worldly honours, and in consequence, a too eager competition for them. The rough edges of one man rub against those of another, if the expression may be allowed; and the friction is often such as to injure the works, and disturb the just arrangements and regular motions of the social machine. But by Christianity all these roughnesses are filed down: every wheel rolls round smoothly in the performance of its appointed function, and there is nothing to retard the several movements, or break in upon the general order. The religious system indeed of the bulk of nominal Christians is satisfied with some appearances of virtue; and accordingly, while it recommends love and beneficence, it tolerates, as has been shewn, pride and vanity in many cases; it even countenances and commends the excessive valuation of character, and it least allows a man's whole soul to be absorbed in the pursuit of the object he is following, be it what it may, of personal or professional success. But though these latter qualities may, for the most part, fairly enough consist with a soft exterior and courtly demeanour, they cannot so well accord with the genuine internal principle of love. Some cause of discontent, some ground of jealousy or of envy will arise, some suspicion will corrode, some disappointment will sour, some slight or calumny will irritate and provoke reprisals. In the higher walks of life, indeed, we learn to disguise our emotions, but such will be the real inward feelings of the soul, and they will frequently betray themselves when we are off our guard, or when we are not likely to be disparaged [belittled] by the discovery. This state of the higher orders, in which men are scuffling eagerly for the same objects, and wearing all the while such an appearance of sweetness and complacency, has often appeared to me to be not ill illustrated by the image of a gaming table. There, every man is intent only on his own profit; the good success of one is the ill success of another, and therefore the general state of mind of the parties engaged may be pretty well conjectured. All this, however, does not prevent, in well-bred societies, an exterior of perfect gentleness and good humour. But let the same employment be carried on among those who are not as well schooled in the art of disguising their feelings; or in places where, by general connivance, people are allowed to give vent to their real emotions; and every passion will display itself, by which the "human face divine" can be distorted and deformed. For those who have never been present at so humiliating a scene, the pencil of Hogarth[1] has provided a representation of it, which is scarcely exaggerated; and the horrid name,[2] by which it is familiarly known among its frequenters, sufficiently attests the fidelity of its resemblance.

But Christianity is not satisfied with producing merely the specious guise of virtue. She requires the substantial reality, which may stand the scrutinizing eye of that Being "who searches the heart" [cf. Psalm 139:1]. Meaning therefore that the Christian should live, and breathe, in an atmosphere, as it were, of benevolence, she forbids whatever can tend to obstruct its diffusion or vitiate its purity. It is on this principle that Emulation is forbidden. For besides that this passion almost insensibly degenerates into envy, and that it derives its origin chiefly from pride and a desire of self-exaltation; how can we easily love our neighbour as ourselves, if we consider him at the same time as our rival, and are intent upon surpassing him in the pursuit of whatever is the subject of our competition?

Christianity, again, teaches us not to set our hearts on earthly possessions and earthly honours, and thereby provides for our really loving, or even cordially forgiving those who have been more successful than ourselves in the attainment of them, or who have even designedly thwarted us in the pursuit. "Let the rich," says the Apostle [James], "rejoice in that he is brought low" [James 1:10]. How can he who means to attempt, in any degree, to obey this precept, be irreconcileably hostile towards any one who may have been instrumental in his depression?

Christianity also teaches us not to prize human estimation at a very high rate, and thereby provides for the practice of her injunction, to love from the heart those who, justly or unjustly may have attacked our reputation, and wounded our character. She commands not the shew but the reality of meekness and gentleness; and by thus taking away the aliment of anger and the fomenters of discord, she provides for the maintenance of peace, and the restoration of good temper among men, when it may have sustained a temporary interruption.

It is another capital excellence of Christianity, that she values moral attainments at a far higher rate than intellectual acquisitions, and proposes to conduct her followers to the height of virtue rather than of knowledge. On the contrary, most of the false religious systems which have prevailed in the world, have proposed to reward the labour of their votary [ardent follower] by drawing aside the veil which concealed from the vulgar eye their hidden mysteries, and by introducing him to the knowledge of their deeper and more sacred doctrines.

This is eminently the case in the Hindoo, and in the Mahometan religion, in that of China, and, for the most part, in the various modifications of ancient Paganism. In systems which proceed on this principle, it is obvious that the bulk of mankind can never make any great proficiency. There was accordingly, among the nations of antiquity, one system, whatever it was, for the learned, and another for the illiterate. Many of the philosophers spoke out, and professed to keep the lower orders in ignorance for the general good, plainly suggesting that the bulk of mankind was to be considered as almost of an inferior species. Aristotle [the Greek philosopher (384–322 B.C.)] himself countenanced this opinion. An opposite mode of proceeding naturally belongs to Christianity, which without distinction professes an equal regard for all human beings, and which was characterized by her first promulgator as the messenger of "glad tidings to the poor" [cf. Luke 7:22].

But her preference of moral to intellectual excellence is not to be praised only because it is congenial with her general character, and suitable to the ends which she professes to have in view. It is the part of true wisdom to endeavour to excel there, where we may really attain to excellence. This consideration might be alone sufficient to direct our efforts to the acquisition of virtue rather than of knowledge.—How limited is the range of the greatest human abilities! how scanty the stores of the richest human knowledge! Those who undeniably have held the first rank, both for natural and acquired endowments, instead of thinking their pre-eminence a just ground of self-exaltation, have commonly been the most forward to confess that their views were bounded and their attainments moderate. Had they indeed been less candid, this is a discovery which we would not have failed to make for ourselves. Experience daily furnishes us with examples of weakness, and short-sightedness, and error, in the wisest and the most learned of men, which might serve to confound the pride of human wisdom.

Not so in morals.—Made at first in the likeness of God, and still bearing about us some faint traces of our high original, we are offered by our blessed Redeemer the means of purification from our corruptions, and of once more regaining the image of our Heavenly Father [cf. Ephesians 2]. In love, the compendious expression for almost every virtue, in fortitude under all its forms, in justice, in humility, and in all the other graces of the Christian character, we are made capable of attaining to heights of real elevation: and were we but faithful in the use of the means of grace which we enjoy, the operations of the Holy Spirit prompting and aiding our diligent endeavours, would infallibly crown our labours with success, and make us partakers of a Divine nature. The writer has himself known some who have been instances of the truth of this remark. To the memory of one,[3] now no more, may he be permitted to offer the last tribute of respectful friendship. His course, short but laborious, has at length terminated in a better world; and his luminous track still shines in the sight, and animates the efforts of all who knew him, and "marshals them the way" to Heavenly glory. Let me not be thought to undervalue any of the gifts of God, or of the fruits of human exertion. But let not these be prized beyond their proper worth. If one of those little industrious reptiles [Wilberforce has mistakenly called ants reptiles, rather than insects], to which we have been well sent for a lesson of diligence and foresight, were to pride itself upon its strength, because it could carry off a larger grain of wheat than any other of its fellow-ants, should we not laugh at the vanity which could be highly gratified with such a contemptible pre-eminence? And is it far different to the eye of reason, when man, weak, short-sighted man, is vain of surpassing others in knowledge, in which at best his progress must be so limited; forgetting the true dignity of his nature, and the path which would conduct him to real excellence?

The unparalleled value of the precepts of Christianity ought not to be passed over altogether unnoticed in this place, though it be needless to dwell on it, since it has been often justly recognized and asserted, and has in some points been ably illustrated and powerfully enforced by the masterly pen of a late writer.[4] It is by no means however the design of this little work to attempt to trace the various excellences of Christianity; but it may not have been improper to point out a few particulars, which, in the course of investigation, have naturally fallen under our notice, and hitherto perhaps may scarcely have been enough regarded. Every such instance, it should always be remembered, is a fresh proof of Christianity being a revelation from God.

It is still less, however, the intention of the writer to attempt to vindicate the Divine origin of our Holy Religion. This task has often been executed by far abler advocates. In particular, every Christian, with whatever reserves his commendations must be qualified, should be forward to confess his obligations *on this head* to the author before alluded to, whose uncommon acuteness has enabled him, in a field already so much trodden, to discover arguments which had eluded the observation of all by whom he was preceded, and whose unequalled perspicuity [clarity of expression] puts his reader in complete possession of the fruits of his sagacity. Anxious, however, in my little measure, to contribute to the support of this great cause, may it be permitted me to state one argument, which impresses my mind with particular force. This is, the great variety of the *kinds* of evidence which have been adduced in proof of Christianity, and the confirmation thereby afforded of its truth:—the proof from prophecy—from miracles—from the character of Christ—from that of his Apostles—from the nature of the doctrines of Christianity—from the nature and excellence of her *practical precepts*—from the accordance we have lately pointed out between the doctrinal and practical system of Christianity, whether considered each in itself or in their mutual relation to each other—from other species of internal evidence, afforded in the more abundance in proportion as the sacred records have been scrutinized with greater care—from the accounts of co-temporary or nearly co-temporary writers—from the impossibility of accounting on any other supposition, than that of the truth of Christianity, for its promulgation [proclamation] and early prevalence: these and other lines of argument have all been brought forward, and ably urged by different writers, in proportion as they have struck the minds of different observers more or less forcibly. Now, granting that some obscure and illiterate men, residing in a distant province of the Roman empire, had plotted to impose a forgery upon the world; though some foundation for the imposture might and indeed must have been attempted to be laid, it seems, at least to my understanding, morally impossible that *so many different species of proofs,* and all so strong, should have lent their *concurrent* aid, and have united their *joint* force in the establishment of the falsehood. It may assist the reader in estimating the value of this argument, to consider upon how different a footing, in this respect, has rested every other religious system, without exception, which was ever proposed to the world; and, indeed, every other historical fact, of which the truth has been at all contested.

Notes ⤳

1. The English engraver and painter William Hogarth (1697–1764).

2. Wilberforce writes, "The *Hell,* so called, be it observed, not by way of reproach, but familiarity, by those who frequent it."

3. Wilberforce writes "The Reverend Matthew Babington, to Temple Rothley, in Leicestershire, who died lately in Lisbon." See also *The Life of William Wilberforce,* vol. 2, p. 159. In a letter written to Zachary Macaulay on July 4, 1796, Wilberforce wrote: "You will have heard from Tom Babington that Matthew at length has fallen asleep. I sincerely believe that a purer spirit scarce ever (I had nearly said never) winged its flight to heaven."

4. Wilberforce may be referring to Philip Doddridge, the author of *The Rise and Progress of Religion in the Soul*—a work which Wilberforce valued very highly.

~Chapter Six

Brief Inquiry into the Present State of Christianity in This Country, with Some of the Causes Which Have Led to its Critical Circumstances—Its Importance to Us as a Political Community, and Practical Hints for Which the Foregoing Considerations Give Occasion

IT MAY NOT BE ALTOGETHER IMPROPER TO REMIND THE reader, that hitherto, our discussion has been concerning the prevailing Religious opinions merely of *professed Christians:* no longer confining ourselves in persons of this description, let us now extend our inquiry, and briefly investigate the *general* state of Christianity in this country.

The tendency of Religion to promote the temporal well-being of political communities, is a fact which depends on such obvious and undeniable principles, and which is so forcibly inculcated by the history of all ages, that there can be no necessity for entering into a formal proof of its truth. It has indeed been maintained, not merely by Schoolmen and Divines, but by the most celebrated philosophers, and moralists, and politicians of every age.

The peculiar excellence in this respect also of Christianity, considered independently of its truth or falsehood, has been recognized by many writers, who, to say the least, were not disposed to exaggerate its merits. Either or both of these propositions being admitted, the state of Religion in a country at any given period, not to mention its connection with the eternal happiness of the inhabitants, immediately becomes a question of great *political* importance: and in particular, it must be material to ascertain whether Religion be in an advancing or in a declining state; and if the latter be the case, whether there be any practicable means for preventing at least its farther declension.

If the representations contained in the preceding chapters, of the state of Christianity among the bulk of professed Christians, be not very erroneous, they may well excite serious apprehension in the mind of every reader, when considered merely in a political view. And this apprehension would be increased, if there should appear reason to believe that, for some time past, Religion has been on the decline among us, and that it continues to decline at the present moment.

When it is proposed, however, to inquire into the actual state of Religion in any country, and in particular to compare that state with its condition at any former period, there is one preliminary observation to be made, if we would not be liable to gross error. There exists, established by tacit consent, in every country, what may be called a general standard or tone of morals, varying in the same community at different periods, and different at the same period in different ranks and situations in society. Whoever falls below this standard, and not unfrequently, whoever also rises above it, offending against this general rule, suffers proportionably in the general estimation. Thus a regard for character, which, as was formerly remarked, is commonly the grand governing principle among men, becomes to a certain degree, though no farther, an incitement to morality and virtue. It follows of course, that where the practice does no more than come up to the required level, it will be no sufficient evidence of the existence, much less will it furnish any just measure of the force of a real internal principle of Religion. Christians, Jews, Turks, Infidels, and Heretics, persons of ten thousand different sorts of passions and opinions, being members at the same time of the same community, and all conscious that they will be examined by this same standard, will regulate their conduct accordingly, and, with no great difference, will all adjust themselves to the required measure.

It must also be remarked, that the causes which lead to raise or to depress this standard, commonly produce their effects by slow and almost insensible decrees; and that it often continues for some time nearly the same, when the circumstances, by which it was fixed have materially altered.

It is a truth which will hardly be contested, that Christianity, whenever it has at all prevailed, has raised the general standard of morals to a height before unknown. Some actions, which among the ancients were scarcely held to be blemishes in the most excellent characters, have been justly considered by the laws of every Christian community, as meriting the severest punishments. In other instances, virtues formerly rare have become common, and in particular a merciful and courteous temper has softened the rugged manners, and humanized the brutal ferocity prevalent among the most polished nations of the heathen world. But from what has been recently observed, it is manifest, that, so far as external appearances are concerned, these effects, when once produced by Christianity, are produced alike in those who deny and in those who admit her divine original; I had almost said in those who reject and those who cordially embrace the doctrines of the Gospel: and these effects might and probably would remain for a while, without any great apparent alteration, however her spirit might languish, or even her authority decline. The form of the temple, as was once beautifully remarked, may continue when the *dii tutelares* [tutelary or guardian deities] have left it. When we are inquiring therefore into the real state of Christianity at any period, if we would not be deceived in this important investigation, it becomes us to be so much the more careful not to take up with superficial appearances.

It may perhaps help us to ascertain the advancing or declining state of Christianity in Great Britain at the present moment, and still more to discover some of the causes by which that state has been produced, to employ a little time in considering what might naturally be expected to be its actual situation; what advantages or disadvantages such a religion might be expected to derive from the circumstances in which it has been placed among us, and from those in which it still continues.

Experience warrants, and reason justifies and explains the assertion, that Persecution generally tends to quicken the vigour and extend the prevalence of the opinions which she would eradicate. For the peace of mankind, it has grown at length almost into an axiom, that "her devilish engine recoils back upon herself." Christianity especially has always thriven under persecution. At such a season she has no lukewarm professors; no adherents concerning whom it is doubtful to what party they belong. The Christian is then reminded at every turn, that his Master's kingdom is not of this world. When all on earth wears a black and threatening aspect, he looks up to heaven for consolation; he learns practically to consider himself as a pilgrim and stranger. He then cleaves to fundamentals, and examines well his foundation, as at the hour of death. When Religion is in a state of external quiet and prosperity, the contrary of all this naturally takes place. The soldiers of the church militant then forget that they are in a state of warfare. Their ardour slackens, their zeal languishes. Like a colony long settled in a strange country,[1] they are gradually assimilated in features, and demeanour, and language, to the native inhabitants, till at length almost every vestige of peculiarity dies away.

If, in general, persecution and prosperity be productive respectively of these opposite effects, this circumstance alone might teach us what expectations to form concerning the state of Christianity in this country where she has long been embodied in an establishment, which is intimately blended, and is generally and justly believed to have a common interest with our civil institutions; which is liberally, though by no means too liberally, endowed, and, not more favoured in wealth than dignity, has been allowed "to exalt her mitred front in courts and parliaments:" an establishment—the offices in which are extremely numerous, and these, not like the priesthood of the Jews, filled up from a particular race, or, like that of the Hindoos, held by a separate caste in entailed succession, but supplied from every class, and branching by its widely extended ramifications into almost every individual family in the community: an establishment—of which the ministers are not, like the Roman Catholic clergy, debarred from forming matrimonial ties, but are allowed to unite themselves, and multiply their holdings to the general mass of the community by the close bonds of family connection; not like some of the severer of the religious orders, immured in colleges and monasteries, but, both by law and custom, permitted to mix without restraint in all the intercourses of society.

Such being the circumstances of the pastors of the church, let the community in general be supposed to have been for some time in a rapidly improving state of commercial prosperity; let is also be supposed to have been making to unequal progress in all those arts, and sciences, and literary productions which have ever been the growth of a polished age, and are the sure marks of a highly finished condition of society. It is not difficult to anticipate the effects likely to be produced on *vital* Religion, both in the clergy and the laity, by such a state of external prosperity as has been assigned to them respectively. And these effects must be infallibly furthered, where the country in question enjoys a free constitution of government. We formerly had occasion to quote the remark of an accurate observer[2] of the stage of human life, that a much looser system of morals commonly prevails in the higher, than in the middling and lower orders of society. Now, in every country, of which the middling classes are daily growing in wealth and consequence, by the success of their commercial speculations; and, most of all, in a country having such a constitution as our own, where the acquisition of riches is the possession also of rank and power; with the comforts and refinements, the vices also of the higher orders are continually descending, and a mischievous uniformity of sentiments, and manners, and morals, gradually diffuses itself throughout the whole community. The multiplication of great cities also, and above all, the habit, ever increasing with the increasing wealth of the country, of frequenting a splendid and luxurious metropolis, would powerfully tend to accelerate the discontinuance of the religious habits of a purer age, and to accomplish the substitution of a more relaxed morality. And it must even be confessed, that the commercial spirit, much as we are indebted to it, is not naturally favourable to the maintenance of the religious principle in a vigorous and lively state.

In times like these, therefore, the strict precepts and self-denying habits of Christianity naturally slide into disuse; and, even among the better sort of Christians, are likely to be softened, so far at least as to be rendered less abhorrent from the general disposition to relaxation and indulgence. In such prosperous circumstances, men, in truth, are apt to think very little about religion. Christianity, therefore, seldom occupying the attention of the bulk of nominal Christians, and being scarcely at all the object of their study, we should expect, of course, to find them extremely unacquainted with its tenets. Those doctrines and principles, indeed, which it contains in common with the law of the land, or which are sanctioned by the general standard of morals formerly described, being brought into continual notice and mention by the common occurrences of life, might continue to be recognized. But whatever she contains peculiar to herself, and which should not be habitually brought into recollection by the incidents of every day, might be expected to be less and less thought of, till at length it should be almost wholly forgotten. Still more might this be naturally expected to become the case, if the peculiarities in question should be, from their very nature, at war with pride, and luxury, and worldly mindedness, the too general concomitants [accompaniments or companions] of rapidly increasing wealth: and this would particularly happen among the laity, if the circumstance of their having been at any time abused to purposes of hypocrisy or fanaticism should have prompted even some of the better disposed of the clergy, perhaps from well intentioned though erroneous motives, to bring them forward less frequently in their discourses on religion.

When so many should thus have been straying out of the right path, some bold reformer might, from time to time, be likely to arise, who should not unjustly charge them with their deviation; but, though right perhaps in the main, yet deviating himself also in an opposite direction, and creating disgust by his violence, or vulgarity, or absurdities, he might fail, except in a few instances, to produce the effect of recalling them from their wanderings.

Still, however, the Divine Original of Christianity would not be professedly disavowed; partly from a real, and more commonly from a political deference for the established faith, but most of all, from the bulk of mankind being not yet prepared, as it were, to throw away the scabbard, and to venture their eternal happiness on the issue of its falsehood. Some bolder spirits, indeed, might be expected to despise the cautious moderation of these timid reasoners, and to pronounce decisively, that the Bible was a forgery, while the generality, professing to believe it genuine, should, less consistently, be satisfied with remaining ignorant of its contents, and when pressed, should discover themselves by no means to believe many of the most important particulars contained in it.

When, by the operation of causes like these, any country has at length grown into the condition which has been here stated, it is but too obvious, that, in the bulk of the community, Religion, already sunk very low, must be hastening fast to her entire dissolution. Causes, energetic and active like these, though accidental hindrances may occasionally thwart their operation, will not at once become sluggish and unproductive. Their effect is sure; and the time is fast approaching, when Christianity will be almost as openly disavowed in the language, as in fact it is already supposed to have disappeared from the conduct of men; when infidelity will be held to be the necessary appendage of a man of fashion, and *to believe* will be deemed the indication of a feeble mind and a contracted understanding.

Something like what have been here premised are the conjectures which we should naturally be led to form, concerning the state of Christianity in this country, and its probable issue, from considering her own nature, and the peculiar circumstances in which she has been placed. That her real condition differs not much from the result of this reasoning from probability, must, with whatever regret, be confessed by all who take a careful and impartial survey of the actual situation of things among us. But our hypothetical delineation, if just, will have approved itself to the reader's conviction, as we have gone along, by suggesting its archetypes; and we may therefore be spared the painful and invidious [likely to cause resentment because of real or imagined injustice] task of pointing out, in detail, the particulars wherein our statements are justified by facts. Every where we may actually trace the effects of increasing wealth and luxury, in banishing one by one the habits, and new-modelling the phraseology of stricter times, and in diffusing throughout the middle ranks those relaxed morals and dissipated manners which were formerly confined to the higher classes of society. We meet, indeed, with more refinement, and more generally with those amiable courtesies which are its proper fruits: those vices also have become less frequent, which naturally infest the darkness of a ruder and less polished age, and which recede on the approach of light and civilization:

> Defluxit numerus Saturnius, & grave
> virus munditiae pepulere. . . .
>
> [Thus the stream of that rude Saturnian
> measure ran
> dry and good taste banished the offensive
> poison. . . .
>
> —Horace][3]

But with these grossnesses, Religion, on the other hand, has also declined; God is forgotten; his providence is exploded; his hand is lifted up, but we see it not; he multiplies our comforts, but we are not grateful; he visits us with chastisements, but we are not contrite. The portion of the week set apart to the service of Religion we give up, without reluctance, to vanity and dissipation. And it is much if, on the periodical

return of a day of national humiliation, having availed ourselves of the certainty of an interval from public business to
secure a meeting for convivial [sociable and lively] purposes, we
do not insult the Majesty of Heaven by feasting and jollity, and
thus deliberately disclaim our begin included in the solemn
services of this season of penitence and recollection.[4]

But when there is not this open and shameless disavowal of Religion, few traces of it are to be found. Improving
in almost every other branch of knowledge, we have become
less and less acquainted with Christianity. The preceding chapters have pointed out, among those who believe themselves to
be orthodox Christians, a deplorable ignorance of the Religion
they profess, an utter forgetfulness of the peculiar doctrines by
which it is characterized, a disposition to regard it as a mere
system of ethics, and, what might seem an inconsistency, at the
same time a most inadequate idea of the nature and strictness
of its practical principles. This declension of Christianity into a
mere system of ethics, may partly be accounted for, as has been
lately suggested, by considering the corruption of our nature,
what Christianity is, and in what circumstances she has been
placed in this country. But it has also been considerably promoted by one peculiar cause, on which, for many reasons, it
may not be improper to dwell a little more particularly.

Christianity in its best days (for the credit of our representations let this be remembered by those who object to our
statement as austere and contracted) was such as it has been
delineated in the present work. This was the Religion of the
most eminent Reformers, of those bright ornaments of our
country who suffered martyrdom under Queen Mary [1516–58];
of their successors in the times of Elizabeth [Queen Elizabeth I
(1533–1603)]; in short, of all the pillars of our Protestant
church; of many of its highest dignitaries; of Davenant, of
Jewell, of Hall, of Reynolds, of Beveridge, of Hooker, of An-
drews, of Smith, of Leighton, of Usher, of Hopkins,[5] of Baxter,[6]
and of many others of scarcely inferior note. In their pages the
peculiar doctrines of Christianity were every where visible, and
on the deep and solid basis of these doctrinal truths were laid
the foundations of a superstructure of morals proportionably
broad and exalted. Of this fact their writings still extant are a
decisive proof, and those who may want leisure, or opportunity,
or inclination, for the perusal of these valuable records, may
satisfy themselves of the truth of the assertion, that, such as we
have stated it, was the Christianity of those times, by consulting

our Articles and Homilies, or even by carefully examining our excellent Liturgy. But from that tendency to deterioration lately noticed, these great fundamental truths began to be somewhat less prominent in the compositions of many of the leading divines before the time of the civil wars. During that period, however, the peculiar doctrines of Christianity were grievously abused by many of the sectaries, who were foremost in the commotions of those unhappy days, who, while they talked copiously of the free grace of Christ, and the operations of the Holy Spirit, were by their lives an open scandal to the name of Christian.[7]

Towards the close of the last century, the divines of the established Church, whether it arose from the obscurity of their own views, or from a strong impression of former abuses, and of the evils which had resulted from them, began to run into a different error. They professed to make it their chief object to inculcate the moral and practical precepts of Christianity, which they conceived to have been before too much neglected; but without sufficiently maintaining, often even without justly laying the grand foundation, of a sinner's acceptance with God, or pointing out how the practical precepts of Christianity grow out of her peculiar doctrines,[8] and are inseparably connected with them. By this fatal error, the very genius and essential nature of Christianity imperceptibly underwent a change. She no longer retained her peculiar characters, or produced that appropriate frame of Spirit by which her followers had been characterized. Facilis defensus ["the defence is easy"]. The example thus set was followed during the present century, and its effect was aided by various causes already pointed out. In addition to these, it may be proper to mention as a cause of powerful operation, that for the last fifty years the press has teemed with moral essays, many of them published periodically, and most extensively circulated, which, being considered either as works of mere entertainment, or, in which at least entertainment was to be blended with instruction, rather than as religious pieces, were kept clear from whatever might give them the air of sermons, or cause them to wear an appearance of seriousness, inconsistent with the idea of relaxation. But in this way the fatal habit of considering Christian morals as distinct from Christian doctrines insensibly gained strength. Thus the peculiar doctrines of Christianity went more and more out of sight, and as might naturally have been expected, the moral system itself also began to wither and decay, being robbed of that which should have supplied it with life and nutriment. At length, in our own days, these peculiar doctrines have almost altogether vanished from our view. Even in many sermons, as we have formerly noticed, scarcely any traces of them are to be found.

But the degree of neglect into which they are really fallen, may perhaps be rendered still more manifest by appealing to another criterion. There is a certain class of publications, of which it is the object to give us exact delineations of life and manners, and when these are written by authors of accurate observation and deep knowledge of human nature (and many such there have been in our times) they furnish a more faithful picture, than can be obtained in any other way, of the prevalent opinions and feelings of mankind. It must be obvious that novels are here alluded to. A careful perusal of the most celebrated of these pieces would furnish a strong confirmation of the apprehension suggested from other considerations concerning the very low state of Religion in this country; but they would still more strikingly illustrate the truth of the remark, that the grand peculiarities of Christianity are almost vanished from the view. In a sermon, although throughout the whole of it there may have been no traces of these peculiarities, either directly or indirectly, the preacher closes with an ordinary form, which, if one were to assert that they were absolutely omitted, would immediately be alleged in contradiction of the assertion, and may just serve to protect them from falling into entire oblivion. But in novels, the writer is not so tied down. In these, people of Religion, and clergymen too, are placed in all possible situations, and the sentiments and language deemed suitable to the occasion are assigned to them. They are introduced instructing, reproving, counselling, comforting. It is often the author's intention to represent them in a favourable point of view, and accordingly he makes them as well-informed and as good Christians as he knows how. They are painted amiable, benevolent, and forgiving; but it is not too much to say, that if all the peculiarities of Christianity had never existed, or had been proved to be false, the circumstance would scarcely create the necessity of altering a single syllable in any of the most celebrated of these performances. It is striking to observe the difference which there is in this respect in similar works of Mahometan [Muslim] authors, wherein the characters, which they mean to represent in a favourable light are drawn vastly more observant of the peculiarities of their religion.[9]

But to make an end of this discussion, concerning the degree in which the peculiarities of Christianity have fallen into neglect, and concerning one of the principal of the causes which have produced it: if this be the state of things even in the case of sermons, and of the compositions of those, whose sphere of information must be supposed larger than that of the bulk of mankind; it must excite less wonder, that in the world in general, though Christianity be not formally denied, people know little about it; and that in fact you find, when you come to converse with them, that, admitting in terms the Divine Revelation of Scripture, they are far from believing the propositions it contains.

It has also been a melancholy prognostic of the state to which we are progressive, that many of the most eminent of the literati of modern times have been professed unbelievers; and that others of them have discovered such lukewarmness in the cause of Christ, as to treat with especial good will, and attention and respect, those men, who, by their avowed publications, were openly assailing, or insidiously undermining the very foundations of the Christian hope; considering themselves as more closely united to them by literature, than severed from them by the widest religious differences.[10] Can it then occasion surprise, that under all these circumstances, one of the most acute and most forward of the professed unbelievers[11] should appear to anticipate, as at no great distance, the more complete triumph of his sceptical principles; and that another author of distinguished name,[12] not so openly professing those infidel opinions, should declare of the writer above alluded to, whose great abilities had been systematically prostituted to the open attack of every principle of Religion, both natural and revealed, "that he had always considered him, both in his life-time and since his death, as approaching as nearly to the idea of a perfectly wise and virtuous man, as perhaps the nature of human frailty will permit?"

Can there then be a doubt, whither tends the path in which we are travelling, and whither at length it must conduct us? If any should hesitate, let them take a lesson from experience. In a neighboring country, several of the same causes have been in action; and they have at length produced their full effect. Manners corrupted, morals depraved, dissipation predominant, above all, Religion discredited, and infidelity grown into repute and fashion,[13] terminated in the public disavowal of every religious principle which had been used to attract the veneration of mankind. The representatives of a whole nation publicly witnessing, not only without horror, but to say the least, without disapprobation, an open unqualified denial of the very existence of God; and at length, as a body, withdrawing their allegiance from the Majesty of Heaven.

There are not a few, perhaps, who may have witnessed with apprehension, and may be ready to confess with pain, the gradual declension of Religion, but who at the same time may conceive that the writer of this tract is disposed to carry things too far. They may even allege, that the degree of Religion for which he contends is inconsistent with the ordinary business of life, and with the well-being of society; that if it were generally to prevail, people would be wholly engrossed by Religion, and all their time occupied by prayer and preaching. Men not being sufficiently interested in the pursuit of temporal objects, agriculture and commerce would decline, the arts would languish, the very duties of common life would be neglected, and, in short the whole machine of civil society would be obstructed, and speedily stopped. An opening for this charge is given by an ingenious writer[14] alluded to in an earlier period of our work, and even somewhat countenanced by an author since referred to, from whom such a sentiment justly excites more surprise.[15]

In reply to this objection it might be urged, that though we should allow it for a moment to be in a considerable degree well founded, yet this admission would not warrant the conclusion intended to be drawn from it. The question would still remain, whether our representation of what Christianity requires be agreeable to the word of God. For if it be, surely it must be confessed to be a matter of small account to sacrifice a little worldly comfort and prosperity, during the short span of our existence in this life, in order to secure a crown of eternal glory, and the enjoyment of those pleasures which are at God's right hand for evermore. It might be added also, that our blessed Saviour had fairly declared, that it would often be required of Christians to make such a sacrifice; and had forwarned us, that in order to be able to do it with cheerfulness whenever the occasion should arrive, we must habitually sit loose to all worldly possessions and enjoyments. And it might farther be remarked, that though it were even admitted, that the *general prevalence of vital Christianity* should somewhat interfere with the views of national wealth and aggrandisement [the increase of power, rank, and wealth]; yet that there is too much reason to believe that, do all we can, this general prevalence needs not to be apprehended, or, to speak more justly, could not be hoped for. But indeed the objection on which we have now been commenting, is not only groundless, but the very contrary to it is the truth. If Christianity, such as we have represented it, were generally to prevail, the world, from being such as it is, would become a scene of general peace and prosperity, and abating the chances and calamities "which flesh is inseparably heir to" [cf. Philippians 3:3], would wear one unwearied face of complacency and joy.

On the first promulgation of Christianity, it is true, some of her early converts seem to have been in danger of so far mistaking the principles of the new Religion, as to imagine that in future they were to be discharged from an active attendance on their secular affairs. But the Apostle [Wilberforce could be referring to Paul of Tarsus or to Simon Peter; see Colossians 3:1–4:6; 1 Peter 2:12–19] most pointedly guarded them against so gross an error, and expressly and repeatedly enjoined them to perform the particular duties of their several stations with increased alacrity and fidelity, that they might thereby do credit to their Christian profession. This he did, at the same time that he prescribed to them that predominant love of God and of Christ, that heavenly-mindedness, that comparative indifference to the things of this world, that earnest endeavour after growth in grace, and perfection in holiness, which have already been stated as the essential characteristics of real Christianity. It cannot therefore be supposed by any who allow to the Apostle even the claim of a consistent instructor, much less by any who admit his Divine authority, that these latter precepts are incompatible with the former. Let it be remembered, that the grand characteristic mark of the true Christian, which has been insisted on, is *his desiring to please God in all his thoughts, and words, and actions; to take the revealed word to be the rule of his belief and practice; to "Let his light shine before men"* [Matthew 5:16]; *and in all things to adorn the doctrine which he professes* [cf. Titus 2:10]. No calling is proscribed, no pursuit is forbidden, no science or art, no pleasure is disallowed, which is reconcilable with this principle. It must be indeed confessed that Christianity would not favour that vehement and inordinate ardour in the pursuit of temporal objects, which tends to the acquisition of immense wealth, or of widely spread renown: nor is it calculated to gratify the extravagant views of those mistaken politicians, the chief object of whose admiration, and the main scope of whose endeavours for their country, are extended dominion, and commanding power, and unrivaled affluence, rather than the more solid advantages of peace, and comfort, and security. These men would barter comfort for greatness. In their vain reveries they forget that a nation consists of individuals, and that true national prosperity is no other than the multiplication of particular happiness.

But in truth, so far is it from being true that the prevalence of *real* Religion would produce a stagnation in life; a man, whatever might be his employment or pursuit, would be furnished with a new motive to prosecute it with alacrity, a motive far more constant and vigorous than any human prospects can supply: at the same time, his solicitude being not so much to succeed in whatever he might be engaged in, as to act from a pure principle and leave the event to God, he would not be liable to the same disappointments as men who are active and laborious from a desire of worldly gain or of human estimation. Thus he would possess the true secret of a life at the same time useful and happy. Following peace also with all men, and looking upon them as members of the same family, entitled not only to the debts of justice, but to the less definite and more liberal claims of fraternal kindness, he would naturally be respected and beloved by others, and be in himself free from the annoyance of those bad passions by which those who are actuated by worldly principles are so commonly corroded. If any country were indeed filled with men, each thus diligently discharging the duties of his own station without breaking in upon the rights of others, but on the contrary endeavouring, so far as he might be able, to forward their views and promote their happiness, all would be active and harmonious in the goodly frame of human society. There would be no jarrings, no, discord. The whole machine of civil life would work without obstruction or disorder, and the course of its movements would be like the harmony of the spheres.

Such would be the happy state of a truly Christian nation within itself. Nor would its condition with regard to foreign countries form a contrast to this its internal comfort. Such a community, on the contrary, peaceable at home, would be respected and beloved abroad. General integrity in all its dealings would inspire universal confidence: differences between nations commonly arise from mutual injuries, and still more from mutual jealousy and distrust. Of the former there would be no longer any ground for complaint; the latter would find nothing to attach upon. But if, in spite of all its justice and forbearance, the violence of some neighboring state should force it to resist an unprovoked attack, for hostilities strictly defensive are those only in which it would be engaged, its domestic union would double its national force, while the consciousness of a good cause, and of the general favour of Heaven, would invigorate its arm, and inspirit its efforts.

It is indeed the position of an author to whom we have frequent occasion to refer, and whose love of paradox has not seldom led him into error, that true Christianity is an enemy to patriotism. If by patriotism be meant that mischievous and domineering quality which renders men ardent to promote, not the happiness, but the aggrandisement of their own country, by the oppression and conquest of every other; to such patriotism, so generally applauded in the Heathen world, that Religion must be indeed an enemy, whose foundation is justice, and whose compendious [succinct] character is "peace and good will toward men" [Luke 2:14]. But if by patriotism be understood that quality which, without shutting up our philanthropy in the narrow bounds of a single kingdom, yet attaches us in particular to the country to which belong; of this true patriotism, Christianity is the most copious source, and the surest preservative. The contrary opinion can indeed only have arisen from not considering the fullness and universality of our Saviour's precepts. Not like the puny productions of human workmanship, which at the best can commonly serve but the particular purpose that they are specially designed to answer, the moral as well as the physical principles of the great Author of all things are capable of being applied at once to ten thousand different uses; thus, amidst infinite complication, preserving a grand simplicity, and therein bearing the unambiguous stamp of their Divine Original. Thus, to specify one out of the numberless instances which might be adduced: the principle of gravitation [gravity], while it is subservient to all the mechanical purposes of common life, keeps at the same time the stars in their courses, and sustains the harmony of worlds.

Thus also in the case before us: society consists of a number of different circles of various magnitudes and uses; and that circumstance, wherein the principle of patriotism chiefly consists, whereby the duty of patriotism is best practiced, and the happiest effect to the general weal [prosperity] produced, is, that it should be the desire and aim of every individual to fill well his own proper circle, as a part and member of the whole, with a view to the production of general happiness. This our

Saviour enjoined when he prescribed the duty of universal love, which is but another term for the most exalted patriotism. Benevolence, indeed, when not originating from Religion, dispenses but from a scanty and precarious fund; and therefore, if it be liberal in the case of some objects, it is generally found to be contracted towards others. Men who, acting from worldly principles, make the greatest stir about general philanthropy or zealous patriotism, are often very deficient in their conduct in domestic life, and very neglectful of the opportunities, fully within their reach, of promoting the comfort of those with whom they are immediately connected. But true Christian benevolence is always occupied in producing happiness to the utmost of its power, and according to the extent of its sphere, be it larger or more limited; it contracts itself to the measure of the smallest; it can expand itself to the amplitude of the largest. It resembles majestic rivers, which are poured from an unfailing and abundant source. Silent and peaceful in their outset, they begin with dispensing beauty and comfort to every cottage by which they pass. In their further progress they fertilize provinces and enrich kingdoms. At length they pour themselves into the ocean, where, changing their names, but not their nature, they visit distant nations and other hemispheres, and spread throughout the world the expansive tide of their beneficence.

It must be confessed that many of the good effects, of which Religion is productive to political societies, would be produced even by a false Religion, which should prescribe good morals, and should be able to enforce its precepts by sufficient sanctions. Of this nature are those effects, which depend on our calling in the aid of a Being who sees the heart, in order to assist the weakness, and in various ways to supply the inherent defects of all human jurisprudence. But the superior excellence of Christianity in this respect must be acknowledged, both in the superiority of her moral code, and in the powerful motives and efficacious means which she furnishes for enabling us to practice it; and in the tendency of her doctrines to provide for the observance of her precepts, by producing tempers of mind which correspond with them.

But, more than all this, it has not perhaps been enough remarked, that true Christianity, from her essential nature, appears peculiarly and powerfully adapted to promote the preservation and healthfulness of political communities. What is in truth their grand malady? The answer is short; Selfishness.

This is that young disease received at the moment their birth, "which grows with their growth, and strengthens with their strength;" and through which at length expire, if not cut off prematurely by some external shock or intestine convulsion.

The disease of selfishness, indeed, assumes different forms in the different classes of society. In the great and the wealthy, it displays itself in luxury, in pomp and parade, and in all the frivolities of a sickly and depraved imagination, which seeks in vain its own gratification, and is dead to the generous and energetic pursuits of an enlarged heart.

In the lower orders, when not motionless under the weight of a superincumbent [overriding] despotism, it manifests itself in pride, and its natural offspring, insubordination, in all its modes. But though the external effects may vary, the internal principle is the same; a disposition in each individual to make self the grand center and end of his desires and enjoyments; to over-rate his own merits and importance, and of course to magnify his claims on others, and in return to under-rate theirs on him; a disposition to under-value the advantages, and overstate the disadvantages, of his condition in life. Thence spring rapacity, and venality, and sensuality. Thence imperious nobles and factious [creating disagreement or division] leaders, and an unruly commonalty [common folk], bearing with difficulty the inconveniences of a lower station, and imputing to the nature or administration of their government the evils which necessarily flow from the very constitution of our species, or which perhaps are chiefly the result of their own vices and follies. The opposite to selfishness is public spirit; which may be termed, not unjustly, the grand principle of political vitality, the very *life's breath* of states, which tends to keep them active and vigorous, and to carry them to greatness and glory.

The tendency of public spirit, and the opposite tendency of selfishness, have not escaped the observation of the founders of states, or of the writers on government, and various expedients have been resorted to and extolled, for cherishing the one, and for repressing the other. Sometimes a principle of internal agitation and dissension, resulting from the very frame of the government, has been productive of the effect. Sparta flourished for more than seven hundred years under the civil institutions of Lycurgus;[16] which guarded against the selfish principle, by prohibiting commerce, and imposing universal poverty and hardship. The Roman commonwealth, in which public spirit was cherished, and selfishness checked, by the principle of the love of glory, was also of long continuance. This passion naturally operates to produce an unbounded spirit of conquest, which, like the ambition of the greatest of its own heroes, was never satiated while any other kingdom was left it to subdue. The principle of political vitality, when kept alive only by means like these, merits the description once given of eloquence:

> [Magna eloquentia,] sicut flamma, materia alitur
> et motibus excitatur et urendo clarescit.

> [Great oratory is like a flame: it needs fuel to
> feed it,
> movement to fan it, and it brightens as it burns.

> —Tacitus][17]

But like eloquence, when no longer called into action by external causes, or fomented by civil broils, it gradually languishes. Wealth and luxury produce stagnation, and stagnation terminates in death.

To provide, however, for the continuance of a state, by the admission of internal dissensions, or even by the chilling influence of poverty, seems to be in some sort sacrificing the end to the means. Happiness is the end for which men unite in civil society; but in societies thus constituted, little happiness, comparatively speaking, is to be found. The expedient, again, of preserving a state by the spirit of conquest, though even this has not wanted its admirers,[18] is not to be tolerated for a moment, when considered on principles of universal justice. Such a state lives, and grows, and thrives by the misery of others, and becomes professedly the general enemy of its neighbours, and the scourge of the human race. All these devices are in truth but too much like the fabrications of man, when compared with the works of the Supreme Being; clumsy, yet weak in the execution of their purpose, and full of contradictory principles and jarring movements.

I might here enlarge with pleasure on the unrivalled excellence, in this very view, of the constitution under which we live in this happy country; and point out how, more perhaps than any which ever existed upon earth, it is so framed as to provide at the same time for keeping up a due degree of public spirit, and yet for preserving unimpaired the quietness, and comfort, and charities of private life; how it even extracts from selfishness itself many of the advantages which, under less happily constructed forms of government, public spirit only can supply. But such a political discussion, however grateful to a British mind, would here be out of place. It is rather our business to remark, how much Christianity in every way sets herself in direct hostility to selfishness, the mortal distemper of political communities, and consequently how their welfare must be inseparable from her prevalence. It might, indeed, be almost stated as the main object and chief concern of Christianity, to root out our natural selfishness, and to rectify the false standard which it imposes on us; with views, however, far higher than any which concern merely our temporal and social well-being; to bring us to a just estimate of ourselves, and of all around us, and to a due impression of the various claims and obligations resulting from the different relations in which we stand. Benevolence, enlarged, vigorous, operative benevolence, is her master principle. Moderation in temporal pursuits and enjoyments, comparative indifference to the issue of worldly projects, diligence in the discharge of personal and civil duties, resignation to the will of God, and patience under all the dispensations of his Providence, are among her daily lessons. Humility is one of the essential qualities, which her precepts most directly and strongly enjoin, and which all her various doctrines tend to call forth and cultivate; and humility, as has been before suggested, lays the deepest and surest grounds for benevolence. In whatever class or order of society Christianity prevails, she sets herself to rectify the particular faults, or, if we would speak more distinctly, to counteract the particular mode of selfishness, to which that class is liable. Affluence she teaches to be liberal and beneficent; authority, to bear its faculties with meekness, and to consider the various cares and obligations belonging to its elevated station as being conditions on which that station is conferred. Thus, softening the glare of wealth, and moderating the insolence of power, she renders the inequalities of the social state less galling to the lower orders, whom also she instructs, in their turn, to be diligent, humble, patient: reminding them that their more lowly path has been allotted to them by the hand of God; that it is their part faithfully to discharge its duties, and contentedly to bear its inconveniences: that the present state of things is very short; that the objects about which worldly men conflict so eagerly, are not worth the contest; that the peace of mind which Religion offers to all ranks indiscriminately, affords more true satisfaction than all the expensive pleasures which are beyond the poor man's reach; that in this view, however, the poor have the advantage, and that if their superiors enjoy more abundant comforts, they are likewise exposed to many temptations from which the inferior classes are happily exempted; that "having food and raiment, they should be therewith content" [1 Timothy 6:8], for that their situation in life, with all its evils, is better than they have deserved at the hand of God; finally, that all human distinctions will soon be done away, and the true followers of Christ will all, as children of the same father, be alike admitted to the possession of the same heavenly inheritance. Such are the blessed effects of Christianity on the temporal well-being of political communities.

But the Christianity which can produce effects like these must be real, not nominal, deep, not superficial. Such then is the Religion we should cultivate, if we would realize these pleasing speculations, and arrest the progress of political decay. But in the present circumstances of this country, it is a farther reason for endeavouring to cultivate this vital Christianity, still considering its effects merely in a political view, that, according to all human appearance, we must either have this or none: unless the prevalence of this be in some degree restored, we are likely not only to lose all the advantages which we might have derived from true Christianity, but to incur all the manifold evils which would result from the absence of all religion.

In the first place, let it be remarked, that a weakly principle of Religion, and even such a one, in a political view, is productive of many advantages; though its existence may be prolonged if all external circumstances favour its continuance, can hardly be kept alive, when the state of things is so unfavourable to vital Religion, as it must be confessed to be in our condition of society. Nor is it merely the ordinary effects of a state of wealth and prosperity to which we here allude. Much also may justly be apprehended, from that change which has taken place in our general habits of thinking and feeling, concerning the systems and opinions of former times. At a less advanced period of society, indeed, the Religion of the state will be generally accepted, though it be not felt in its vital power. It was the Religion of our forefathers. With the bulk it is on that account entitled to reverence, and its authority is admitted without question. The establishment in which it subsists pleads the same prescription, and obtains the same respect. But in our days, things are very differently circumstanced. Not merely the blind prejudice in favour of former times, but even the proper respect for them, and the reasonable presumption in their favour, has abated. Still less will the idea be endured of any system being kept up, when the imposture is seen through by the higher orders, for the sake of retaining the common people in subjection. A system, if not supported by a real persuasion of its truth, will fall to the ground. Thus it not infrequently happens, that in a more advanced state of society, a religious establishment must be indebted for its support to that very Religion which in earlier times it fostered and protected; as the weakness of some aged mother is sustained, and her existence lengthened, by the tender assiduities of the child whom she had reared in the helplessness of infancy. So in the present instance, unless there be reinfused into the mass of our society, something of that principle, which animated our ecclesiastical system in its earlier days, it is vain for us to hope that the establishment will very long continue: for the anomaly will not much longer be borne, of an establishment, the *actual* principles of the bulk of whose members, and even teachers, are so extremely different from those which it professes. But in proportion as vital Christianity can be revived, in that same proportion the church establishment is strengthened; for the revival of vital Christianity is the very reinfusion of which we have been speaking. This is the very Christianity on which our establishment is founded; and that which her Articles, and Homilies, and Liturgy, teach throughout.

But if, when the reign of prejudice, and even of honest prepossession, and of grateful veneration, is no more (for by these almost any system may generally be supported, before a state, having passed the period of its maturity, is verging to its decline) if there are any who think that a dry, unanimated Religion, like that which is now professed by nominal Christians, can hold its place, much more, that it can be revived among the general mass of mankind, it may be affirmed, that, arguing merely on human principles, they know little of human nature. The kind of Religion which we have recommended, whatever opinion may be entertained concerning its truth, and to say nothing of the agency of Divine Grace, must at least be conceded to be the only one at all suited to make impression upon the lower orders, by strongly interesting the passions of the human mind. If it be thought that a system of ethics may regulate the conduct of the higher classes, such a one is altogether unsuitable to the lower, who must be worked upon by their affections, or they will not be worked upon at all. The ancients were wiser than ourselves, and never thought of governing the community in general by their lessons of philosophy. These lessons were confined to the school of the learned, while for the million, a system of Religion, such as it was, was kept up as, alone adapted to their grosser natures. If this reasoning fail to convince, we may safely appeal to experience. Let the Socinian and the moral teacher of Christianity come forth, and tell us what effects *they* have produced on the lower orders. They themselves will hardly deny the inefficacy of their instructions. But, blessed be God, the Religion which we recommend has proved its correspondence with the character generally given of Christianity, that it was calculated for the poor, by changing the whole condition of the mass of society in many of the most populous districts in this and other countries; and by bringing them from being scenes of almost unexampled wickedness and barbarism, to be eminent for sobriety, decency, industry, and, in short, for whatever can render men useful members of civil society.

If indeed through the blessing of Providence, a principle of true Religion should in any considerable degree gain ground, there is no estimating the effects on public morals, and the consequent influence on our political welfare. These effects are not merely negative: though it would be much, merely to check the farther progress of a gangrene, which is eating out the very vital principles of our social and political existence. The general standard of morality formerly described, would be raised, it would at least be sustained and kept for a while from further depression. The esteem which religious characters would personally attract, would extend to the system which they should hold, and to the establishment of which they should be members. These are all merely natural consequences. But to those who believe in a superintending Providence, it may be added, that the blessing of God might be drawn down upon our country, and the strokes of his anger be for a while suspended.

Let us be spared the painful task of tracing, on the contrary, the fatal consequences of the extinction of Religion among us. They are indeed such as no man, who is ever so little interested for the welfare of his country, can contemplate without the deepest concern. The very loss of our church establishment, though, as in all human institutions, some defects may be found in it, would itself be attended with the most fatal consequences. No prudent man dares hastily pronounce how far its destruction might not greatly endanger our civil institutions. It would not be difficult to prove, that the want of it would also be in the highest degree injurious to the cause of Christianity; and still more, that it would take away what appears from experience to be one of the most probable means of its revival. To what a degree might even the avowed principles of men, not altogether without Religion, decline, when our inestimable Liturgy should no longer remain in use: a Liturgy justly inestimable, which continually sets before us a faithful model of the Christian's belief, and practice, and language, restraining us, as far as restraint is possible, from excessive deviations; furnishing us with abundant instruction when we would return to the right path; affording an advantage-ground of no little value to such instructors as still adhere to the good old principles of the Church of England; in short, daily shaming us, by preserving a living representation of the opinions and habits of better times, as some historical record, which reproaches a degenerate posterity, by exhibiting the worthier deeds of their progenitors. In such a state of things, to what a depth public morals might sink, may be anticipated by those who consider what would then be the condition of a society; who reflect how bad principles and vicious conduct mutually aid each other's operation, and how, in particular, the former make sure the ground which the latter may have gained; who remember, that in the lower orders, the system of honour, and the responsibility of character, are wanting, which in the superior classes, in some poor degree supply the place of higher principles. It is well for the happiness of mankind, that such a community could not long subsist. The cement of society being no more, the state would soon be dissolved into individuality.

Let it not be vainly imagined, that our state of civilization must prevent the moral degeneracy here threatened. A neighbouring nation [France] has lately furnished a lamentable proof, that superior polish and refinement may well consist with a very large measure of depravity. But to appeal to a still more decisive instance: it may be seen in the history of the latter years of the most celebrated of the Pagan nations, that the highest degrees of civilization and refinement are by no means inseparable from the most shocking depravity of morals. The fact is certain, and the obvious inference with regard to ourselves cannot be denied. The cause of this strange phaenomenon (such it really appears to our view) for which the natural corruption of man might hardly seem to account sufficiently, has been explained by an inspired writer [Paul]. Speaking of the most polished nations of antiquity, he observes: "Because when they knew God, they glorified him not as God, and were not *solicitous*[19] to retain him in their knowledge, he gave then over to a reprobate mind" [Romans 1:28]. Let us then beware, and take warning from their example: let us not suffer our self-love to beguile us: let us not vainly persuade ourselves, that although prosperity and wealth may have caused us to relax a little too much, in those more serious duties which regard our Maker, yet that we shall stop where we are; or, at least, that we can never sink into the same state of moral depravation. Doubtless we should sink as low, if God were to give us up also to our own imaginations. And what ground have we to think he will not? If we would reason justly, we should not compare ourselves with the state of the Heathen world when at its worst, but with its state at that period, when, for its forgetfulness of God, and its ingratitude towards him, it was suffered to fall, till at length it reached that worst, its ultimate point of depression. The Heathens had only reason and natural conscience to direct them: we enjoy, superadded to these, the clear light of Gospel revelation, and a distinct declaration of God's dealings with them, to be a lesson for our instruction. How then can we but believe that if we, enjoying advantages so much superior to theirs, are alike forgetful of our kind Benefactor, we shall also be left to ourselves: and if so left, what reason can be assigned why we should not fall into the same enormities?

What then is to be done? The inquiry is of the first importance, and the general answer to it is not difficult.—The causes and nature of the decay of Religion and morals among us sufficiently indicate the course, which, on principles of sound policy, it is in the highest degree expedient for us to pursue. The distemper of which, as a community, we are sick, should be considered rather as a moral than a political malady. How much has this been forgotten by the disputants of modern times: and accordingly, how transient may be expected to be the good effects of the best of their publications! We should endeavour to tread back our steps. Every effort should be used to raise the depressed tone of public morals. This is a duty particularly incumbent on all who are in the higher walks of life; and it is impossible not to acknowledge the obligations, which in this respect we owe as a nation to those exalted characters whom God is his undeserved mercy to us still suffers to continue on the throne, and who set to their subjects a pattern of decency and moderation rarely seen in their elevated station.

But every person of rank, and fortune, and abilities, should endeavour in like manner to exhibit a similar example, and to recommend it to the imitation of the circle in which he moves. It has been the opinion of some well-meaning people, that by giving, as far as they possibly could with innocence, into the customs and practices of irreligious men, they might soften the prejudices too frequently taken up against Religion, of its being an austere gloomy service, and thus secure a previous favourable impression against any time when they might have an opportunity of explaining or enforcing their sentiments. This is always a questionable, and, it is to be feared, a dangerous policy. Many mischievous consequences necessarily resulting from it might easily be enumerated. But it is a policy particularly unsuitable to our inconsiderate and dissipated times, and to the lengths at which we are arrived. In these circumstances, the most likely means of producing the *revulsion* which is required, must be boldly to proclaim the distinction between "the adherents of God and Baal" [Baal is one of the many ancient near Eastern gods mentioned in the Bible]. The expediency of this conduct in our present situation is confirmed by another consideration, to which we have before had occasion to refer. It is this—that when men are aware that something of difficulty is to be effected, their spirits rise to the level of the encounter; they make up their minds to bear hardships and brave dangers, and to persevere in spite of fatigue and opposition: whereas in a matter which is regarded as of easy and and ordinary operation, they are apt to slumber over their work, and to fail in what a small effort might have been sufficient to accomplish, for want of having called up the requisite degree of energy and spirit. Conformably to the principle which is hereby suggested, in the circumstances in which we are placed, the line of demarcation between the friends and the enemies of Religion should now be made clear; the separation should be broad and obvious. Let him then, who wishes well to his country, no longer hesitate what course of conduct to pursue. The question now is not, in what liberties he might warrantably indulge himself in another situation, but what are the restraints on himself which the exigencies of the present times render it advisable for him to impose. Circumstanced as we now are, it is more than ever obvious that *the best man is the truest patriot.*

Nor is it only by their personal conduct, though this mode will always be the most efficacious, that men of authority and influence may promote the cause of good morals. Let them in their several stations encourage virtue and discountenance vice in others. Let them enforce the laws by which the wisdom of our forefathers has guarded against the grosser infractions of morals, and congratulate themselves, that in a leading situation on the bench of justice there is placed a man who, to his honour be it spoken, is well disposed to assist their efforts.[20] Let them favour and take part in any plans which may be formed for the advancement of morality. Above all things, let them endeavour to instruct and improve the rising generation; that, if it be possible, an antidote may be provided for malignity of that venom which is storing up in a neighbouring country. This has long been to my mind the most formidable feature of the present state of things in France; where, it is to be feared, a brood of moral vipers, as it were, is now hatching, which, when they shall have attained their mischievous maturity, will go forth to poison the world. But fruitless will be all attempts to sustain, much more to revive, the fainting cause of morals, unless you can in some degree restore the prevalence of Evangelical Christianity. It is in morals as in physics; unless the source of practical principles be elevated, it will be in vain to attempt to make them flow on a high level in their future course. You may force them for a while into some constrained position, but they will soon drop to their natural point of depression. By all, therefore, who are studious of their country's welfare, more particularly by all who desire to support our ecclesiastical establishment, every effort should be used to revive the Christianity of our better days.

The attempt should especially be made in the case of the pastors of the Church, whose situation must render the principles which they hold a matter of supereminent [outstanding] importance. Wherever these teachers have steadily and zealously inculcated the true doctrines of the Church of England, the happiest effects have commonly rewarded their labours. And it is worth observing, in the view which we are now taking, that these men, as might naturally be expected, are, perhaps without exception, friendly to our ecclesiastical and civil establishments;[21] and consequently, that their instructions and influence tend *directly,* as well as *indirectly,* to the maintenance of

the cause of order and good government. Nor should it be
forgotten by any, who, judging with the abstract coldness of
mere politicians, might doubt whether, by adopting the measures here recommended, a religious warmth would not be
called into action, which might break out into mischievous
irregularities, that experience proves and establishment affords, from its very nature, the happy means of exciting a
considerable degree of fervour and animation, and at the same
time restraining them within due bounds. The duty of encouraging vital Religion in the Church particularly devolves on all
who have the disposal of ecclesiastical preferment, and more
especially on the dignitaries of the sacred order. Some of these
have already sounded the alarm, justly censuring the practice
of suffering Christianity to degenerate into a mere system of
ethics, and recommending more attention to the peculiar doctrines of our Religion. In our schools, in our universities, let the
study be encouraged of the writings of those venerable divines
who flourished in the purer times of Christianity. Let even a
considerable proficiency in their writings be required of candidates for ordination. Let our churches no longer witness that
unseemly discordance, which has too much prevailed, between
the prayers and the sermon which follows.

But it may be enough to have briefly hinted at the
course of conduct, which, in the present circumstances of this
country, motives merely political should prompt us to pursue.
To all who have at heart the national welfare, the above suggestions are solemnly submitted. They have not been urged without misgivings, lest it should appear, as though the concern of
Eternity were melted down into a mere matter of temporal
advantage, or political expediency. But since it has graciously
pleased the Supreme Being so to arrange the constitution of
things, as to render the prevalence of true Religion and of pure
morality conducive to the well-being of states, and the preservation of civil order; and since these subordinate inducements
are not infrequently held forth, even by the sacred writers, it
seemed not improper, and scarcely liable to misconstruction, to
suggest inferior motives to readers, who might be less disposed
to listen to considerations of a higher order.

Would to God that the course of conduct here suggested might fairly be pursued: would to God that the happy
consequences, which would result from the principles we have
recommended could be realized; and above all, that the influence of true Religion could be extensively diffused: it is the best

wish which can be formed for his country, by one who is deeply anxious for its welfare:—

> Lucem redde tuam, dux bone, patriae!
> Instar veris enim vultus ubi tuus
> Affulsit populo, gratior it dies,
> Et soles melius nitent.

> [Restore thy light, O excellent chief,
> to thy country; for it is like spring
> where thy countenance has
> appeared; to the people the day
> passes more pleasantly, and
> the sun shines more brightly.

> —Horace][22]

Notes ⌒

1. Wilberforce writes, "the author must acknowledge himself indebted to Dr. [John] Owen for this illustration."

2. It is likely that Wilberforce is referring here to the political economist Adam Smith (1723–90). Wilberforce quoted previously from Smith's book entitled *Theory of Moral Sentiments.*

3. This Latin passage cited by Wilberforce is taken from Book II, lines 158–59 of *Epistles,* a work by the Roman poet Horace (65–8 B.C.). I have inserted an English translation by H. Rushton Fairclough. Fairclough's translation is part of the Loeb Classical Library edition of *Satires, Epistles, Ars Poetica* (Cambridge, Mass.: Harvard University Press, 1970), p. 411. I have also corrected Wilberforce's slightly inacurate rendering of this passage. Again, it appears he may have quoted this passage from memory. NOTE: The Saturnian measure was an ancient Italian poetic meter. Following the introduction of Greek literature into Rome, the Saturnian neasure was superceded by Greek metrical forms.

4. Wilberforce writes,

> The author here alludes to what happened within his own knowledge; and he has been assured by others, on whose testimony he can rely, of several similar instances. But to prevent misconstruction as to the incident which mainly gives rise to the remark, he thinks it necessary to declare, that the account which appeared in some of the news-papers, of an entertainment having been given by Mr. [William] Pitt on the Fast Day, is untrue; and he is glad of the opportunity, which the mention of this subject affords him, of contradicting a statement which he can positively affirm to have been false. This one of the many instances which should

enforce on the readers of news-papers, the *duty* of not *hastily* giving credit to reports to the disadvantage of *any* man, of *any* party. A person in a public station must often aquiesce under the grossest calumnies, unless he will undertake the vain and endless task of contradicting all the falsehoods which prejudice may conceive, and malignity propagate against him.—The writer may perhaps express himself with the more feeling on this subject; because he as often been, and, indeed, at this very moment is, in the circumstances which he has stated.

5. These men are John Davenant (Bishop of Salisbury, 1576–1641), John Jewel (Bishop of Salisbury, 1522–71), Joseph Hall (Bishop of Norwich, 1574–1656), Edward Reynolds (Bishop of Norwich, 1599–1676), William Beveridge (Bishop of St. Asaph, 1637–1708), Richard Hooker (theologian, 1554–1600), Lancelot Andrewes (Bishop of Winchester, 1555–1626), Robert Leighton (Archbishop of Glasgow, 1611–84), Archbishop James Ussher (Archbishop of Armagh, 1581–1656), Ezekiel Hopkins (Bishop of Derry, 1634–90), and Richard Baxter (Presbyterian divine, 1615–91). The Smith that Wilberforce refers to has been very difficult to identify; candidates for this person could be: George Smith (nonjuring divine, 1693–1756), Henry Smith (Puritan divine, also known as "silver-tongued Smith," 1550?–91), John Smith (divine, 1563–1616), Samuel Smith (ejected divine, 1584–1662?), Thomas Smith (Bishop of Carlisle, 1615–1702), and Thomas Smith (nonjuring divine and scholar, 1638–1710).

6. Wilberforce writes,

> I must beg leave to class among the brightest ornaments of the church of England, this great man [Richard Baxter], who with his brethren was so shamefully ejected from the church in 1666, in violation of the royal word, as well as of the clear principles of justice. With his controversial pieces I am little acquainted: but his practical writings [i.e. the 1707 edition of Baxter's *Practical Works*], in four massy folios, are a treasury of Christian wisdom, and it would be a most valuable service to mankind to revise them, and perhaps to abridge them, so as to render them more suited to the taste of modern readers. This has already been done in the case of his *Dying Thoughts,* a beautiful little piece, and of his *Saints' Rest.* His *Life* also, written by himself, and in a separate volume, contains much useful matter, and many valuable particulars of the history of the times of Charles I, [Oliver] Cromwell, &c. &c.

7. Wilberforce writes,

> Let me by no means be understood to censure all the sectaries without discrimination. Many of them, and some who by the unhappy circumstances of the times became objects of notice in a political view, were men of great erudition, deep views of Religion, and unquestionable piety: and though the writings of the Puritans are prolix, and according to the fashion of their age,

rendered rather perplexed than clear by multiplied divisions and subdivisions; yet they are a mine of wealth, in which any one who will submit to some degree of labour will find himself well rewarded for his pains. In particular the writings of Dr. [John] Owen, Mr. [John] Howe, and Mr. [John] Flavel, well deserve this character; of the first mentioned author, there are two pieces which I would especially recommend to the reader's perusal, one on *Heavenly Mindedness*, abridged by Dr. Mayo: the other, on the *Mortification of Sin in Believers*. While I have been speaking in terms of such high, and, I trust, such just eulogium of many of the teachers of the Church of England; this may not be an improper place to express the high obligations we owe to the Dissenters, for many excellent publications. Of this number are Dr. Evans' *Sermons on the Christian Temper;* and that most useful book, *The Rise and Progress of Religion in the Soul,* by Dr. [Philip] Doddridge; also, his [Doddridge's] *Life,* by [Job] Orton, and [Doddridge's] *Letters;* and two volumes of *Sermons,* one on Regeneration, the other on the Power and Grace of Christ. May the writer be permitted to embrace this opportunity to recommending two volumes, published separately, of *Sermons,* by the late Dr. [John] Witherspoon, president of the College of New Jersey [what is now Princeton University].

8. Wilberforce writes, "Vide [See] section 6 of the fourth chapter, where we have expressly and fully treated of this most important truth."

9. Wilberforce writes, "No exceptions have fallen within my own reading, but the writings of [Samuel] Richardson [flourished 1643–58]."

10. Wilberforce writes,

It is with pain that the author finds himself compelled to place so great a writer as Dr. [William] Robertson [1721–93] in this class. But to say nothing of his phlegmatic account of the [R]eformation, a subject which we should have thought likely to excite in any one, who united the character of a Christian Divine with that of an Historian, some warmth of pious gratitude for the good providence of God: to pass over also the ambiguity, in which he leaves his readers as to his opinion of the authenticity of the Mosaic chronology, in his disquisitions on the trade of India; his letters to Mr. [Edward] Gibbon [1737–94, author the *The Rise and Fall of the Roman Empire*], lately published, cannot but excite emotions of regret in every sincere Christian. The author hopes that he has so far explained his sentiments as to render it almost unnecessary to remark, what, however, to prevent misconstruction, he must here declare, that so far from approving, he must be understood decidedly to condemn, a hot, a contentious, much more an abusive manner of opposing or of speaking of the assailants of Christianity. The Apostle's direction in this respect can not be too much attended to. "The servant of the Lord must not strive; but be gentle unto all men, apt to teach, patient, in meekness instructing those that oppose themselves: if God peradventure will give them repentance to the acknowledging of the truth." 2 Timothy 2:24, 25.

11. Mr. David Hume (1711–76).

12. Wilberforce writes, "Vide [See] Dr. A. Smith's *Letter to W. Strahan, Esq.*"

13. Wilberforce writes, "What is stated here must be acknowledged by all, be their political opinions concerning French events what they may; and it makes no difference in the writer's view of the subject, whether the state of morals was or was not, quite, or nearly, as bad, before the French Revolution."

14. Wilberforce writes, "Soame Jenyns." See chapter 1, note 1.

15. Wilberforce refers the reader to "Paley's *Evidence.*" The author is William Paley (1743–1805). The full title of this work is *Evidences of Christianity,* and it was first published in 1794.

16. Lycurgus, a legislator of the ancient Greek city-state of Sparta, is thought to have lived sometime between the eleventh and the ninth century B.C. Scholars seem to disagree as to whether Lycurgus was a historical person, but he was written about by many important figures of the classical age, including Aristotle, Plutarch, Xenophon, and Herodotus. In addition, it is said that he had a temple in Sparta and was worshipped there as a hero. To him is attributed the framing of the Spartan constitution, a document distinguished for its delineation of governmental powers.

17. This Latin passage cited by Wilberforce is taken from Book XXXVI of *Dialogus De Oratoribus,* a work by the Roman writer Tacitus (c. A.D. 55–c. 117). I have inserted an English translation by Sir W. Peterson. Peterson's translation appears in the Loeb Classical Library's edition of *Dialogus De Oratoribus* (Cambridge, Mass.: Harvard University Press, 1980), p. 329. It appears that Wilberforce may have cited this passage slightly inacurately from memory. I have corrected the Latin citation by inserting the words "Magna eloquentia."

18. Wilberforce writes, "See especially that great historian, Ferguson, who, in his *Essay on Civil Society,* endeavors to vindicate the cause of heroism from the censure conveyed by the poet: 'From Macedonia's madman to the Swede'." Wilberforce is referring here to Adam Ferguson (1723–1816), a professor of philosophy at the University of Edinburgh. Ferguson's *Essay on Civil Society* was published in 1766.

19. Wilberforce writes, "Such seems to be the just rendering of the word which our testament translates, 'did not like to retain God in their knowledge.' " See Romans 1:28.

20. Wilberforce writes, "It is a gratification to the writer's personal as well as public feelings, to pay this tribute of respect to the character of Lord Chief Justice Kenyon."

21. Wilberforce writes, "This is not thrown out rashly, but asserted on the writer's own knowledge."

22. Horace, *Odes,* Book 4, 5, 5.

$\sim$Chapter Seven

Practical Hints to Various
Descriptions of Persons

SECTION ONE $\sim$

THUS HAVE WE ENDEAVOURED TO TRACE THE CHIEF defects of the religious system of the bulk of professed Christians in this country. We have pointed out their low idea of the importance of Christianity in general, their inadequate conceptions of all its leading doctrines, and the effect hereby naturally produced in relaxing the strictness of its practical system; more than all, we have remarked their grand fundamental misconception of its genius and essential nature. Let not therefore the difference between them and true believers be considered as a minute difference, as a question of forms or opinions. The question is of the very substance of Religion; the difference is of the most serious and momentous amount. We must speak out. *Their Christianity is not Christianity.* It wants the radical principle. It is mainly defective in all the grand constituents. Let them no longer be deceived by names in a matter of infinite importance; but with humble prayer to the source of all wisdom, that he would enlighten their understanding, and clear their hearts from prejudice, let them seriously examine by the Scripture standard their real belief and allowed practice, and they will become sensible of the shallowness of their scanty system.

If through the blessing of Providence on any thing which may have been here written, there should be any whom it has disposed to this important duty of self-inquiry, let me previously warm them to be well aware of our natural proneness to think too favourably of ourselves. Selfishness of one of the principal fruits of the corruption of human nature; and it is obvious that selfishness disposes us to overrate our good qualities, and to overlook or extenuate our defects. The corruption of human nature therefore being admitted, it follows undeniably, that in all our reckonings, if we would form a just estimate of our character, we must make allowance for the effects of selfishness. It is also another effect of the corruption of human nature, to cloud our moral sight, and blunt our moral sensibility. Something must therefore be allowed for this effect likewise. Doubtless, the perfect purity of the Supreme Being makes him see in us stains far more in number, and deeper in dye, than we ourselves can discover. Nor should another awful consideration be forgotten. When we look into ourselves, those sins only, into which we have lately fallen are commonly apt to excite any lively impression. Many individual acts of vice, or a continued course of vicious or dissipated conduct, which, when recent, may have smitten us with deep remorse, after a few months or years leave very faint traces in our recollection; at least, those acts alone continue to strike us strongly, which were of very extraordinary magnitude. But the strong impressions which they first excited, not the faded images which they subsequently present to us, furnish the true measure of their guilt. And to the pure eyes of God, this guilt must always have appeared far greater than to us. Now to the Supreme Being we must believe that there is no past or future; as whatever *will be,* so whatever *has been,* is retained by him in a present and unvarying contemplation, continuing always to appear just the same as at the first moment of its happening. Well may it then humble us in the sight of that Being who is of purer eyes than to behold iniquity [cf. Habakkuk 1:13], to call to mind that, unless our offences have been blotted out by our obtaining an interest in the satisfaction of Christ, through true repentance and lively faith, we appear before him clothed with the sins of our whole lives, in all their original depth of colouring, and with all the aggravations which we no longer particularly remember, but which, in general, we, may perhaps recollect to have once filled us with shame and confusion of face. The writer is the rather desirous of enforcing this reflection; because he can truly declare that he has found no consideration so efficacious in producing in his own mind the deepest self-abasement.

In treating of the sources of the erroneous estimates which we form of our religious and moral character, it may not, perhaps, be without its uses to take this occasion of pointing out some other common springs of self-deception. Many persons, as was formerly hinted, are misled by the favourable opinions entertained of them by others; many, it is to be feared, mistake a hot zeal for orthodoxy, for a cordial acceptance of the great truths of the Gospel; and almost all of us, at one time or other, are more or less misled by confounding the suggestions of the understanding with the impulses of the will, the assent which our judgment gives to religious and moral truths, with a hearty belief and approbation of them.

There is another frequent source of self-deception, productive of so much mischief in life that though it may appear to lead to some degree of repetition, it would be highly improper to omit the mention of it in this place. That we may be the better understood, it may be proper to premise, that certain particular vices, and likewise that certain particular good and amiable qualities, seem naturally to belong to certain particular periods and conditions of life. Now, if we would reason fairly in estimating our moral character, we ought to examine ourselves with reference to that particular "sin which does most easily beset us" [cf. Hebrews 12:1–2], not to some other sin to which we are not so much liable. And in like manner, on the other hand, we ought not to account it matter of much self-complacency, if we find in ourselves that good and amiable quality which naturally belongs to our period or condition; but rather look for some less ambiguous sign of a real internal principle of virtue. But we are very apt to reverse these rules of judging: we are very apt, on the one hand, both in ourselves and in others, to excuse "the besetting sin" [cf. Hebrews 12:1–2], taking and giving credit for being exempt from others, to which we or they are less liable; and on the other hand, to value ourselves extremely on our possession of the good or amiable quality which naturally belongs to us, and to require no more satisfactory evidence of the *sufficiency* at least of our moral character. The bad effects of this partiality are aggravated by the practice, to which we are sadly prone, of being contented, when we take a hasty view of ourselves, with negative evidences of our state, thinking it very well if we are not shocked by some great actual transgression, instead of looking for the positive signs of a true Christian, as laid down in the holy Scripture.

But the source of self-deception, which it is more particularly our present object to point out, is a disposition to consider as a conquest of any particular vice, our merely forsaking it on our quitting the period or condition of life to which that vice belongs, when perhaps also we substitute for it the vice of the new period or condition on which we are entering. We thus mistake merely outgrowing our vices, or our relinquishing them from some change in our worldly circumstances, for a thorough, or at least for a sufficient reformation.

But this topic deserves to be viewed a little more closely. Young people may, without much offence, be inconsiderate and dissipated; the youth of one sex may indulge occasionally in licentious excesses; those of the other may be supremely given up to vanity and pleasure: yet, provided that they are sweet tempered, and open, and not disobedient to their parents or other superiors, the former are deemed *good hearted* young men, the latter, *innocent* young women. Those who love them best have no solicitude about their spiritual interests: and it would be deemed strangely strict in themselves, or in others, to doubt of their becoming more religious as they advance in life; to speak of them as being actually under the divine displeasure; or, if their lives should be in danger, to entertain any apprehensions concerning their future destiny.

They grow older, and marry. The same licentiousness which was formerly considered in young men a venial frailty, is now no longer regarded in the husband and the father as compatible with the character of a decently religious man. The language is of this sort; "they have sown their wild oats, they must now reform, and be regular." Nor perhaps is the same manifest predominance of vanity and dissipation deemed innocent in the matron: but if they are kind respectively in their conjugal and parental relations, and are tolerably regular and decent, they pass for *mighty good sort of people,* and it would be altogether unnecessary scrupulosity in them to doubt of their coming up to the requisitions of the divine law, as far as in the present state of the world can be expected from human frailty. Their hearts, however, are no more than before supremely set on the great work of their salvation, but are chiefly bent on increasing their fortunes, or raising their families. Meanwhile they congratulate themselves on having amended from vices, which they are no longer strongly tempted to commit, or abstaining from which ought not to be assumed as a test of the strength of the religious principle, since the commission of them would prejudice their characters, and perhaps injure their fortune in life.

Old age has at length made its advances. Now, if ever, we might expect that it would be deemed high time to make eternal things the *main* object of attention. No such thing! There is still an appropriate good quality, the presence of which calms the disquietude, and satisfies the requisitions both of themselves of those around them. It is now required of them that they should be good natured and cheerful, indulgent to frailties and the follies of the young, remembering, that when young themselves they gave in to the same practices: how opposite this to that dread of sin, which is the sure characteristic of the true Christian; which causes him to look back upon the vices of his own youthful days with shame and sorrow, and which, instead of conceding to young people to be wild and thoughtless, as a privilege belonging to their age and circumstances, prompts him to warn them against what has proved to himself matter of such bitter retrospection. Thus, throughout the whole of life, some means or other are devised for stifling the voice of conscience. "We cry peace, while there is no peace" [Jeremiah 6:14], and both to ourselves and others that complacency is furnished which ought only to proceed from a consciousness of being reconciled to God, and a humble hope of our possessing his favour.

I know that these sentiments will be termed uncharitable; but I must not be deterred by such an imputation. It is time to have done with that senseless cant [insincere talk] of charity, which insults the understandings, and trifles with the feelings of those who are really concerned for the happiness of their fellow-creatures. What matter of keen remorse and of bitter self-reproaches are they storing up for their future torment, who are themselves its miserable dupes, or who, being charged with the office of watching over the eternal interests of their children or relations, suffer themselves to be lulled asleep, or beguiled by such shallow reasonings into sparing themselves the momentary pain of executing their important duty. Charity, indeed, is partial to the object of her regard, and where actions are of a doubtful quality, this partiality disposes her to refer them to a good, rather than to a bad motive. She is apt also somewhat to exaggerate merits, and to see amiable qualities in a light more favourable than that which strictly belongs to them. But true charity is wakeful, fervent, full of solicitude, full of good offices, not so easily satisfied, not so ready to believe that every thing is going on well, as a matter of course; but jealous of mischief, apt to suspect danger, and prompt to extend relief. These are the symptoms by which genuine regard will manifest itself in a wife or in a mother, in the case of the *bodily* health of the object of her affections. And where there is any real concern for the *spiritual* interests of others, it is characterized by the same infallible marks. That wretched quality, by which the sacred name of charity is now so generally and so falsely usurped, is no other than indifference, which, against the plainest evidence, or at least where there is strong ground of apprehension, is easily contented to believe that all goes well, because it has no anxieties to allay, no fears to repress. It undergoes no alternation of passions; it is not at one time flushed with hope, nor at another chilled by disappointment.

To a considerate and feeling mind there is something deeply afflicting, in seeing the engaging cheerfulness and cloudless gaiety incident to youth, welcomed as a sufficient indication of internal purity by the delighted parents, who, knowing the deceitfulness of these flattering appearances, should eagerly avail themselves of this period, when once wasted never to be regained, of good humored acquiescence and dutiful docility: a period when the soft and ductile [pliable or flexible] temper of the mind renders it more easily susceptible of the impressions we desire, and when, therefore, habits should be formed, which may assist our natural weakness to resist the temptations to which we shall be exposed in the commerce of maturer life. This more especially affecting in the female sex, because that sex seems, by the very constitution of its nature, to be more favourably disposed than ours to the feelings and offices of Religion; being thus fitted by the bounty of Providence, the better to execute the important task which devolves on it, of the education of our earliest youth. Doubtless, this more favourable disposition to Religion in the female sex, was graciously designed also to make women doubly valuable in the wedded state: and it seems to afford to the married man the means of rendering an active share in the business of life more compatible than it would otherwise be with the liveliest devotional feelings: that when the husband should return to his family, worn and harassed by worldly cares or professional labours, the wife, habitually preserving a warmer and more unimpaired spirit of devotion, than is perhaps consistent with being immersed in the bustle of life, might revive his languid [lacking vigor] piety, and that the religious impressions of both might derive new force and tenderness from the animating sympathies of conjugal affection. Can a more pleasing image be presented to a considerate mind, than that of a couple, happy in each other and in the pledges of their mutual love, uniting in an act of grateful adoration to the author of all their mercies: recommending each other, and the objects of their common care, to the divine protection; and repressing the solicitude of conjugal and parental tenderness by a confiding hope, that, through all the changes of this uncertain life, the Disposer [God as the determiner of the courses of events] of all things will assuredly cause all to work together for the good of them that love and put their trust in him [cf. Romans 8:28]; and that, after this uncertain state shall have passed away, they shall be admitted to a joint participation of never-ending happiness. It is surely no mean or ignoble office which we would allot to the female sex, when we would thus commit to them the charge of maintaining in lively exercise whatever emotions most dignify and adorn human nature; when we would make them as it were the medium of our intercourse with the heavenly world, the faithful repositories of the religious principle, for the benefit both of the present and of the rising generation.

Must it not then excite our grief and indignation, when we behold mothers forgetful at once of their own peculiar duties, and of the high office which Providence designed their daughters to fulfill; exciting, instead of endeavouring to moderate in them, the natural sanguineness [optimism] and inconsiderateness of youth; hurrying them night after night to the resorts of dissipations, thus teaching them to despise the *common* comforts of the family circle, and instead of striving to raise their views, and to direct their affections to their true object, acting as if with the express design studiously to extinguish every spark of a devotional spirit, and to kindle in its stead an excessive love of pleasure, and, perhaps, a principle of extravagant vanity, and ardent emulation.

Innocent young women! Good hearted young men! Wherein does this *goodness of heart* and this *innocence* appear? Remember that we are fallen creatures, born in sin, and naturally depraved. Christianity recognizes no *innocence* or *goodness of heart*, but in the remission of sin, and in the effects of the operation of divine grace. Do we find in these young persons the characters which the holy Scriptures lay down as the only satisfactory evidences of a safe state? Do we not, on the other hand discover the specified marks of a state of alienation from God? Can the

blindest partiality persuade itself that *they* are loving, or striving "to love God with all their hearts, and minds, and souls,
and strength?" [Mark 12:33]. Are *they* "seeking first the kingdom
of God, and his righteousness?" [Matthew 6:33]. Are *they* "working out their salvation with fear and trembling?" [Philippians
2:12]. Are *they* "clothed with humility?" [1 Peter 5:5]. Are *they* not,
on the contrary, supremely given up to self-indulgence? Are
they not at least "lovers of pleasure more than lovers of God?"
[2 Timothy 3:4]. Are the offices of Religion *their* solace or *their*
task? Do *they* not come to these sacred services with reluctance,
continue in them by constraint, and quit them with gladness?
And of how many of *these* persons may it not be affirmed in the
spirit of the prophet's language: "The harp and the viol, the
tabret and pipe, and wine, are in their feasts: but they regard
not the work of the Lord, neither consider the operation of his
hands?" [Isaiah 5:12]. Are not the youth of one sex often
actually committing, and still more often wishing for the opportunity to commit those sins of which the Scripture says
expressly, "that they which do such things *cannot* inherit the
kingdom of God?" [Galatians 5:21]. Are not the youth of the
other mainly intent on the gratification of vanity, and looking
for their chief happiness to the resorts of gaiety and fashion, to
all the multiplied pleasures which public places, or the still
higher gratifications of more refined circles, can supply?

    And then, when the first ebullitions [enthusiastic spir-
its] of youthful warmth are over, what is their boasted reformation? They may be decent, sober, useful, respectable, as
members of the community, or amiable in the relations of
domestic life. But is *this* the change of which the Scripture
speaks? Hear the expressions which it uses, and judge for
yourselves—"Except a man be *born again,* he cannot enter into
the kingdom of God" [cf. John 3:3]. —"The *old man* is corrupt
according to the deceitful lusts" [Ephesians 4:22]; an expression but too descriptive of the vain delirium of youthful dissipation, and of the false dreams of pleasure which it inspires; but
"the *new man*" is awakened from this fallacious estimate of
happiness; "*he* is renewed in knowledge after the image of
him that created him" [Colossians 3:10]. —"He is created after
God in righteousness and true holiness" [Ephesians 4:24]. The
persons of whom we are speaking are no longer, indeed, so
thoughtless, and wild, and dissipated, as formerly; so negligent
in their attention to objects of real value; so eager in the
pursuit of pleasure; so prone to yield to the impulse of appe-

tite. But this is no more than the change of which a writer of no very strict cast speaks, as naturally belonging to their riper age:

> Conversis studiis aetas, animusque virilis
> quaerit opes, & amicitias: inservit honori:
> co mmisisse cavet, quod mox mutare laboret.

> [With altered aims, the age and spirit of the man
> seeks wealth and friends, becomes a slave to ambition,
> and is fearful of having done what it will soon be
> eager to change.]

—Hor[ace][1]

This is a point of infinite importance: let it not be thought tedious to spend even yet a few more moments in the discussion of it. Put the question to another issue, and try it by appealing to the principle of life being a state of probation; a proposition, indeed, true in a certain sense, though not exactly in that which is sometimes assigned to it, and you will still be led to no very different conclusion. Probation implies resisting, in obedience to the dictates of Religion, appetites which we are naturally prompted to gratify. Young people are not tempted to be churlish, interested, covetous, but to be inconsiderate and dissipated, "lovers of pleasure more than lovers of God" [2 Timothy 3:4]. People again in middle age are not so strongly tempted to be thoughtless, and idle, and licentious. From excesses of this sort they are sufficiently withheld, particularly when happily settled in domestic life, by a regard to their characters, by the restraints of family connections, and by a sense of what is due to the decencies of the married state. *Their* probation is of another sort; *they* are tempted to be supremely engrossed by worldly cares, by family interests, by professional objects, by the pursuit of wealth or of ambition. Thus occupied, they are tempted to "mind earthly rather than heavenly things" [Colossians 3:1–2], forgetting "the one thing needful" [Luke 10:42]; to "set their affections" [Colossians 3:2] on temporal rather than eternal concerns, and to take up with "a form of godliness" [2 Timothy 3:5], instead of seeking to experience the power thereof: the foundations of this nominal Religion being laid, as was formerly explained more at large, in the forgetfulness, if not in the ignorance, of the peculiar doctrines of Christianity, These are the *ready-made* Christians formerly spoken of, who consider Christianity as a geographical term,

properly applicable to all those who have been born and edu-
cated in a country wherein Christianity is professed; not as
indicating a renewed nature, as expressive of a peculiar character, with its appropriate desires and aversions, and hopes, and
fears, and joys, and sorrows. To people of this description, the
solemn admonition of Christ is addressed: "I know thy works;
that thou hast a name—that thou livest, and art dead.—Be
watchful, and strengthen the things which remain that are
ready to die; for I have not found thy works perfect before
God" [Revelation 3:2].

If there be any one who is inclined to listen to this
solemn warning, who is awakened from his dream of false
security, and is disposed to be not only *almost* but *altogether* a
Christian—O! let him not stifle or dissipate these beginnings of
seriousness, but sedulously cherish them as the "workings of
the Divine Spirit" [cf. Psalm 16:11 and Proverbs 5:6], which
would draw him from the "broad" and crowded "road of destruction into the narrow" and thinly peopled path "that leadeth to
life" [Matthew 7:13]. Let him retire from the multitude—Let
him enter into his closet, and on his bended knees implore, for
Christ's sake and in reliance on his mediation, that God would
"take away from him the heart of stone, and give him a heart of
flesh" [Ezekiel 11:19]; that the Father of light would open his
eyes to his true condition, and clear his heart from the clouds
of prejudice, and dissipate the deceitful medium of self-love.
Then let him carefully examine his past life, and his present
course of conduct, comparing himself with God's word: and
considering how any one might reasonably have been expected
to conduct himself, to whom the Holy Scriptures had been
always open, and who had been used to acknowledge them to
be the revelation of the will of his Creator, and Governor, and
Supreme Benefactor; let him there peruse the awful denunciations against impenitent sinners; let him labour to become
more and more deeply impressed with a sense of his own
radical blindness and corruption; above all, let him steadily
contemplate, in all its bearings and connections, that stupen-
dous truth, *the incarnation and crucifixion of the only begotten Son
of God, and the message of mercy proclaimed from the cross to repenting sinners.*—"Be ye reconciled unto God" [2 Corinthians 5:20].
—"Believe in the Lord Jesus Christ, and thou shalt be saved"
[Acts 16:31].

When he fairly estimates the guilt of sin by the costly
satisfaction which was required to atone for it, and the worth of

his soul by the price which was paid for its redemption, and contrasts both of these with his own sottish [drunken] inconsiderateness; when he reflects on the amazing love and pity of Christ, and on the cold and formal acknowledgements with which he has hitherto returned this infinite obligation, making light of the precious blood of the Son of God, and trifling with the gracious invitations of his Redeemer: surely, if he be not lost to sensibility, mixed emotions of guilt, and fear, and shame, and remorse, and sorrow, will nearly overwhelm his soul; he will smite upon his breast, and cry out in the language of the publican, "God be merciful to me a sinner" [Luke 18:13]. But, blessed be God, such an one needs not despair—it is to persons in this very situation, and with these very feelings, that the offers of the Gospel are held forth, and its promises assured; "to the weary and heavy laden" [Matthew 11:28] under the burthen of their sins; to those who thirst for the water of life; to those who feel themselves tied and bound by the chain of their sins; "who abhor their captivity, and long earnestly for deliverance." Happy, happy souls! which the grace of God has visited, "has brought out of darkness into his marvellous light" [1 Peter 2:9], and "from the power of Satan unto God" [Acts 26:18]. Cast yourselves then on his undeserved mercy; he is full of love, and will not spurn you: surrender yourselves into his hands, and solemnly resolve, through his Grace, to dedicate henceforth all your faculties and powers to his service.

It is yours now "to work out your own salvation with fear and trembling" [Philippians 2:12], relying on the fidelity of him who has promised to "work in you both to will and to do of his good pleasure" [Philippians 2:13]. Ever look to him for help: your own safety consists in a deep and abiding sense of your own weakness, and in a firm reliance on his strength. If you "give all diligence" [2 Corinthians 8:7], his power is armed for your protection, his truth is pledged for your security. You are enlisted under the banner of Christ—"Fear not, though the world, and the flesh, and the devil are set in array against you" [Ephesians 6:12]. —"Faithful is he that hath promised" [Hebrews 10:23]; —"be ye also faithful unto death, and ye shall possess a crown of life" [Revelation 2:10]. —"He that endureth to the end, the same shall be saved" [Matthew 10:22]. In such a world as this, in such a state of society as ours, especially if in the higher walks of life, you must be prepared to meet with many difficulties—arm yourselves, therefore, in the first place, with determined resolution not to rate human estimation beyond its true value; not to dread the charge of of particularity, when it shall be necessary to incur it; but as was before recommended, let it be your constant endeavour to retain before your mental eye, that bright assemblage of invisible spectators, who are the witnesses of your daily conduct, and "to seek that honour which cometh from God" [John 5:44]. You cannot advance a single step till you are in some good measure possessed of this comparative indifference to the favour of men. We have before explained ourselves too clearly to render it necessary to declare, that no one should needlessly affect singularity: but to aim at incompatible advantages, to seek to please God and the world, where their commands are really at variance, is the way to be neither respectable, nor good, nor happy. Continue to be ever aware of your own radical corruption and habitual weakness. In truth, if your eyes are really opened, and your heart truly softened, "hungering and thirsting after righteousness" [Matthew 5:6], rising in your ideas of true holiness, and proving the genuineness of your hope by desiring "to purify yourself even as God is pure" [1 John 3:3]; you will become daily more and more sensible of your own defects, and wants, and weaknesses, and more and more impressed by a sense of the mercy and long-suffering of that gracious Saviour, "who forgiveth all your sins, and healeth all your infirmities" [Psalm 103:3].

This is the solution of what to a man of the world might seem a strange paradox, that in proportion as the Christian grows in grace, he grows also in humility. Humility is indeed the vital principle of Christianity; that principle by which from first to last she lives and thrives, and in proportion to the growth or decline of which she must decay or flourish. *This* first disposes the sinner in deep self-abasement to accept the offers of the Gospel; *this,* during his whole progress, is the very ground and basis of his feelings and conduct, both in relation to God, his fellow-creatures, and himself; and when at length he shall be translated into the realms of glory, *this* principle shall still subsist in undiminished force: "he shall fall down and cast his crown before the lamb, and ascribe blessing, and honour, and glory, and power, to him that sitteth upon the throne, and to the lamb, for ever and ever" [Revelation 5:13]. The *practical* benefits of this habitual lowliness of spirit are too numerous, and at the same time too obvious, to require enumeration. It will lead you to dread the beginnings, and fly from the occasions of sin, as that man would shun some infectious distemper, who should know that he was predisposed to take the contagion [the spreading of disease by contact or close association]. It will prevent a thousand difficulties, and decide a thousand questions concerning worldly compliances, by which those persons are apt to be embarrassed, who are not duly sensible of their own exceeding frailty, whose views of the Christian character are not sufficiently elevated, and who are not enough possessed with a continual fear of "grieving the Holy Spirit of God" [Ephesians 4:30], and of thus provoking him to withdraw his gracious influence. But if you are really such as we have been describing, you need not be urged to set the standard of practice high, and to strive after universal holiness. It is the desire of your hearts to act in all things with a single eye to the favour of God, and thus the most ordinary actions of life are raised into offices of Religion. This is the purifying, the transmuting principle which realizes the fabled touch, which changes all to gold [Wilberforce is making a reference to King Midas].[2] But it belongs to this desire of pleasing God, that we should be continually solicitous to discover the path of duty; that we should not indolently wait, satisfied with not refusing occasions of glorifying God, when they are forced upon us, but that we should pray to God for wisdom and spiritual understanding, that may be acute in discerning opportunities of serving him in the world, and judicious in selecting and wise in improving them. Guard indeed against the distraction of worldly cares, and cultivate heavenly mindedness, and a spirit of continual prayer, and neglect not to watch incessantly over the workings of your deceitful heart: but be active also, and useful. Let not your precious time be wasted "in shapeless idleness;" an admonition which, in our days, is rendered but too necessary by the relaxed habits of persons even of real piety: but wisely husband and improve this fleeting treasure. Never be satisfied with your present attainments; but forgetting the things which are behind, labour still to "press forward" [Philippians 3:13–14] with undiminished energy, and to run the race that is set before you without flagging in your course [Hebrews 12:1–2].

Above all, measure your progress by your improvement in love to God and man. "God is Love" [1 John 4:8]. This is the sacred principle which warms and enlightens the heavenly world, that blessed seat of God's visible presence. There it shines with unclouded radiance. Some scattered beams of it are graciously lent to us on earth, or we had been benighted and lost in darkness and misery; but a larger portion of it is infused into the hearts of the servants of God, who thus "are renewed in the divine likeness" [cf. Romans 6:5], and even here exhibit some faint traces of the image of their heavenly Father. It is the principle of love which disposes them to yield themselves up without reserve to the service of him, "who has bought them with the price of his own blood" [cf. Hebrews 9:22].

Servile, and base, and mercenary, is the notion of Christian practice among the bulk of nominal Christians. They give no more than they *dare* not with-hold; they abstain from nothing but what they *must* not practice. When you state to them the doubtful quality of any action, and the consequent obligation to desist from it, they reply to you in the very spirit of Shylock, "they cannot find it in the bond."[3] In short, they know Christianity only as a system of restraints. She is despoiled of every liberal and generous principle: she is rendered almost unfit for the social intercourses of life, and is only suited to the gloomy walls of that cloister [a monastery or convent], in which they would confine her. But *true Christians* consider themselves not as satisfying some rigorous creditor, but as discharging a debt of gratitude. Theirs is accordingly not the stinted return of a constrained obedience, but the large and liberal measure of a voluntary service. This principle, therefore, as was formerly remarked, and as has been recently observed of true Christian humility, prevents a thousand *practical* embarrassments by which they are continually harassed, who act from a less generous motive, and who require it to be clearly ascertained to them, that any gratification or worldly compliance, which may be in question, is beyond the allowed boundary line of Christian practice.[4] *This* principle regulates the true Christian's choice of companions and friends, where he is at liberty to make an option; *this* fills him with the desire of promoting the temporal well-being of all around him, and still more, with pity, and love, and anxious solicitude for their spiritual welfare. Indifference indeed in this respect is one of the surest signs of a low or declining state in Religion. *This* animating principle it is, which in the true Christian's happier hour inspires his devotions, and causes him to delight in the worship of God; which fills him with consolation, and peace, and gladness, and sometimes even enables him "to rejoice with joy unspeakable and full of glory" [1 Peter 1:8].

But this world is not his resting-place: here, to the very last, he must be a pilgrim and a stranger; a soldier, whose warfare ends only with life, ever struggling and combating with the powers of darkness, and with the temptations of the world around him, and the still more dangerous hostilities of internal depravity. The perpetual vicissitudes of this uncertain state, the peculiar trials and difficulties with which the life of a Christian is chequered, and still more, the painful and humiliating re-membrance of his own infirmities, teach him to look forward, almost with outstretched neck, to that promised day, when he shall be completely delivered from the bondage of corruption, and sorrow and sighing shall flee away [Isaiah 35:10]. In the anticipation of that blessed period, and comparing this churl-ish and turbulent world, where competition, and envy, and anger, and revenge, so vex [to irritate] and agitate the sons of men, with that blissful region where Love shall reign without disturbance, and where all being knit together in bonds of indissoluble friendship, shall unite in one harmonious song of praise to the Author of their common happiness, the true Christian triumphs over the fear of death: he longs to realize these cheering images, and to obtain admission into that blessed company.—With far more justice than it was originally used, he may adopt the beautiful exclamation—

> O praeclarum illum diem,
> cum ad illud divinum animorum concilium
> coetumque profsiciscar,
> atque ex hac turba et colluvione discedam.

> [O greatest of days, when I shall hasten to
> that divine assembly and gathering of souls,
> and when I shall depart from this crowd
> and rabble of life!

> —Cicero][5]

What has been now as well as formerly remarked, con-cerning the habitual feelings of the real believer, may suggest a reply to an objection common in the mouths of the nominal Christians, that we would deny men the innocent amusements and gratifications of life; thus causing our Religion to wear a gloomy forbidding aspect, instead of her true and natural face of cheerfulness and joy. This is a charge of so serious a nature, that although it may lead into a digression, it may not be improper to take some notice of it.

In the first place, Religion prohibits no amusement or gratification which is *really* innocent. The question, however, of its innocence, must not be tried by the loose maxims of worldly morality, but by the spirit of the injunctions of the word of God, and by the indulgence being conformable or not conformable to the genius of Christianity, and to the tempers and dispositions of mind enjoined on its professors. There can be no dispute concerning the true end of recreations. They are intended to refresh our exhausted bodily or mental powers, and to restore us, with renewed vigour, to the more serious occupations of life. Whatever, therefore, fatigues either body or mind, instead of refreshing them, is not fitted to answer the designed purpose. Whatever consumes more time, or money, or thought, than it is expedient (I might say *necessary*) to allot to mere amusement, can hardly be approved by any one who considers these talents [units of money used in biblical times] as precious deposits for the expenditure of which he will have to give account. Whatever directly or indirectly must be likely to injure the welfare of a fellow-creature, can scarcely be a suitable *recreation* for a Christian, who is "to love his neighbour as himself" [Mark 12:31]; or a very consistent *diversion* for any one, the business of whose life is to diffuse happiness.

But does a Christian never relax? Let us not so wrong and vilify the bounty of Providence, as to allow for a moment that the sources of innocent amusement are so rare, that men must be driven, almost by constraint, to such as are of a doubtful quality. On the contrary, such has been the Creator's goodness, that almost every one, both of our physical, and intellectual, and moral faculties, and the same may be said of the whole creation which we see around us, is not only calculated to answer the proper end of its being, by its subserviency to some purpose of solid usefulness, but to be the instrument of administering pleasure.

> Not content
> With every food of life to nourish man,
> Thou mak'st all nature beauty to his eye
> And music to his ear.

Our Maker also, in his kindness, has so constructed us, that even mere vicissitude is grateful and refreshing—A consideration which should prompt us often to seek, from a prudent *variation* of *useful pursuits,* that recreation for which we are apt to resort to what is altogether *unproductive and unfruitful.*

Yet rich and multiplied are the springs of innocent relaxation. The Christian relaxes in the temperate use of all the gifts of Providence. Imagination, and taste, and genius, and the beauties of creation, and the works of art, lie open to him. He relaxes in the feast of reason, in the intercourses of society, in the sweets of friendship, in the endearments of love, in the exercise of hope, of confidence, of joy of gratitude, of universal good will, of all the benevolent and generous affections, which, by the gracious ordination of our Creator, while they disinterestedly intend only happiness to others, are most surely productive to ourselves of complacency and peace. 0! little do they know of the true measure of enjoyment, who can compare these delightful complacencies with the frivolous pleasures of dissipation, or the course gratifications of sensuality. It is no wonder, however, that the nominal Christian should reluctantly give up, one by one, the pleasures of the world, and look back upon them, when relinquished, with eyes of wistfulness and regret, because he knows not the sweetness of the delights with which true Christianity repays those trifling sacrifices, and is greatly unacquainted with the *nature* of that pleasantness which is to be found in the ways of Religion.

It is indeed true, that when any one, who has long been going on in the gross and unrestrained practice of vice, is checked in his career, and enters at first on a religious course, he has much to undergo. Fear, guilt, remorse, shame, and various other passions, struggle and conflict within him. His appetites are clamorous for their accustomed gratification, and inveterate habits are scarcely to be denied. He is weighed down by a load of guilt, and almost overwhelmed by the sense of his unworthiness. But all this ought in fairness to be charged to the account of his past sins, and not to that of his present repentance. It rarely happens, however, that this state of suffering continues very long. When the mental gloom is the blackest, a ray of heavenly light occasionally breaks in, and suggests the hope of better days. Even in this life it commonly holds true, "They that sow in tears shall reap in Joy" [Psalm 126:5].

Neither, when we maintain, that the ways of Religion are ways of pleasantness, do we mean to deny that the Christian's internal state is, through the whole of his life, a state of discipline and warfare. Several of the causes which contribute to render it such have been already pointed out, together with the workings of his mind in relation to them: but if he has solicitudes and griefs peculiar to himself, he has "joys also with which a stranger intermeddles not" [Proverbs 14:10].

"Drink deep," however, "or taste not," is a direction full as applicable to Religion, if we would find it a source of pleasure, as it is to knowledge. A little Religion is, it must be confessed, apt to make men gloomy, as a little knowledge to render them vain: hence the unjust imputation often brought upon Religion by those whose degree of Religion is just sufficient, by condemning their course of conduct, to render them uneasy; enough merely to impair the sweetness of the pleasures of sin, and not enough to compensate for the relinquishment of them by its own peculiar comforts. Thus these men bring up, as it were, an ill report of that land of promise,[6] which, in truth, abounds with whatever, in our journey through life, can best refresh and strengthen us.

We have enumerated some sources of pleasure which men of the world may understand, and must knowledge to belong to the true Christian; but there are others, and those of a still higher class, to which they must confess themselves strangers. To say nothing of a qualified, I dare not say entire, exemption form those distracting passions and corroding cares by which he must naturally be harassed, whose treasure is within the reach of mortal accidents, there is the humble quiet-giving hope of being reconciled to God, and of enjoying his favour; with that solid peace of mind, which the world can neither give nor take away [cf. John 14:27], which results from a firm confidence in the infinite wisdom and goodness of God, and in the unceasing care and kindness of a gracious Saviour: and there is the persuasion of the truth of the divine assurance, that all things shall work together for good [Romans 8:28].

When the pulse indeed beats high, and we are flushed with youth, and health, and vigour, when all goes on prosperously, and success seems almost to anticipate our wishes; then we feel not the want of the consolations of Religion: but when fortune frowns, or friends forsake us, when sorrow, or sickness, or old age comes upon us, then it is, that the superiority of the pleasures of Religion is established over those of dissipation and vanity, which are ever apt to fly from us when we are most in want of their aid. There is scarcely a more melancholy sight to a considerate mind, than that of an old man, who is a stranger to those only true sources of satisfaction. How affecting, and at the same time how disgusting is it to see such a one awkwardly catching at the pleasures of his younger years, which are now beyond his reach, or feebly attempting to retain them: while they mock his endeavours and elude his grasp. To such a one, *gloomily* indeed does the evening of life set in! All is sour and cheerless. He can neither look backward with complacency nor forward with hope: while the aged Christian, relying on the assured mercy of his Redeemer, can calmly reflect that his dismission is at hand; that his redemption draweth nigh: while his strength declines and his faculties decay, he can quietly repose himself on the fidelity of God: and at the very entrance of the valley of the shadow of death [Psalm 23:4] he can lift up an eye, dim, perhaps, and feeble, yet occasionally sparkling with hope, and confidently looking forward to the near possession of his heavenly inheritance, "to those joys which eye hath not seen, nor ear heard, neither hath it entered into the heart of man to conceive" [1 Corinthians 2:9].

Never were there times which inculcated more forcibly, than those in which we live, the wisdom of seeking happiness beyond the reach of human vicissitudes. What striking lessons have *we* had of the precarious tenure of all sublunary [earthly] possessions. Wealth, and power, and prosperity, how peculiarly transitory and uncertain! But Religion dispenses her choicest cordials in the seasons of exigence, in poverty, in exile, in sickness, and in death. The essential superiority of that support which is derived from Religion is less felt, at least it is less apparent, when the Christian is in full possession of riches, and splendour, and rank, and all the gifts of nature and fortune. But when all these are swept away by the rude hand of time, or the rough blasts of adversity, the true Christian stands, like the glory of the forest, erect and vigorous; stripped indeed of his summer foliage, but more than ever discovering to the observing eye the solid strength of his substantial texture:

> Pondere fixa suo est, nudosque per aera ramos
> Attollens, trunco non frondibus efficit umbram.

> [It is fixed by its own weight and raising its bare
> branches to the air,
> it produces shade with its trunk and not its leaves.]

SECTION TWO

Advice to Some Who Profess Full Assent to the Fundamental Doctrines of the Gospel

In a former chapter we largely insisted on what may be termed the fundamental practical error of the bulk of professed

Christians in our days; their either overlooking or misconceiving the peculiar method which the Gospel has provided for the renovation of our corrupted nature, and for the attainment of every Christian grace.

But there are mistakes on the right hand and on the left; and our general proneness, when flying from one extreme to run into an opposite error, renders it necessary to superadd another admonition. The generally prevailing error of the present day, indeed, is that fundamental one which was formerly pointed out. But while we attend, in the first place, to this, and, on the warrant both of Scripture and experience, prescribe hearty repentance and lively faith, as the only root and foundation of all true holiness; we must at the same time guard against a practical mistake of another kind. They who, with penitent hearts, have humbled themselves before the cross of Christ, and who, pleading his merits as their only ground of pardon and acceptance with God, have resolved henceforth, through the help of his Spirit, to bring forth the fruits of righteousness, are sometimes apt to conduct themselves as if they considered their work as done, or at least as if this were the whole they had to do, as often as, by falling afresh into sin, another act of repentance and faith may seem to have become necessary. There are not a few in our relaxed age, who thus satisfy themselves with what may be termed *general* Christianity; who feel *general* penitence and humiliation from a sense of their sinfulness in *general,* and *general* desires of universal holiness; but who neglect that vigilant and jealous care, with which they should labour to extirpate [to root out and destroy completely] every *particular* corruption, by studying its nature, its root, its ramifications, and thus becoming acquainted with its secret movements, with the means whereby it gains strength, and with the most effectual methods of resisting it. In like manner, they are far from striving with persevering alacrity for the acquisition and improvement of every Christian grace. Nor is it unusual for ministers, who preach the truths of the Gospel with fidelity, ability, and success, to be themselves also liable to the charge of dwelling altogether in their instructions on this *general* Religion, instead of tracing and laying open the secret motions of inward corruption, and instructing their hearers how best to conduct themselves in every distinct part of the Christian warfare; how best to strive against each particular vice, and to cultivate each grace of the Christian character. Hence it is, that in too many persons, concerning the sincerity of whose general professions of Religion we should be sorry to entertain a doubt, we see little progress made in the regulation of their tempers, in the improvement of their time, in the reform of their plan of life, or in ability to resist the temptation to which they are particularly exposed. They will confess themselves, in general terms, to be *"miserable sinners:"* this is a tenet of their creed, and they feel even proud in avowing it. They will occasionally also lament particular failings: but this confession is sometimes obviously made, in order to draw forth a compliment for the very opposite virtue; and where this is not the case, it is often not difficult to detect, under this false guise of contrition, a secret self-complacency, arising from the manifestations they have afforded of their acuteness or candour in discovering the infirmity in question, or of their frankness or humility in acknowledging it. This will scarcely seem an illiberal suspicion to any one who either watches the workings of his own heart, or who observes that the faults confessed in these instances are very seldom those with which the person is most clearly and strongly chargeable.

We must mainly warn these men, and the consideration is seriously pressed on their instructors also, *that they are in danger of deceiving themselves. Let them beware lest they be nominal Christians of another sort.* These persons require to be reminded that there is no *short compendious method of holiness,* but that it must be the business of their whole lives to grow in grace, and continually adding one virtue to another, as far is may be, "to go on towards perfection" [Hebrews 6:1]. "He only that doeth righteousness is righteous" [1 John 3:7]. Unless "they bring forth the fruits of the spirit" [cf. Galatians 5:22], they can have no such sufficient evidence that they have received that "Spirit of Christ," "without which they are none of his" [Romans 8:9]. But where, on the whole, our unwillingness to pass an unfavourable judgment may lead us to indulge a hope that "the root of the matter is in them" [Job 19:28], yet we must at least declare to them, that instead of adorning the doctrine of Christ, they disparage and discredit it. The world sees not their secret humiliation, nor the exercises of their closets, but it is acute in discerning practical weaknesses: and if it observe that they have the same eagerness in the pursuit of wealth or ambition, the same vain taste for ostentation and display, the same ungoverned tempers, which are found in the generality of mankind; it will treat with contempt their pretences to superior sanctity, and indifference to worldly things, and will be hardened in its prejudices against the only mode which God has provided for our escaping the wrath to come, and obtaining eternal happiness.

Let him, then, who would be indeed a Christian, watch over his ways and over his heart with unceasing circumspection. Let him endeavour to learn, both from men and books, particularly from the lives of eminent Christians,[7] what methods have been actually found most effectual for the conquest of every particular vice, and for improvement in every branch of holiness. Thus studying his own character, and observing the most secret workings of his own mind, and of our common nature, the knowledge which he will acquire of the human heart in general, and especially of his own, will be of the highest utility in enabling him to avoid or to guard against the occasions of evil: and it will also tend, above all things, to the growth of humility, and to the maintenance of that sobriety of spirit and tenderness of conscience which are eminently characteristic of the true Christian. It is by this unceasing diligence, as the Apostle [Peter] declares, that the servants of Christ must make their calling sure [2 Peter 1:10]. Their labour will not be thrown away; "an entrance shall at length be ministered unto them abundantly, into the everlasting kingdom of our Lord and Savior Jesus Christ" [2 Peter 1:11].

SECTION THREE ⌁

Brief Observations Addressed to Sceptics and Unitarians

There is another class of men, an increasing class, it is to be feared, in this country, that of absolute unbelievers, with which this little work has properly no concern; but may the writer, sincerely pitying their melancholy state, be permitted to ask them one plain question? If Christianity be not in their estimation true, yet is there not at least a presumption in its favour sufficient to entitle it to a serious examination; from its having been embraced, and that not blindly and implicitly, but upon full inquiry and deep consideration, by Bacon, and Milton, and Locke, and Newton,[8] and much the greater part of those, who, by the reach of their understandings, or the extent of their knowledge, and by the freedom of their minds, and their daring to combat existing prejudices, have called forth the respect and admiration of mankind. It might be deemed scarcely fair to insist on Churchmen, though some of them are among the greatest names this country has ever known. Can the sceptic in general say with truth, that he has either prosecuted an examination into the evidences of Revelation at all, or at least with a seriousness and diligence in any degree proportioned to the importance of the subject. The fact is, and it is a fact which redounds to the honour of Christianity, that infidelity is not the result of sober inquiry and deliberate preference. It is rather the slow production of a careless and irreligious life, operating together with prejudices and erroneous conceptions concerning the nature of the leading doctrines and fundamental tenets of Christianity.

Take the case young men of condition, bred up by what we have termed nominal Christians. When children, they are carried to church, and thence they become acquainted with such parts of Scripture as are contained in our public service. If their parents preserve still more of the customs of better times, they are taught their Catechism, and furnished with a little farther religious knowledge. After a while, they go from under the eyes of their parents; they enter into the world, and move forward in the path of life, whatever it may be, which has been assigned to them. They yield to the temptations which assail them, and become, more or less, dissipated and licentious. At least they neglect to look into their Bible; they do not enlarge the sphere of their religious acquisitions; they do not even endeavour, by reflection and study, to turn into what may deserve the name of knowledge and rational conviction, the opinions which, in their childhood, they had taken on trust.

They travel, perhaps, into foreign countries; a proceeding which naturally tends to weaken their nursery, prejudice in favour of the Religion in which they were bred, and by removing them from all means of public worship, to relax their practical habits of Religion. They return home, and commonly are either hurried round in the vortex [a whirlpool or whirlwind] of dissipation, or engage with the ardour of youthful minds in some public or professional pursuit. If they read or hear any thing about Christianity, it is commonly only about those tenets which are subjects of controversy: and what reaches their ears of the Bible, in their occasional attendance at church, though it may sometimes impress them with an idea of the purity of Christian morality, contains much which, coming thus detached, perplexes and offends them, and suggests various doubts and startling objections, which a farther acquaintance with the Scripture would remove. Thus, growing more and more to know Christianity only by the difficulties it contains; sometimes tempted by an ambition of shewing themselves superior to vulgar prejudice, and always prompted by the natural pride of the human heart to cast off subjection to dogmas [doctrines put forward by some authority (especially the church), to be accepted as true without question] imposed on them; disgusted, perhaps, by the immoral lives of some professed Christians, by the weaknesses and absurdities of others, and by what they observe to be the implicit belief of numbers, whom they see and know to be equally ignorant with themselves, many doubts and suspicions of greater or less extent spring up within them. These doubts enter into the mind at first almost imperceptibly: they exist only as vague indistinct surmises, and by no means take the precise shape or the substance of a formed opinion. At first, probably, they even offend and startle by their intrusion; but by degrees the unpleasant sensations they once excited wear off: the mind grows more familiar with them. A confused sense (for such it is, rather than a formed idea) of its being desirable that their doubts should prove well founded, and of the comfort and enlargement which would be afforded by that proof, lends them much secret aid. The impression becomes deeper, not in consequence of being reinforced by fresh arguments, but merely by dint [means] of having longer rested in the mind; and as they increase in force, they creep on and extend themselves. At length they diffuse themselves over the whole of Religion, and possess the mind in undisturbed occupancy.

It is by no means meant that this is universally the process. But, speaking generally, this might be termed, perhaps not unjustly, the *natural history* of scepticism. It approves itself to the experience of those who have with any care watched the progress of infidelity in persons around them; and it is confirmed by the written lives of some of the most eminent unbelievers. It is curious to read their own accounts of themselves, the rather as they accord so exactly with the result of our own observation—we find that they once perhaps gave a sort of implicit hereditary assent to the truth of Christianity, and were what, by a mischievous perversion of language, the world denominates *believers*. How were they then awakened from their sleep of ignorance? At what moment did the light of truth beam in upon them, and dissipate the darkness in which they had been involved? The period of their infidelity is marked by no such determinate boundary. Reason, and thought, and inquiry had little or nothing to do with it. Having for many years lived careless and irreligious lives, and associated with companions equally careless and irreligious; not by force of study and reflection, but rather by the lapse of time, they at length attained to their infidel maturity. It is worthy of remark, that where any are reclaimed from infidelity, it is generally by a process much more rational than that which has been here described. Something awakens them to reflection. They examine, they consider, and at length yield their assent to Christianity on what they deem sufficient grounds.

From the account here given, it appears plainly that infidelity is generally the offspring of prejudice, and that its success is mainly to be ascribed to the depravity of the moral character. This fact is confirmed by the undeniable truth, that in *societies* which consist of individuals, infidelity is the natural fruit, not so much of a studious and disputatious, as of a dissipated and vicious age. It diffuses itself in proportion as the general morals decline, and it is embraced with less apprehension, when every infidel is kept in spirits, by seeing many around him who are sharing fortunes with himself.

To any fair mind this consideration alone might be offered, as suggesting a strong argument against infidelity, and in favour of Revelation. And the friends of Christianity might justly retort the charge, which their opponents often urge with no little affectation of superior wisdom, that we implicitly surrender ourselves to the influence of prejudice, instead of examining dispassionately the ground of our faith, and yielding our assent only according to the degree of evidence.

In our own days, when it is but too clear that infidelity increases, it is not in consequence of the reasonings of the infidel writers having been much studied, but from the progress of luxury, and the decay of morals: and, so far as this increase maybe traced at all to the works of sceptical writers, it has been produced, not by argument and discussion, but by sarcasms and points of wit, which have operated on weak minds, or on nominal Christians, by bringing gradually into contempt, opinions which, in their case, had only rested on the basis of blind respect and the prejudices of education. It may therefore be laid down as an axiom [an accepted general truth], that *infidelity is in general a disease of the heart more than of the understanding.* If Revelation were assailed only by reason and argument, it would have little to fear. The literary opposers of Christianity, from Herbert to Hume,[9] have been seldom read. They made some stir in their day: during their brief span of existence they were noisy and noxious [unpleasant and harmful]; but like the locusts of the east, which for a while obscure the air, and destroy the verdure [green plant life], they were soon swept away and forgotten. Their very names would be scarcely found if Leland[10] had not preserved them from oblivion.

The account which has been given, of the secret, but grand source of infidelity, may perhaps justly be extended, as being not seldom true in the case of those who deny the fundamental doctrines of the Gospel.

In the course which we lately traced from nominal orthodoxy to absolute infidelity, Unitarianism[11] is indeed, a sort of half-way house, if the expression may be pardoned, a stage on the journey, where sometimes a person indeed finally stops, but where, not infrequently, he only pauses for a while, and then pursues his progress.

The Unitarian teachers by no means profess to absolve their followers from the unbending strictness of Christian morality. They prescribe the predominant love of God, and an habitual spirit of devotion: but it is an unquestionable fact; a fact which they themselves almost admit, that this class of religionist is not in general distinguished for superior purity of life, and still less for that frame of mind which, by the injunction "to be spiritually, not carnally, minded" [Romans 8:6], the word of God prescribes to us, as one of the surest tests of our experiencing the vital power of Christianity. On the contrary, in point of fact, *Unitarianism* seems to be resorted to, not merely by those who are disgusted with the peculiar doctrines of Christianity, but by those also who are seeking a refuge from the strictness of her practical precepts; and who, more particularly, would escape from the obligation which she imposes on her adherents, rather to incur the dreaded charge of singularity, than fall in with the declining manners of a dissipated age.

Unitarianism, where it may be supposed to proceed from the understanding rather than from the heart, is not infrequently produced by a confused idea of the difficulties, or, as they are termed, the impossibilities which orthodox Christianity is supposed to involve. It is not our intention to enter into the controversy:[12] but it may not be improper to make one remark as a guard to persons in whose way the arguments of the Unitarians maybe likely to fall; namely, that one great advantage possessed by Deists [those who believe in the existence of a god without accepting revelation], and perhaps in a still greater degree by Unitarians, in their warfare with the Christian system, results from the very circumstances of their being the assailants. They urge what they state to be powerful arguments against the truth of the fundamental doctrines of Christianity, and then call upon men to abandon them as posts no longer tenable. But they who are disposed to yield to this assault, should call to mind, that it has pleased God so to establish the constitution of all things, that perplexing difficulties and plausible objections may be adduced against the most established truths; such, for instance, as the being of a God, and many others both physical and moral. In all cases, therefore, it becomes us, not on a partial view to reject any proposition, because it is attended with difficulties, but to compare the difficulties which it involves, with those that attend the alternative proposition which must be embraced on its rejection.

We should put to the proof the alternative proposition in its turn, and see whether it be not still less tenable than that which we are summoned to abandon. In short, we should examine circumspectly on all sides, and abide by that opinion which, on carefully balancing all considerations, appears fairly entitled to our preference. Experience, however, will have convinced the attentive observer of those around him, that it has been for want of adverting to this just and obvious principle,that the Unitarians in particular have gained most of their proselytes [converts] from the Church, so far as argument has contributed to their success. If the Unitarians, or even the Deists, were considered in their turn as masters of the field, and were in their turn attacked, both by arguments tending to disprove their system directly, and to disprove it indirectly, by shewing the high probability of the truth of Christianity, and of its leading and peculiar doctrines, it is most likely that they would soon appear wholly unable to keep their ground. In short, reasoning fairly, there is no medium between absolute *Pyrrhonism* [extreme skepticism] and true Christianity: and if we reject the latter on account of its difficulties, we shall be still more loudly called upon to reject every other system which has been offered to the acceptance of mankind. This consideration might, perhaps, with advantage be more attended to than it has been, by those who take upon them to vindicate the truth of our holy Religion: as many, who from inconsideration, or any other cause, are disposed to give up the great fundamentals of Christianity, would be startled by the idea, that on the same principle on which they did this, they must give up the hope of finding any rest for the sole of their foot on any ground of Religion, and not stop short of unqualified Atheism.

Besides the class of those who professedly reject revelation, there is another, and that also, it is to be feared, an increasing one, which may be called the class of half-unbelievers, who are to be found in various degrees of approximation to a state of absolute infidelity. The system, if it deserve the name, of these men, is grossly irrational. Hearing many who assert and many who deny the truth of Christianity, and not reflecting seriously enough to consider that it must be either true or false, they take up a strange sort of middle opinion of its qualified truth. They conceive that there must be something in it, though by no means to the extent to which it is pushed by orthodox Christians. They grant the reality of future punishment, and even that they themselves cannot altogether expect to escape it; yet "they trust it will not go so hard with them as the churchmen state;" and, as was formerly hinted, though disbelieving almost every material doctrine which Christianity contains, yet, even in their own minds, they by no means conceive themselves to be inlisted [enlisted] under the banners of infidelity, or to have much cause for any great apprehension lest Christianity should prove true.

But let these men be reminded, that there is no middle way. If they can be prevailed on to look into their Bible, and do not make up their minds absolutely to reject its authority; they must admit that there is no ground whatever for this vain hope, which they suffer themselves to indulge, of escaping with a slight measure of punishment. Nor let them think their guilt inconsiderable. Is it not grossly criminal to trifle with the long-suffering of God, to despise alike his invitations and his threatenings, and the offer of his spirit of grace, and the precious blood of the Redeemer? Far different is the Scripture estimate. "How shall we escape if we neglect so great salvation?" "It shall be more tolerable for Sodom and Gomorrah, in the day of judgment" [see Matthew 10:15], than for those who voluntarily shut their eyes against that full light, which the bounty of Heaven has poured out upon them. These half-

unbelievers are even more reprehensible than downright sceptics, for remaining in this state of careless uncertainty, without
endeavouring to ascertain the truth or falsehood of revelation.
The probability which they admit, that it may be true, imposes
on them an additional and undeniable obligation to inquiry.
But both to them and to decided sceptics it must be plainly
declared, that they are in these days less excusable than ever,
for not looking into the grounds and proofs on which is rested
the truth of Christianity; for never before were these proofs *so
plainly, and at so easy a rate,* offered to the consideration of
mankind. Through the bounty of Providence, the more widely
spread poison of infidelity has in our days been met with more
numerous and more powerful antidotes. One of these has
already been pointed out: it should be a matter of farther
gratitude to every real Christian, that in the very place on
which modern infidelity had displayed the standard of victory,
a warrior[13] in the service of Religion, a man of the most acute
discernment and profound research, has been raised up by
Providence to quell their triumph. He was soon taken from us;
but happily for him and for ourselves, not till he had announced, that, like the Magi of old, he had seen the star of
Christ in the East, and had fallen down and worshipped him.
Another[14] should be mentioned with honour, who is pursuing
the track which that great man had pointed out. Henceforth let
all objectors against Christianity, on the ground of its being
disproved by the oriental records, be put to silence. The
strength of their cause consisted in their ignorance, and in our
own, of oriental learning. They availed themselves for a while
of our being in a state of darkness; but the light of day has at
length broken in and exposed to deserved contempt their
superficial speculations.

    The infatuation of these unbelievers upon trust would
be less striking, if they were able altogether to decline Christianity, and were at liberty to relinquish their pretensions to its
rewards, on condition being exempted from its punishments.
But that is not the case; they must stand the risk of the
encounter, and their eternal happiness or misery is suspended
upon the issue.[15] What must be the emotions of these men, on
first opening their eyes in the world of spirits, and being
convinced, too late, of the aweful reality of their impending
ruin. May the mercy and the power of God awaken them from
their desperate slumber, while life is yet spared, and there is yet
space for repentance!

SECTION FOUR ↗

Advice Suggested by the State of the Times to True Christians

To those who really deserve the appellation of true Christians, much has been said incidentally in the course of the present work. It has been maintained, and the proposition will not be disputed by any sound or experienced politician, that they are always most important members of the community. But we may boldly assert, that there never was a period wherein, more justly than in the present, this could be affirmed of them, whether the situation, in all its circumstances, of our own country be attentively considered, or the general state of society in Europe. Let them on their part seriously weigh the important station which they fill, and the various duties it now peculiarly enforces on them. If we consult the most intelligent accounts of foreign countries which have been recently published, and compare them with the reports of former travellers, we must be convinced, that Religion and the standard of morals are every where declining, abroad even more rapidly than in our own country. But still, the progress of irreligion, and the decay of morals at home, is such as to alarm every considerate mind, and to forebode the worst consequences, unless some remedy can be applied to the growing evil. We can depend only upon true *Christians* for effecting, in any degree, this important service. Their system, as was formerly stated, is that of our national church: and in proportion, therefore, as their system prevails, or as it increases in respect and estimation, from the manifest good conduct of its followers, in that very proportion the church is strengthened in the foundations on which alone it can be much longer supported, the esteem and attachment of its members, and of the nation at large. Zeal is required in the cause of Religion; they only can feel it. The charge of singularity must be incurred; they only will dare to encounter it. Uniformity of conduct, and perseverance in exertion, will be requisite; among no others can we look for those qualities.

Let true Christians then, with becoming earnestness, strive in all things to recommend their profession, and to put to silence the vain scoffs of ignorant objectors. Let them boldly assert the cause of Christ in an age when so many, who bear the name of Christians are ashamed of Him: and let them consider as devolved [passed down] on Them the important duty of suspending for a while the fall of their country, and, perhaps, of performing a still more extensive service to society at large; not by busy interference in politics, in which it cannot but be confessed there is much uncertainty, but rather by that sure and radical benefit of restoring the influence of Religion, and of raising the standard of morality.

Let them be active, useful, generous towards others; manifestly moderate and self-denying in themselves. Let them be ashamed of idleness, as they would be of the most acknowledged sin. When Providence blesses them with affluence, let them withdraw from the competition of vanity, and, without sordidness or absurdity, shew by their modest demeanour, and by their retiring from display, that, without affecting singularity, they are not slaves to fashion; that they consider it as their duty to set an example of moderation and sobriety, and to reserve for nobler and more disinterested purposes, that money which others selfishly waste in parade, and dress, and equipage. Let them evince, in short, a manifest moderation in all temporal things, as becomes those whose affections are set on higher objects than any which this world affords, and who possess, within their own bosoms, a fund of satisfaction and comfort which the world seeks in vanity and dissipation. Let them cultivate a catholic spirit of universal good will, and of amicable fellowship towards all those, of whatever sect or denomination, who, differing from them in non-essentials, agree with them in the grand fundamentals of Religion. Let them countenance men of real piety wherever they are found, and encourage in others every attempt to repress the progress of vice, and to revive and diffuse the influence of Religion and virtue. Let their earnest prayers be constantly offered, that such endeavours may be successful, and that the abused long-suffering of God may still continue to us the invaluable privilege of vital Christianity.

Let them pray continually for their country in this season of national difficulty. We bear upon us but too plainly the marks of a declining empire. Who can say but that the Governor of the universe, who declares himself to be a God who hears the prayers of his servants, may, in answer to their intercessions, for a while avert our ruin, and continue to us the fullness of those temporal blessings, which in such abundant measure we have hitherto enjoyed.[16] Men of the world, indeed, however they may admit the natural operation of natural causes, and may therefore confess the effects of Religion and morality in promoting the well-being of the community; may yet, according to their humour, with a smile of complacent pity, or a sneer of supercilious [haughty, scornful] contempt, read of the service which real Christians may render to their country, by conciliating the favour and calling down the blessing of Providence. It may appear in their eyes in instance of the same superstitious weakness, as that which prompts the terrified inhabitant of Sicily to bring forth the image of his tutelar saint, in order to stop the destructive ravages of Aetna [Mount Aetna, an active volcano].[17] We are, however, sure, if we believe the Scripture, that God will be disposed to favour the nation to which his servants belong; and that, in fact, such as They, have often been the unknown and unhonoured instruments of drawing down on their country the blessings of safety and prosperity.

But it would be an instance in myself of that very false shame which I have condemned in others, if I were not boldly to avow my firm persuasion, that *to the decline of Religion and morality our national difficulties must both directly and indirectly be chiefly ascribed; and that the only solid hopes for the well-being of my country depend not so much on her fleets and armies, not so much on the wisdom of her rulers or the spirit of her people, as on the persuasion that she still contains many, who, in a degenerate age, love and obey the Gospel of Christ, on the humble trust that the intercession of these may still be prevalent, that for the sake of these, Heaven may still look upon us with an eye of favour.*

Let the prayers of the Christian reader be also offered up for the success of this feeble Endeavour in the service of true Religion. God can give effect to the weakest effort; and the writer will feel himself too much honoured, if by that which he has now been making, but a single fellow creature should be awakened from a false security, or a single Christian, who deserves the name, be animated to more extensive usefulness. He may seem to have assumed to himself a task which he was ill qualified to execute.

He fears he may be reproached with arrogance and presumption for taking upon him the office of a teacher. Yet, as formerly suggested, it cannot be denied, that it belongs to his public situation to investigate the state of the national Religion and morals; and that it is the part of a real patriot to endeavour to retard their decline, and promote their revival. But if the office, in which he has been engaged, were less intimately connected with the duties of his particular station, the candid and the liberal mind would not be indisposed to pardon him. Let him be allowed to offer in his excuse a desire not only to discharge a duty to his country, but to acquit himself of what he deems a solemn and indispensible obligation to his acquaintance and his friends. Let him allege the unaffected solicitude which he feels for the welfare of his fellow creatures. Let him urge the fond wish he gladly would encourage, that while, in so large a part of Europe, a false philosophy having been preferred before the lessons of revelation, Infidelity has lifted up her head without shame, and walked abroad boldly and in the face of day: while the practical consequences are such as might be expected, and licentiousness and vice prevail without restraint: here at least there might be a sanctuary, a land of Religion and piety, where the blessings of Christianity might be still enjoyed, where the name of the Redeemer might still be honoured; where mankind might be able to see what is, in truth, the Religion of Jesus, and what are its blessed effects; and whence, if the mercy of God should so ordain it, the means of religious instruction and consolation might be again extended to surrounding countries and to the world at large.

§

FINIS

§

Notes ⌐

1. This passage is taken from lines 166–68 of *Ars Poetica,* a work by the Latin poet Horace (65–8 B.C.). I have used H. Ruston Fairclough's English translation, taken from The Loeb Classical Library's edition of Horace's *Satires, Epistles, Ars Poetica* (Cambridge, Mass.: Harvard University Press, 1970), p. 465. NOTE: I have also corrected the capitalization and punctuation originally used by

Wilberforce in this Latin citation to avoid any possible confusion on the part of the reader.

2. According to Greek mythology, King Midas was granted a favor as a reward for service performed for the god, Dionysus. In an act of great folly, he requested that everything that he touched turn to gold. Eventually, Midas was freed from what amounted to a curse by bathing in the source of the waters called Pactolus, near Mount Tmolus.

3. Shylock is a character in William Shakespeare's play *The Merchant of Venice*. Shylock uttered the words "I cannot find it, 'tis not in the bond" in act 4, scene 1, line 262 of this play.

4. Wilberforce writes,

> "Neither will I offer burnt-offerings unto the Lord my God," (says David) "of that which doth cost me nothing." 2 Sam. 24:24. "They" (the Apostles) "departed from the presence of the council, rejoicing that they were counted worthy to suffer shame of the name of Jesus." Acts 5:41. See also 1 Peter 4:13–14; James 1:2; Heb. 10:34; 1 Thess. 1:6. Such are the marks exhibited in Scripture of a true love to God; and though our regard for our common Lord is not put to the same severe test as that of the Apostles and first Christians was, yet if the same principle existed in us also, it would surely dispose us to act in the *spirit* of that conduct, and prompt us rather to be willing to exceed in self denials and labours for Christ's sake, than to be so forward as we are to complain, whenever we are called upon to perform or to abstain from any thing, though in an instance ever so little contrary to our inclinations.

5. Cicero. *De Senectute*, 23, 85.

6. Wilberforce is making an allusion here to the story of Joshua, Caleb, and the Israelite spies who investigated the promised land. Joshua and Caleb brought back a favorable report saying that the promised land was one "flowing with milk and honey." While their fellow spies agreed that the land was indeed good, they were more impressed with the fact that it was a land filled with fierce peoples and asserted that the land could not be settled by Israel. See the book of Numbers, chapter 13.

7. Wilberforce writes,

> It may not be amiss to mention a few useful publications of this sort. Walton's *Lives*, particularly the last edition by Mr. Zouch; Gilpin's *Lives;* the *Lives of Bishop Bedell* and *Bishop Bull;* of Archbishop Usher; some extracts from Burnet of the life of the incomparable Leighton, prefixed to a volume of the latter's *Sermons; Passages of the Life of Lord Rochester,* by Burnet; the *Life of Sir Matthew Hale;* of the excellent Doddridge, by Orton; of Henry, father and son, of Mather; of Halyburton; Hamson's & Whitehead's *Life of Wesley; Life of Baxter,* by himself, &c. &c. &c.

The books, authors, and editors Wilberforce is listing are, in order: Izaak Walton (1593–1683), author of the *Lives of John Donne, H. Wotton, Richard Hooker, George Herbert and Robert Sanderson,* Thomas Zouch (1737–1815); William Gilpin's *Lives;* the *Lives of Bishop Bedell and Bishop Bull;* Archbishop Ussher; Gilbert Burnet (1643–1715), author of *History of My Own Time;* Robert Leighton (1611–84), Archbishop of Glasgow; *Passages of the Life of Lord Rochester,* by Gilbert Burnet; the *Life of Sir Matthew Hale;* Philip Doddridge (1702–51); Job Orton (1717–83); of Philip Henry (1631–96) and Matthew Henry (1662–1714), author of *Exposition of the Old and New Testaments;* Cotton Mather (1663–1728); Halyburton; Hamson & Whitehead's *Life of John Wesley;* and Richard Baxter's autobiography *Reliquiae Baxterianae.*

8. These men are philosopher and essayist Francis Bacon (1561–1626), poet John Milton (1608–74), the English philosopher John Locke (1632–1704), and scientist Sir Issac Newton (1642–1727).

9. Wilberforce is referring here to philosopher, deist, and poet Edward Herbert (1583–1648), and the Scottish philosopher and historian David Hume (1711–76).

10. Wilberforce is referring to English divine and scholar John Leland (1691–1766). Leland's most important work was his *A View of the Principal Deistical Writers that Have Appeared in England During the Last and Present Century.*

11. Wilberforce writes,

> The author is aware, that he may perhaps be censured for conceding this term to the class of persons now in question, since orthodox Christians equally contend for the unity of the Divine Nature. And it perhaps may hardly be a sufficient excuse, that, it not being his object particularly to refute the errors of Unitarianism, he uses the term in its popular sense rather than give needless offence. He thus guards, however, against any false construction being drawn from his use of it.

12. Wilberforce writes,

> The author of this treatise has, since its completion, perused a work entitled, *Calvinism and Socinianism Compared,* by A[ndrew] Fuller [1754–1815]; and, without reference to the peculiarities of Calvinism, he is happy to embrace this opportunity of confessing the high obligation which, in common with all the friends of true Religion, he owes to the author of that highly valuable publication for his masterly defence of the doctrines of Christianity, and his acute refutation of the opposite errors.

13. Wilberforce writes, "It is almost superfluous to state, that Sir William Jones is here meant, who, from the testimony borne to his extraordinary talents by Sir John Shore [Lord Teignmouth], in his first address to the Asiatic Society of Calcutta, appears to have been a man of most extraordinary genius and astonishing erudition."

14. Wilberforce refers the reader to "Mr. Maurice." He is referring to oriental scholar and historian Thomas Maurice (1754–1824). Among his many interdisciplinary works, Maurice published a work entitled *Observations Connected With Astronomy.*

15. Wilberforce writes, "This argument is pressed with uncommon force in [Blaise] PASCAL'S *Thoughts on Religion,* a work highly valuable, though not in every part to be approved; abounding in particular with those deep views of Religion, which the name of its author prepares us to expect."

16. Wilberforce writes, "Vide [See] some exquisitely beautiful lines in the last book of Cowper's *Task,* wherein this sentiment is introduced." The last book of "The Task" to which Wilberforce refers (Book Six) is entitled "The Winter Walk At Noon."

17. Mount Aetna is located on the east coast of Sicily. According to Greek mythology, this volcanic mountain was believed to be the place where Hephaestus and the Cyclops made thunderbolts for Zeus, king of the gods.

⌐A̶ppendix One

Wilberforce's 1789 Memorandum of
Reasons Pro and Con for Publishing a
Work on "Practical Christianity"

Reasons for Delaying the Publication of
"Practical Christianity," etc.

Forncett, Dec. 6th, 1789

FOR PUBLISHING (with name):

1st. Some careless people alarmed, credit of my name, and general operation.

2nd. Even to the careless whom I know, I can hardly open myself with plainness, in private.

3rd. The really well-disposed [could be] taught the difference between being almost and altogether Christians.

4th. Things may be said to those in high stations, bishops, &c., which could hardly be personally to them in private.

5th. My way cleared of many difficulties by this explicit avowal of my sentiments; unjust conclusions will no longer be drawn from my cheerfulness, or my not making religion the matter of frequent conversation.

6th. Perhaps an association of serious people produced, labouring for national reform.[1]

CONTRA:

1, 2, 3, 4. I can now speak to my private friends, both of the careless and well-disposed, and even of the bishops.

A. The dread of an over-righteous man would deter people from co-operating with me for national reform.

B. My influence with P[itt], Chancellor [of the Exchequer], present and future, and other great men, even [King] G[eorge] himself, would be lessened: few if any [clerical] livings: few great men would attend to my recommendations in all the ways wherein I now have influence: few private men, &c. I should be looked upon as morose and uncharitable. Bishops would fear me.

5th. I may effect this without such a publication by private conversation with friends, and by public declarations.

6th. Such an association [of serious people labouring for national reform] would not now do good; the times would not bear it—the courts of law would set their faces against it.

C. To publish in defence of religion not my particular province.

D. Were I to express all I think I should be deemed an enthusiast, and were I to withhold I might mislead. Form might be substituted in the place of religion.

E. My connexion with P[itt] and my parliamentary situation put me into the capacity of doing much good in the private talks: I may carry bills of reform, I may get a bishop.[2]

In the end, Wilberforce decided not to write and publish his book in 1789:

I resolve on the whole not to publish, but I may at leisure write, and leave an injunction to publish if I die. Then much of the good may be done by the work, at least some of it, and none of the evil accrue. Meanwhile, let me remember to clear my way more, with due regard to preserving of influence, and to speak to friends of all sorts as plainly as I can safely; distribute proper books, &c.

Notes ↰

1. Robert Isaac Wilberforce and Samuel Wilberforce, *The Life of William Wilberforce*, Vol. 2, pp. 399–400.

2. Ibid. Wilberforce's list order (i.e. the structure of numbers and letters) may be a bit confusing, or leave the impression that I have omitted some part of his list. I have not. The reasons for and against are presented just as they appear in *The Life of Wilberforce*.

$\sim$ Appendix Two

An Excerpt from The Life of William
Wilberforce *on the Impact of*
A Practical View of Christianity
Following its Publication in 1797

UPON THE 12TH OF APRIL HIS WORK WAS PUBLISHED—
"My book out to day" [an entry in Wilberforce's diary]. Many
were those who anxiously watched the issue. Dr. [Isaac] Milner
had strongly dissuaded his attempt. "A person who stands so
high for talent," wrote David Scott, "must risk much in point of
fame at least, by publishing upon a subject on which there have
been the greatest exertions of the greatest genius." His publisher was not devoid of apprehensions as to the safety of his own
speculation. There was then little demand for religious publications, and "he evidently regarded me an amiable enthusiast."[2]
"You mean to put your name to the work? Then I think we may
venture upon 500 copies," was Mr. [Thomas] Cadell's conclusion. Within a few days it was out of print, and within half a
year five editions (7500 copies) had been called for. His friends
were delighted with the execution of the work, as well as with its
reception. "I heartily thank you for your book," wrote Lord
Muncaster [author of the book *Historical Sketches on the Slave
Trade*]. "As a friend I thank you for it; as a man I doubly thank
you; but as a member of the Christian world, I render you all
gratitude and acknowledgment. I thought I knew you well, but
I know you better now, my dearest excellent Wilber." "I see no
reason," said his friend James Gordon,[3] "why you should wish
to have given it another year's consideration; the world would
only have been so much the worse by one year." "I send you

herewith," Mr. Henry Thornton writes to Mr. [Zachary] Macaulay, "the book on religion lately published by Mr. Wilberforce; it excites even more attention than you would have supposed, amongst all the graver and better disposed people. The bishops in general much approve of it, though some more warmly, some more coolly. Many of his gay and political friends admire and approve of it; though some do but dip into it. Several have recognised the likeness of themselves. The better part of the religious world, and more especially the Church of England, prize it most highly, and consider it as producing an era in the history of the church. The Dissenters, many of them, call it legal,[4] and point at particular parts. Gilbert Wakefield has already scribbled something against it. "I myself am amongst those who contemplate it as a most important work."

This was the universal feeling amongst those who looked seriously around them on the face of things. "I am truly thankful to Providence," wrote Bishop Porteus,[5] "that a work of this nature has made its appearance at this tremendous moment. I shall offer up my fervent prayers to God, that it may have a powerful and extensive influence on the hearts of men, and in the first place on my own, which is already humbled, and will I trust in time be sufficiently awakened by it." "I deem it," Mr. Newton told him,[6] "the most valuable and important publication of the present age, especially as it is yours:" and to Mr. [Charles] Grant he wrote, "What a phenomenon has Mr. Wilberforce sent abroad! Such a book by such a man, and at such a time! A book which must and will be read by persons in the higher circles, who are quite inaccessible to us little folk, who will neither hear what we can say, nor read what we may write. I am filled with wonder and with hope. I accept it as a token for good; yea, as the brightest token I can discern in this dark and perilous day. Yes, I trust that the Lord, by raising up such an incontestable witness to the truth and power of the gospel, has a gracious purpose to honour him as an instrument of reviving and strengthening the sense of real religion where it already is, and of communicating it where it is not."

The aspect of the times, in which, says Mr. Hey,[7] "hell seems broke loose in the most pestiferous doctrines and abominable practices, which set the Almighty at defiance, and break the bonds of civil society," led even the less thoughtful to look to its effect with some anxiety. "I sincerely hope," wrote the Lord Chancellor, (Loughborough,)[8] "that your book will be read by many, with that just and proper temper which the awful circumstances in which we stand ought to produce." Its tone was well calculated to create these hopes. There was an air of entire reality pervading its addresses, which brought them closely home to the heart and conscience of the reader. It was not the fine-spun theory of some speculative declaimer, but the plain address of one who had lived amongst and watched those to whom he spoke. "Let me recommend you to open on the last section of the fourth chapter," was his advice to Mr. Pitt;[9] "you will see wherein the religion which I espouse differs practically from the common system. Also the sixth chapter has almost a right to a perusal, being the basis of all politics, and particularly addressed to such as you." "I desired my book-seller," he tells Mr. Newton,[10] "to leave at your house a copy of my publication; and though I scarcely suppose that your leisure will be sufficient to enable you to fight through the whole of it, you may perhaps look into it occasionally. If so, let me advise you to dip into the third or fourth chapters, and perhaps the concluding one. I cannot help saying it is a great relief to my mind to have published what I may call my manifesto; to have plainly told my worldly acquaintance what I think of their system and conduct, and where it must end. I own I shall act in my parliamentary situation with more comfort and satisfaction than hitherto. You will perceive that I have laboured to make my book as acceptable to men of the world as it could be made without a dereliction of principle; and I hope I have reason to believe not without effect. I hope also that it may be useful to young persons who with general dispositions to seriousness are very ignorant about religion, and know not where to apply for instruction. It is the grace of God, however, only that can teach, and I shall at least feel a solid satisfaction from having openly declared myself as it were on the side of Christ, and having avowed on what my hopes for the well-being of the country bottom."

But whilst thus addressed in the first instance to his personal acquaintance, it reasoned on the common principles of human nature. It was devotional, not controversial. It spoke the language of no sect or party, but brought out clearly and forcibly the great outlines of the revealed gospel, contrasting them keenly but soberly with the ordinary practice of the day. It was therefore well fitted, like the Manual of a Kempis [Thomas a Kempis, author of *The Imitation of Christ*], to spread throughout the whole church, and call on every side into practical efficiency admitted, though long dormant, principles. Its composition would naturally increase its influence. As a literary work it might be judged to need greater condensation; but its style was the best suited to produce effect. "I was purposely," he has said, "more diffuse than strict taste prescribed, because my object was to make an impression upon men in general." "Do not curtail too much," he once said to a friend, "portable [concentrated] soup must be diluted before it can be used." There is in truth throughout the volume a rich and natural eloquence, which wins its way easily with every reader. Its illustrations are happy; its insight into motives clear; and above all, its tone is every where affectionate and earnest. It was seen to be "the produce of his heart as well as of his understanding."

He addressed his fellow-countrymen moreover from an eminence on which he could be heard; as a layman safe from the imputation of professional bias; and as one who lived in the public eye, and was seen to practise what he taught. He raised indeed a strict, but his own example proved that it was a practicable, standard. His life had long been a puzzle to observers. Some had even thought him mad, because they could not comprehend the strange exhibition of his altered habits; but his work supplied the rationale of his conduct, whilst his conduct enforced the precepts of his work. Any one might now examine the staff of the Wizard and learn the secrets of his charmed book. "How careful ought I to be," was his own reflection,[11] "that I may not disgust men by an inconsistency between the picture of a Christian which I draw, and which I exhibit! How else can I expect the blessing of God on my book? May His grace quicken me." "That he acted up," is the judgment of a shrewd observer, "to his opinions as nearly as is consistent with the inevitable weakness of our nature, is a praise so high that it seems like exaggeration; yet in my conscience I believe it, and I knew him well for at least forty years."[12]

The effect of this work can scarcely be overrated. Its circulation was at that time altogether without precedent. In 1826 fifteen editions (and some very large impressions) had issued from the press in England. "In India," says [The Reverend] Henry Martyn in 1807, "Wilberforce is eagerly read." In America the work was immediately reprinted, and within the same period twenty-five editions had been sold. It has been translated into the French, Italian, Spanish, Dutch, and German languages. Its influence was proportionate to its diffusion. It may be affirmed beyond all question, that it gave the first general impulse to that warmer and more earnest spring of

piety which, amongst all its many evils, has happily distinguished the last half century.

As soon as his book was published he set off for Bath,
where he was followed by the congratulations of many of his
friends. "My book," he says,[13] "is universally well received,
especially by the Archbishop of Canterbury, and the Bishops of
London, Durham, Rochester, and Llandaff, the Duchess of
Gloucester, Sir J. Scott. Much pleased by a letter from Lord St.
Helen's, most highly commending it as adapted to the good of
worldly men." From Mr. Newton he heard again:

> To W. Wilberforce, Esq.
>
> My very dear Sir,
>
> I can converse with you as often as I please by your late
> publication, which I have now read through with increasing
> satisfaction a third time. I mean not to praise you, but I must
> and will praise the Lord for your book, which I cannot doubt
> will be accompanied by a Divine blessing and productive of
> happy effects. I hope it will be useful to me, and of course to
> those who attend on my ministry. I have been near fifty years
> in the Lord's school: during this space He has graciously
> taught me many things of which I was once no less ignorant
> than the beasts of the field. He has made me a debtor to
> many ministers, and to many books, but still I had something
> to learn from your book. You have not only confirmed but
> enlarged my views of several important points. One thing
> strikes me much, and excites my praise to the Lord on your
> behalf, that a gentleman in your line of life, harassed with a
> multiplicity of business and surrounded on all sides with
> snares, could venture to publish such a book, without fearing
> a retort either from the many friends or the many enemies
> amongst whom you have moved so many years. The power of
> the Lord in your favour seems to be little less remarkable
> than in the three young men who lived unhurt and unsinged
> in the midst of the fire, or of Daniel, who sat in peace in the
> den when surrounded by lions. It plainly shows that His
> grace is all-sufficient to keep us in any situation which His
> providence appoints us.
>
> I believe I must in future alter the tone of my quarterly
> payments [at this time, John Newton was accustomed to
> write to Wilberforce at least four times every year], if I
> continue to make them. Though I have long been well
> satisfied that the Lord had in mercy set you apart for
> Himself, yet I thought an occasional hint of the dangers to

which you were exposed might not be unseasonable. But now I shall be glad to look to you (at least to your book) for cautions against the evils that beset my own path, and for considerations to strengthen my motives for running the uncertain remainder of my race with alacrity. May the wisdom and power of the Most High guide, strengthen, and protect you. I am with the most sincere regard,

My dear Sir,

Your much obliged and affectionate

John Newton.

"Reading June 7, 1797."

There were other letters which gave him even greater and more enduring satisfaction. Not a year passed throughout his after-life, in which he did not receive fresh testimonies to the blessed effects which it pleased God to produce through his publication. . . . Men of the first rank and highest intellect, clergy and laity, traced to it their serious impressions of religion; and tendered their several acknowledgments in various ways; from the anonymous correspondent "who had purchased a small freehold in Yorkshire, that by his vote he might offer him a slight tribute of respect," down to the grateful message of the expiring [Edmund] Burke. That great man was said by Mr. [The Right Honourable William] Windham in the House of Commons, when he had arranged his worldly matters, to have amused his dying hours with the writings of [Joseph] Addison. He might have added what serious minds would have gladly heard: "Have you been told," Mr. Henry Thornton asks Mrs. Hannah More,[14] "that Burke spent much of the two last days of his life in reading Wilberforce's book, and said that be derived much comfort from it and that if he lived he should thank Wilberforce for having sent such a book into the world? So says Mrs. Crewe,[15] who was with Burke at the time." Before his death Mr. Burke summoned Dr. Laurence to his side, and committed specially to him the expression of these thanks.

Notes ↲

1. See Robert Isaac Wilberforce and Samuel Wilberforce, *The Life of William Wilberforce* Vol. 2 (London: John Murray, 1838), pp. 199–209.

2. Conversational Memoranda.

3. Letter from J. Gordon, Esq.

4. In the year 1818, he (Wilberforce) was assailed in the "Scotsman" by an exactly opposite insinuation. "Mr. Wilberforce is man of rigid Calvinistic principles." In the margin of the paper he wrote, "False."

5. Beilby Porteous (Bishop of London) to W. Wilberforce, Esq. May 10.

6. John Newton to W. Wilberforce, April 21.

7. William Hey to W. Wilberforce, Esq., April 29.

8. Lord Loughborough (afterwards Earl of Rosslyn), Letter to W. Wilberforce, Esq., May 5.

9. Letter from W. Wilberforce to the Right Hon. William Pitt (at that time Prime Minster of England), April 16.

10. W. Wilberforce to John Newton, April 19.

11. Journal, April 9.

12. Entry on a blank page of the "Practical View," by J. B. S. Morritt, Esq.

13. Diary, May 28.

14. Hannah More was an author and playwright whose works were even more widely published than Wilberforce's *A Practical View of Christianity*. Wilberforce possessed a great fondness for her writings, especially her morality tale *The Shepherd of Salisbury Plain*.

15. Afterwards Lady Crewe.

Recommended Bibliography

Ashwell, A. R., *Life of the Right Reverend Samuel Wilberforce, D.D. Lord Bishop of Oxford and Afterwards of Winchester with Selections from His Diaries and Correspondence.* 3 vols. London: John Murray, 1880.

Belmonte, Kevin Charles, "William Wilberforce: The Making of an Evangelical Reformer." M.A. Thesis, Gordon-Conwell Theological Seminary, South Hamilton, Mass., 1995.

Buxton, Travers, *William Wilberforce: The Story of a Great Crusade.* London: The Religious Tract Society, 1903.

Colquhoun, John Campbell, *Wilberforce, His Friends and Times.* London: Longmans, Green, Reader, & Dyer, 1866.

Cormack, Patrick, *Wilberforce, The Nation's Conscience.* London: Pickering, 1983.

Coupland, Reginald, *Wilberforce: A Narrative.* London: Collins, 1945.

Furneaux, Robin, *William Wilberforce.* London: Hamish Hamilton, 1974.

Gurney, Joseph John, *Familiar Sketch of the Late William Wilberforce.* Norwich: Josiah Fletcher, 1838.

Harford, A. M., ed., *Harford Annals.* Privately printed, c. 1906.

Harford, John S., *Recollections of William Wilberforce, Esq.* London: Longman, Green, Longman, Roberts, & Green, 1864.

Lean, Garth, *God's Politician.* Colorado Springs, Colo.: Helmers & Howard, 1987.

Ludwig, Charles, *He Freed Britain's Slaves.* Scottdale, Pa.: Herald, 1977.

Newsome, David, *The Parting of Friends: The Wilberforces and Henry Manning.* Grand Rapids, Mich.: William B. Eerdmans, 1993.

Patten, John A. *These Remarkable Men: The Beginnings of a World Enterprise.* London: Lutterworth, 1945.

Pollock, John, *Wilberforce.* New York: St. Martin's, 1977.

Sheppard, Thomas, *William Wilberforce, Emancipator of the Slaves.* Wheaton: Exeter, 1937.

_____, *William Wilberforce.* Hull: Hull Municipal Technical College School of Printing, 1940.

Silvester, James, *William Wilberforce, Christian Liberator: A Centenary Biography.* Mitre, 1934.

Stoughton, John, *William Wilberforce.* London: Hodder & Stoughton, 1880.

Warner, Oliver, *William Wilberforce and His Times.* London: B. T. Batsford, 1962.

Wheeler, H. M., *The Slaves' Champion.* London, 1859.

Wilberforce, A. M., ed., *Private Papers of William Wilberforce.* London: T. Fisher Unwin, 1897.

Wilberforce, Robert Isaac, and Samuel Wilberforce, *The Life of William Wilberforce.* 5 vols. London: John Murray, 1838.

Wilberforce, Yvette, *William Wilberforce: An Essay.* Privately printed, 1967.

Wildridge, T. Tindall, *The Wilberforce Souvenir.* Hull: M. C. Peck, 1884.

Writings of William Wilberforce ↗

Wilberforce, William, *An Appeal to the Religion, Justice, and Humanity of the Inhabitants of the British Empire on Behalf of the Negro Slaves in the West Indies.* London: J. Hatchard & Son, 1823.

_____, *A Letter on the Abolition of the Slave Trade; Addressed to the Freeholders and Other Inhabitants of Yorkshire.* London: T. Cadell, 1807.

_____, *A Letter to His Excellency the Prince of Talleyrand Perigord on the Subject of the Slave Trade.* London, 1814.

_____, *A Practical View of the Prevailing Religious System of Professed Christians in the Higher and Middle Classes in This Country, Contrasted with Real Christianity.* London: T. Cadell, 1797.

_____, "A Recommendation of Richard Baxter's *Saints' Rest.*" (Wilberforce wrote this piece for an 1814 edition of Baxter's book.)

_____, "An Introductory Essay for John Witherspoon's *Essay on Justification.*" (This piece by Wilberforce appeared in an 1840 [British?] edition of Witherspoon's *Essay on Justification.*)

_____, "An Introductory Essay for John Witherspoon's *Essay on Regeneration.*" (This piece by Wilberforce appeared in an 1823 edition of the Witherspoon book.)

_____, *The Correspondence of William Wilberforce.* Ed. Robert Isaac Wilberforce and Samuel Wilberforce. London: John Murray, 1840, 2 vols.

_____, *Family Prayers.* Ed. Robert Isaac Wilberforce. London, 1834.

_____, *Letters to the Gentlemen, Clergy, and Freeholders of the County of York, Occasioned by the Election for Their County,* 1807.

_____, "On the Duty of Great Britain to Christianize India." *Christian Observer.* May, 1812, pp. 261–72. (Pagination is from the hardcover edition for the year 1812. Wilberforce did not identify himself as the author of this piece, he used the pen name "Christian.")

_____, *The Speech of William Wilberforce, Esq., Representative for the County of York, on the Question of the Abolition of the Slave Trade.* London: The Logographic, 1789.

_____, *Substance of the Proceedings in the House of Commons on Thursday, July 25, 1822, on the Occasion of Two Addresses to His Majesty: One Moved by Mr. Wilberforce . . .* London, 1822.

Index

A

Abuse of things, unfairness of arguing from it against their use, 41

Acceptance with God, commonly prevailing notions respecting it, 62–64; Scripture and Church of England, doctrine respecting it, 64–67; practical consequences, of common notions respecting it, 64–65; true doctrine vindicated from objection, 67

Adam, the first man, 18, 176

Addison, Joseph, 178, 265

Adultery, 133, 134, 177

Affections, of their admission into religion, 43–44; their admission into religion reasonable, 44–47; true test and measure of them in religion, 47–49; in religion, not barely allowable, but highly necessary, 49–51; our Savior the just object of them, 52; objection that they are impossible towards an invisible being, 52–58; little excited by public misfortunes, 56–57; towards our Savior, special grounds for them, 57–58; divine aid promised for exciting them, 58; our statements respecting them in religion verified by facts, 59–60; religious, St. Paul a striking instance of them, 46

Alexis, character from Virgil's *Eclogues*, 30

Allah, 70

Ambition, votaries of, 92–93

Amiable tempers, 128–42; substituted for religion, 128–29; value of, estimated by the standard of mere reason, 129–30; false pretenders to them, 129–30; real nature, when not grounded in religion, 130; precarious nature, 130–31; value of, on Christian principles, 133; life, Christians most so, 135, 137–40; its just praise, 140–41; apt to deceive us, 141

Anaxarchus, 173, 181

B

C

D

F

G

I

J

K

L

M

N

O

P

R

S

W

Y

Z